Working with
Bereaved Children
and Young People

Brenda Mallon

Working with Bereaved Children and Young People

Los Angeles | London | New Delhi
Singapore | Washington DC

SAGE Publications Ltd
1 Oliver's Yard
55 City Road
London EC1Y 1SP

SAGE Publications Inc.
2455 Teller Road
Thousand Oaks, California 91320

SAGE Publications India Pvt Ltd
B 1/I 1 Mohan Cooperative Industrial Area
Mathura Road
New Delhi 110 044

SAGE Publications Asia-Pacific Pte Ltd
33 Pekin Street #02-01
Far East Square
Singapore 048763

Library of Congress Control Number: 2010925152

British Library Cataloguing in Publication data

A catalogue record for this book is available from
the British Library

ISBN 978-1-84920-370-8
ISBN 978-1-84920-371-5 (pbk)

Typeset by C&M Digitals (P) Ltd, Chennai, India
Printed by CPI Antony Rowe, Chippenham, Wiltshire
Printed on paper from sustainable resources

Contents

Introduction

Working with Bereaved Children and Young People brings together new research into the worlds of bereaved children. In the chapters which follow we will hear the voices of children and young people who have been bereaved. We will explore issues concerned with resilience, mental health difficulties and learning disability, spirituality, the impact of trauma, suicide and gang culture on young people's lives and the ways we can support young people whose lives have been fractured. Throughout, there will be the opportunity to reflect on what you have read and exercises to help you increase your self-awareness which is vital if you are to serve these young people well.

Bereavement is a personal, social and cultural event. In the grieving process personal attitudes, beliefs and knowledge come into play, as do the social resources available to the bereaved, as well as the culture in which they live. These help the person make sense of their loss and this is particularly the case for bereaved children who will look to the adults around them to give a lead in how they should respond to loss.

For some families there is no need for any intervention following a bereavement since they have a robust network of support though family, friends and community. In other instances, the support networks may be more insubstantial or non-existent. Where the latter is the case, more support may be required through, befriending, volunteer support or bereavement counselling. Children need non-stigmatising support which 'acknowledges the bereaved child is grieving and not ill' (Willis, 2004: 4). It is important not to make assumptions about what a grieving child needs.

It is often the case that the extent to which children are bereaved is not recognised. In the UK a child under 18 is bereaved of a parent every 30 minutes (Ross and Hayes, 2004). This works out at 53 children a day which is 20,000 every year (Meltzer 1999). According to the Child Bereavement Network, more than 3000 people between the ages of one and nineteen die each year in the UK from illness or accidents. Each year around 5000 families are bereaved by suicide (Williams, 2004).

The Joseph Rowntree Foundation conducted a review of the literature on the way in which loss and bereavement affected young people. The report highlighted the fact that those who had experienced multiple bereavements or bereavement when they had other disadvantages in their life were statistically more likely to experience negative outcomes. These were found in difficulties with education, reduced self-esteem, depression and increased risk-taking behaviour.

The Harvard Bereavement Study found that two years after a death, one quarter of the children were admonished for not showing enough grief, while another quarter were told they should have finished grieving. In this latter group were children and young people who were still crying a lot in the second year after their bereavement (Worden, 1996). The point here is that there is no definitive path for grief nor a time limit. Each person expresses their feelings in their own way and, while we will look at bereavement theories and strategies to help the bereaved child, we need to bear in mind the unique journey of grief that the child or young person travels.

Robert Neimeyer said that 'grief therapy begins with who we are, and extends to what we do' (Trinder, 2008: 1). *Working with Bereaved Children and Young People* explores the theories, skills and personal attributes that we use to support children and young people. Those working with the bereaved may have no formal counselling training yet they may provide 'embedded counselling'. This involves using core counselling skills as central to their role. Such people may not be trained counsellors yet these skills are 'embedded in their work, people such as nurses, chaplains, emergency workers and funeral directors. Embedded counselling allows for flexibility so that conversations may take place outside the counselling room' (McLeod, 2008: 14).

It is vital that we listen to the children and young people who have experienced loss. Once we do that we can offer what they need rather than what we think they need. 'Grieving children don't need to be fixed. Grief is not an illness that needs to be cured. It is not a task with definable, sequential steps. It is not a bridge to cross, a burden to bear, or an experience to 'recover' from. It is a normal, healthy and predictable response to loss. We can get caught up in fixing and instructing when the skills of evoking and listening better suit the need' (Schuurman, 2002: 9). However, we also need to be aware of the impact working with bereaved young people has on the listener or counsellor, which is why regular, consistent supervision is essential to maintain emotional well-being and professional clarity.

William Worden says of the children he worked with as part of the Harvard Child Bereavement Study, 'In the end it is their wisdom, born of experience, that is the best "Counselling" for all of us' (1996: 171). I hope that *Working with Bereaved Children and Young People* will help us to listen to these bereaved children with our hearts as well as our heads. In the process we may find that our lives are transformed just as those children and young people we support are transformed through their experience. The wisdom and courage of those children I have worked with and their resilience in the face of great sorrow and loss, have taught me so much and I am in their debt. I hope that by sharing some of their stories that you too will be helped in your role of working with the bereaved.

All names and identifying factors have been changed to maintain the anonymity of the children and young people included in the book.

Reflexive Exercises

At the end of each chapter you will find reflexive exercises. These personal awareness exercises are to enable you to learn more about yourself and your feelings and beliefs about dying, death and bereavement. These notes are for yourself though you may choose to share them with others, particularly if you are completing them as part of bereavement support training. Wherever possible have someone available to whom you can talk if the exercise causes you distress or puts you in touch with unexpected or disturbing feelings. It is important that you address these now rather than when they emerge when working with a bereaved child or young person.

Keep a record of the exercises and your responses in a notebook specifically chosen for these activities. Set aside some private time so that you can complete each exercise and allow an hour for each one, though some may be completed more quickly than others. Do build in time to reflect on what you have written and consider what it means to you and your work with others. Give yourself several days between each exercise so that you have time to consider the thoughts and feeling that emerge over time.

Early Attachment and the Building of Resilience: The Theoretical Basis of Bereavement Counselling

'When I'm trying to hide the sadness it makes my throat hurt more. I cry because I don't feel like myself, I'm completely different. A big chunk of me has gone, it's like I've got a big hole inside me. My Dad shouts at me to go to school but I need him because I feel dizzy and so sad every morning. My heart feels weak.' T., aged eleven. His mother died after a long illness.

There have been many changes in the theoretical foundations of bereavement counselling over the past century that, in many ways, reflect the changes in society. From Freud's 'Mourning and Melancholia' in 1917, Bowlby's seminal work on attachment theory, through Elisabeth Kubler-Ross, Colin Murray Parkes and William Worden to the most recent work of Kari and Atle Dyrgrov (2008). From linear tasks and stages of mourning we have moved to the development of Continuing Bonds from Klass, Silverman and Nickman (1996) and the dynamic Dual Process model of Stroebe and Schut (1999). Life and death in the twenty-first century is underpinned by family, society and cultural factors which play a part in our work with bereaved children and young people (Klass, 1999b). As in all bereavement, whilst we recognise the importance of theories which form the foundation of our knowledge, each child and young person has their own unique response to bereavement (Alexander, 2002).

Early writers, such as Freud, were of the psychoanalytic tradition which focused on the individual and his response to grief and its impact on his inner psychic world. More recent theories are influenced by systems theory, which focuses less on the individual perspective. The inter-relationships of the bereaved person, their family, friends and wider community are all seen to play an integral part in our response to death. This is exquisitely summed up in the words of John Donne:

No man is an island, entire of itself. Every man is a piece of the continent, a part of the main. If a clod be washed away by the sea, Europe is the less, as well as if a promontory were, as well as is a manor of thy friend and mine were. Any man's death diminishes me, because I am involved in mankind and therefore, never send to know for whom the bells tolls, it tolls for thee. ('Meditation XVII')

Donne believed that everyone was connected by their community bonds as well as spiritual bonds. When misfortune happens to one person, it impacts on all those who take part in the same society or who are interconnected by the same system.

Attachment Theory

John Bowlby (1907–1990), a British psychiatrist, was a pioneer in recognising the significance of child–mother attachment or child–care-giver attachment in the development of the child. He may have been influenced by his own experiences as a child. He grew up in an upper middle-class family and his beloved nanny, his primary care-giver, left when he was four years old. He later described this as being as tragic as if his mother had died. This experience, compounded by being sent to boarding-school at the age of seven, may account for his deeply felt concern about loss in children's lives.

Working with Mary Ainsworth, Bowlby recognised that if we are to understand the child's behaviour we need to understand his environment (Wiener, 1989). He showed how the early family environment influenced the emotional and physical development of the child and he brought the idea of attachment theory to prominence in the early 1950s. 'The mother is the most important person in a baby's life for its physical and psychosocial care, and the psychosocial interaction between baby and mother is as important as the physical feeding and contact and babies become distressed when their mother does not respond to their signals.' (Graham and Orley, 1998: 272)

After World War II, the WHO invited Bowlby to write a report on the fate of children made homeless by the conflict. *Maternal Care and Mental Health* was published in 1951. In it he concluded that 'care in a family was the most appropriate form of care for children and much preferred to living in an institution' (Graham and Orley, 1998: 268). He concluded that emotional deprivation and frequent separations were a major contribution to delinquency and to psychiatric disorders, which is relevant for children and young people in public care, and this is expanded in Chapter 4. He revealed how early separation from the mother, main care-giver or significant attachment figure, produced adverse reactions in babies and young children and, against the popular view of the time, he advocated that mothers should visit their child in hospital to maintain the attachment. In passing, the practice of separating babies from their mothers at the time of the birth in hospital was roundly condemned. Bowlby emphasised the fact that each child needs to have a secure base from which to explore.

Unlike other analysts of his time, Bowlby believed, after long-standing research and observation of children, that excessive separation anxiety was the result of adversive family experiences including threats of being abandoned, rejection by parent(s), illness of parents or siblings or death of parents or siblings. He recognised that children often blamed themselves for these family events. He was influenced by a series of films made by Joyce and James Robertson, who studied the effects on young children who were briefly separated from their mothers. They filmed children in nurseries and those placed in foster care and concluded that, although separation from a mother (or mother-figure) provoked anxiety, children adapted to foster placements where a nurturing substitute mother was present (Shapland, 1976). One of the films, *A Two-Year-Old Goes to the Hospital*, documented the impact of loss and suffering by the young child separated from her primary care-giver and influenced a change in policy allowing parents to stay with their children in hospital.

Bowlby's views are powerfully reflected in the work of Camila Batmanghelidjh, founder of Kids Company, a charity that works with violent, rejected and disenfranchised young people. As she says, 'If the attachment is inconsistent and unpredictable and is not in tune with the infant's needs, the child develops an ambivalent or insecure attachment' (Batmanghelidjh, 2007: 25).

Attachment is essential to the development of emotional well-being and resilience (Frayley and Shaver, 1999; Huertas, 2005; Machin, 2009). Without attachment to a significant person, usually a parent or constant carer, a child may fail to thrive, fail to relate to others and be unable to feel empathy for others. If the attachment relationship is robust and sensitive, the child gains a sense of security which can sustain him in the face of adversity.

Bowlby and Parkes (1970) defined four main stages in the grieving process:

1   Numbness, shock and denial which may cause the bereaved to feel a sense of unreality.
2   A phase of yearning and protest in which grief may come in waves of crying, sighing, anxiety and the child or young person may sense the presence of the dead person.
3   Disorganisation, low mood and hopelessness.
4   Re-organisation involving letting go of the attachment and investing in the future.

This model was interpreted as by many as linear, which did not allow for the way in which the bereaved move backwards and forwards in their responses.

Recent research by Linda Machin (2009) has extended our understanding of attachment and its role in relationships in adult life as well as its role in resilience or vulnerability, security or insecurity, when faced with bereavement. Though there is ongoing research into the links between early attachment and response to bereavement, Machin states, 'What is clear is that relationships, their meanings and consequences for self-perception are key to the nature of grief responses' (2009: 39).

Elisabeth Kubler-Ross (1926–2004)

> Watching the peaceful death of a human being reminds us of a falling star; one of a million lights in a vast sky that flares up for a brief moment only to disappear into the endless night forever. (Kubler-Ross, 1969: 276)

Swiss born physician and psychiatrist, Elisabeth Kubler-Ross was the first person to carry out extensive research with terminally ill patients. Her seminal work, *On Death and Dying* (1969), describes how those who are dying pass through a number of 'stages'.

- Denial – the patient does nor accept that he has a terminal illness.
- Anger – anger towards self because their body has let them down; anger towards others including medical staff because the patient feels they have been failed in some way.
- Bargaining – the patient may bargain with God or another unseen force, for extra time to live longer or become well again.

- Depression – the patient may feel low and dejected as they face their mortality.
- Acceptance – given the chance to grieve, the patient may come to accept their forthcoming demise and go through a period of contemplation, reflection and accept the inevitability of their situation.

Kubler-Ross went on to apply these stages to people who had been bereaved.

Kubler-Ross (1975) added greatly to our understanding of terminally ill patients and bereavement and her model was widely accepted and used to explain the pattern of grief, and was included in the training of medical personnel. In fact, it became so widely known it featured on the TV programme 'The Simpsons' as DABDA (Denial, anger, bargaining, depression and acceptance) (DeSpelder and Strickland, 2002). However, the model later lost favour. Subsequent researchers found no evidence to support these stages and found conflicting reactions among the dying and bereaved (Stroebe and Schut, 1999). As with the Bowlby's and Parkes' model, Kubler-Ross's was interpreted as a linear model and did not allow for the fluidity of most people's experience of bereavement. People may alternate between these stages and may never feel resolution or acceptance.

William Worden's Task Model

J. William Worden, psychologist and grief specialist, was, with Phyllis Silverman, co-director of the Harvard Child Bereavement Study. The longitudinal study, which began in 1987, revealed that for many bereaved children the negative consequences of the death of a parent do not appear until after the end of the second year following the death. His book based on the findings of the study, *Children and Grief: When a Parent Dies* (1996), changed the way we think of children and bereavement.

J. William Worden's four-stage Task Model is based on the idea that following bereavement there are a series of psychological tasks that have to be undertaken (Worden, 1991). In this way he continues Freud's concept of grief as a job of work that the bereaved must accomplish. The stages are:

- Accepting the reality of the loss.
- Working through the pain of grief.
- Adjusting to a changed environment in which the deceased is missing.
- Emotionally relocating the deceased and moving on with life.

This model was later extended by psychologist Therese Rando, who adds that readjustment includes moving adaptively into the new world, without forgetting the old attachments, to form a new identity and to reinvest in life (Rando, 1993).

From the research of Worden and Silverman in the Harvard Bereavement Study grew the theory of 'Continuing Bonds', discussed later in this chapter, which is now a strong theme in bereavement. Continuing Bonds were clearly prevalent in the children they interviewed (Hospice Foundation, 2010).

Colin Murray Parkes

Colin Murray Parkes has been a highly important figure in bereavement research, as his many influential texts show. His most recent works concentrate on grieving as a reconstruction process in which the bereaved make a 'psychosocial transition' (1996). This grows out of his earlier concept which introduced the term 'Assumptive World' (1988). We each live in a world where we 'assume' life will carry on as it always has, without major transformations. Children assume they will live with their family, go to school, do their homework and have friends; however, this assumptive world may be shattered when a parent dies. Their security is split asunder, they may have to move house because of a change in financial resources, then move school and lose friends. Their world is turned upside down yet they have to learn how to negotiate their new world. This transition is the 'work' of grieving and mourning and children and young people will look to adults to find out how to move through this territory that has no map and to learn to make some meaning out of it (Neimeyer, 2005).

Continuing Bonds

> The dead are an active, positive resource to be drawn on by the living.
> (Riches and Dawson, 2000: 37)

The theory of Continuing Bonds was introduced by Klass, Silverman and Nickman in 1996 and was developed from findings of the Harvard Child Bereavement Study. It maintains that the bereaved keep links with the deceased person and these continue over time. The bonds move into the future life of the bereaved (Holland, 2001). This model encompasses what many feel is the reality of grief; that is, it is not something to be worked through or resolved because in reality grief is not so easily resolved. Previously, with the stage models of grief, people felt they were somehow inadequate because they could not get to the final stage of acceptance or resolution. The Continuing Bonds model, like the Dual Process Model, discussed later in this chapter, reflects the actual experience of the bereaved in which they incorporate the lost loved one in their ongoing life (Stroebe et al., 1995).

Children also maintain links with the deceased through memories, objects that they keep, photographs and so on (Silverman et al., 1995). Children also think about what their dead parent or sibling would advise them to do or behave in a way the deceased would have approved of. Many children do not want to forget or say goodbye. 'You don't have to say goodbye; say "See you later." You always think about them but you do get over it,' was the hopeful counsel of an eleven-year-old girl' (Worden, 1996: 172).

In many cultures continuing bonds with the dead are woven into the fabric of the culture (Deeken, 2004; Valentine, 2009). In Japan the ancestral tradition, *sosen suhai*, fosters continuing bonds between the living and the dead through a complex system of rituals, which ensure the smooth journey of the deceased to the world of the ancestors. They include rites at the funeral, in memorial services, visits to the grave and the erection of a home altar, known as *butsudan*. 'These attachments are based on reciprocity and mutual dependency, the living providing care and comfort to their dead who, in turn, look out for the living' (Valentine, 2009: 7).

Continuing bonds are particularly important in Japanese culture (Ishii, 2008). Ishii describes four main aspects of grieving which include firstly, the custom of offering food daily at the home altar or shrine and yearly visits to the grave; secondly conversing with the dead person at the home altar and at the grave; thirdly the home altar and grave are for the extended family not only the immediate family; and fourthly the living attend Buddhist rites for the dead for many years after the death. These connections are maintained in traditional ways and 'provide a safe way for bereaved Japanese, a people who are known for their reluctance to show their feelings, to express their emotions' (Ishii, 2008: 11). This cultural tradition may influence the behaviour of bereaved Japanese children who may present with school-related difficulties, such as refusal to attend, rather than sadness, for example.

African beliefs about life involve continuity through ancestors, so death is viewed as a transition from one form of life to another and responsibility for the care of children is delegated through the extended family system (Richter, 2008). These kinship networks also give the primary safety net for bereaved children and young people. However, it is vital to know the cultural traditions the child lives within, so, for example, in Australia, indigenous Aboriginal people do not use the dead person's name, so using a memory book, for example, might be quite problematic (Lansdown, 1999).

Early theorists, including Freud, proposed that those who are bereaved should work towards detachment from the bereaved. However, when his friend, Ludwig Binswanger's son died, he wrote, 'Although we know after such a loss the acute state of mourning will subside, we also know we shall remain inconsolable and will never find a substitute. No matter what may fill the gap, even if it to be filled completely, it nevertheless remains something else. And, actually this is how it should be, it is the only way of perpetuating that love that we do not wish to relinquish' (Freud, 1960: 386). We maintain the bonds to those we love and learn to live with the loss rather than 'get over it' or achieve 'closure'. The voice of the deceased may continue to influence present day choices even though the person is not physically present (Hedtke, 2001).

In a study by Hogan, bereaved adolescents were asked what they would want to say to their deceased sibling if they could ask something. Eighty-one-per cent said they would say, 'I love you and miss you' – statements in the present tense indicating that the siblings maintained continuing bonds with the deceased (Hogan, 2006). In earlier research (Hogan and DeSantis, 1994) this was described as 'ongoing attachment'.

Dual Process Model

Margaret Stroebe and Henk Schut first published their 'Dual Process Model' of coping with bereavement in 1999. Its emphasis is on how individuals cope with bereavement and it relates to the processes, styles and strategies of managing bereavement rather than defined stages. They describe it as a dynamic model and it is sometimes known as the Oscillation Model. It describes how a person moves between Loss-oriented behaviour and Restoration-oriented behaviour. Loss-oriented coping includes intrusive grief, breaking of bonds and focusing on the past, while Restorative-orientation includes avoiding grief, focusing on the future and gives respite from dwelling on the loss and the stress of avoiding it (Abdelnoor and Hollins, 2004b). It demonstrates how the grieving person alternates between grief focus and dealing with changes in life (Stroebe and Schut, 2008). Current ideas on grief include both the letting go of bonds and holding on to the attachment (Klass et al., 1996).

Stroebe and Schut describe how this model is reflected in children's grieving: 'Children shift back and forth between grief and engagement – a dual process of "loss orientation" dealing with and processing various aspects of the loss experience, and "restoration orientation" of adapting to the demanding changes triggered by the loss while trying to cope with the many activities of daily life' (1999: 216).

Narrative Approaches

> The dead help us to write their stories – ours as well. In a sense every story
> has a ghost writer. (Becker and Knudson, 2003: 714)

Robert Neimeyer, Professor of Psychology at the University of Memphis, developed
a new paradigm of grief theory in which meaning reconstruction is central (Neimeyer,
2005). It is described as a constructivist or narrative approach. This social constructivist
model is based on the view that a person's assumptive world is radically altered following major loss. The world we know has altered: there is a loss of sense of meaning. We
need to re-establish or re-construct meaning for our lives using all the resources that are
available to us. A child or young person needs those in their immediate family and wider
community to help them in this re-construction process. Neimeyer says of his view: 'The
narratives that people draw on are as varied as their personal biographies, and as complex
as the overlapping cultural belief systems that inform their attempts at meaning making'
(Neimeyer, 2005: 28).

When someone a child or young person loves dies, it changes their life story. The world
they existed in previously is changed, the characters in the life story have changed roles
and one is physically absent. At that point, the plot is altered and in making sense of the
loss, the child and family have to make meaning of the changes. Part of the process of
making meaning may be in telling and re-telling the story of the death, events leading
up to it and subsequent developments. Sociologist Tony Walter suggests that in using
biography and stories as we grieve allows us to 'keep' those who have died as we talk to
family and friends about the person who has died (Walter, 1996). In addition, families try
to make sense of death in the stories they exchange (Nadeau, 1997).

Research indicates that young children remember more than previously thought (Gopnik
et al., 1999). Families who speak together about the dead person and their time together
enable the child to build his memories and the bonds with the dead person (Traylor et al.,
2003). Founder of the bereavement charity Winston's Wish, Julie Stokes, in her remarkable book *Then, Now and Always* (2004), writes of the importance of working at memories
and likens the process to kneading bread, so that in the shared warmth, memories can gently rise to the surface and help in the grieving process. Revisiting memories brings benefits
to the child (Monroe, 2001; Kraus, 2010). The narratives that develop help bring meaning
into the child's life which has been disrupted by death (Eakon, 1999; Neimeyer, 2001)
Narrative therapy includes themes of strength, resilience, hopefulness and appreciation as
well as ongoing connections (Hedtke, 2001).

> 'It's a struggle, but you can survive it. It gets easier as memories come in
> and grief goes out.' Twelve-year-old boy, two years after the death of his
> father. (Worden, 1996: 172)

For the child 'the "voice" of the deceased continues to influence present day choices and
actions' (Hedtke, 2001: 5) A person who is approaching death may be helped to think
about what stories and memories they wish to be remembered by after death. In this
ways, bonds are actively nurtured so that death does not mean the end of the relationship
(Stokes, 2004). For the bereaved, continuing bonds brings solace. As Emeritus Professor
Thomas Attig says in *The Heart of Grief: Death and the Search for Lasting Love:*

> Grieving persons who want their loved ones back need to look for some other way to love them while they are apart. Desperate longing prevents their finding that different way of loving. Letting go of having them in the flesh is painful and necessary. But it is not the same as completely letting go. We still hold the gifts they gave us, the values and meanings we found in their lives. We can still have them as we cherish their memories and treasure their legacies in our practical lives, souls and spirits. (2000: xii)

Theories are important, but as Carl Jung said, 'Learn your theories well, but lay them aside when you touch the reality of the living soul' (Schuurman, 2008: 2).

Physical Influences on Early Development

Early experiences within the womb and during the first years of life shape a child's 'social brain', their emotional character and emotional responses (Gerhardt, 2004: 3). This emotional, cognitive and physical development is important because when a child or young person is bereaved, these early experiences will come into play. As Gerhardt says, 'It is as babies that we first feel and learn what to do with our feelings, when we start to organise our experiences and thinking capacities' (Gerhardt, 2004: 10).

As we return to earlier theories about attachment, recent research shows how attachment impacts on the development of the brain. 'New theories tie maladaptive attachment patterns directly to dysfunctional brain development that may inhibit integrative connections in the developing child's brain' (Silberg, 2003: 4). As Di Ciacco so cogently argues: 'Research has confirmed that changes can occur in the brain on a cellular level and result in altered pathway conduction, abnormal changes in hormones and neurotransmitters, lower immune system response and the risk of permanently altered brain function' (2008: 58). These changes can affect the child for the rest of his life and increase his vulnerability to both physical and emotional distress (Hofer, 1996; Personen et al., 2007; Scaer, 2005; van der Kolk et al., 2006).

Research into neuropsychological dimensions of grief have become more prevalent in recent years because of the increased sophistication of devices which can record brain activity. 'Significant loss, especially the death of a parent early in development, becomes "hardwired" into a child's physical body, emotional responses, moral understanding, cognitive reasoning and perceptions and social skills' (Di Ciacco, 2008: 14). Early experiences of loss have a significant effect on how the brain develops (Gunnar, 2006).

There is much evidence to show that increased stress leads to higher levels of mental distress in bereaved children (Silverman and Worden, 1992) and there 'is considerable evidence that the mental health problems of bereaved parents are associated with the mental health problems of their children' (Kalter et al., 2002–2003; Lin et al., 2004: 674).

Resilience and Childhood Bereavement

> Coping in bereavement is a balance between the factors that guard against the medical and physical health consequences of grief and those that provide sources of strength and resilience. (Chaplin et al., 2008: 55)

Resilience in children helps to protect them from the adverse affects of bereavement (Cicchetti et al., 1993; Hurd, 2004). As Professor of Child Psychiatry, Richard Harrington, states, 'Factors in the child include temperament, scholastic competence, high self-esteem and the capacity to form supportive relationships. Developmental stage is also important. The relative immaturity of children may help to protect them from what is in adults one of the major complications of bereavement, depressive disorder. Children are much less prone to depressive disorder than adolescents or adults' (Harrington and Harrison, 1999: 223; Stokes, 2009a).

Recent research advocates that the use of a strength-based approach to supporting bereaved children in school as opposed to the deficit-based approach which is prominent in the literature on parental loss in childhood (Bonnano, 2004). It focuses on helping the child tell their grief story from a resiliency point of view (Eppler, 2008). Children who were asked about their grief experiences following parental death spoke and wrote about their sadness but also about having a full range of emotional experiences from being happy, helpful and having fun. 'There were themes of support from immediate family, extended family, school and some peers. These children, with their full range of emotions and with helpful support systems, do not seem adequately described by a deficit-based model that focuses only on grief's sadness, anger, fear and isolation' (Eppler, 2008: 196). The children in the study stressed that they wanted others to see them as strong, resilient and normal in spite of their bereavement.

Resilience

> The roots of resilience and the capacity to withstand emotionally adversive situations without resorting to defensive exclusion are to be found in the sense of being understood by and existing in the mind and heart of a loving, attuned, and self-possessed other. (Foscha, 2000: 60).

Resilience, the ability to withstand and recover from adversity, has become an important concept in mental health theory and bereavement research in recent years (Luthar et al., 2000). Mandleco and Peery (2000) describe resilience as the ability to adjust, adapt and bounce back in spite of trauma and stresses in life. Sandler et al. (2008) talks of resilience rather than recovery after bereavement. Children and young people can be helped to build a 'resilient mind-set' to strengthen their ability to withstand and manage stress (Brooks and Goldstein, 2001, 2002) and this has important implications for all who work with bereaved children.

In recent years there has been a change of focus in bereavement research to examine the significance of resilience rather than focus on vulnerability and the negative physical and mental health consequences following bereavement (Lin et al., 2004; Stroebe, 2009). Resilience research considers the factors that protect the individual from being over-whelmed by grief and seeks to find out what sources of strength and positive strategies help the young person adapt to the loss. Bonnano, in his research into resilience, found that the majority of bereaved people experience short-lived distress reactions and are able to continue functioning at the same level during bereavement as they had prior to the loss' (Bonnano, 2009).

As was discussed earlier, resilience is founded on secure attachments to and positive relationships with significant carers, be these parents or others. It also includes strong social support networks, positive school experiences, feelings of high self-esteem, and self-belief, the ability to reframe adverse experiences and learn from them – turning 'stumbling blocks into stepping stones' – and the opportunity to contribute to others. (Newman, 2002; 2003). When working with bereaved children and young people it is helpful to ascertain their earlier experiences and the quality and nature of their attachment to significant others.

Recent research has become more focused on how children and young people 'survive and thrive in spite of stressful circumstances' (Eppler et al., 2009: 2). The research has indicated that individual attributes such as intelligence, communication skills, the ability to engage with their peers, to show empathy for others, internal locus of control, positive self-esteem, family cohesion and external support systems, such as the community or church, enhance the ability to thrive in difficult circumstance (Baldwin et al., 1990; Carver, 1998; Howard et al., 1999).

Resilience following bereavement is not only about past attachments but is affected by present family relationships as well factors in the child (Levy and Wall, 2000; Luthar et al., 2000). 'The environment of the child's life may be changed following a bereavement with additional and cumulative stressors impacting on his ability to cope. Higher levels of caregiver warmth and discipline and lower levels of caregiver mental health problems were family-level variables that significantly differentiated resilient children from affected children (Eppler, 2008; Heikes, 1997) In addition, 'The interplay between trauma and poor attachment relationships has been recognized as having an impact on resilience and recovery' (Batmanghelidjh, 2007: 109).

Bereaved children's perceptions of less threat in response to negative events and greater personal efficacy in coping with stress were 'child-level variables that differentiated resilient children from affected status' (Lin et al., 2004: 673). Schuurman found that 'the key at-risk factor bereaved children demonstrate in greater proportion than their non-bereaved peers is an external locus of control. Resilient children have a strong belief that they can control their fates by their own actions; bereaved children show a higher evidence of externalising control, believing that their fate is in someone else's hands. No wonder they display higher levels of anxiety, depression, health problems, pessimism, underperformance and lower self-esteem' (Schuurman, 2003: 130–1).

The study of resilience focuses on discovering those processes which account for positive outcomes in the face of adversity (Luthar et al., 2000). Resilience is bound up with positive and humorous memories (Lohnes, 1994). As the child grows, memories that are nurtured and cherished will enable him to build and maintain a secure attachment to a dead parent and, in so doing, enhance his resilience (Brewer and Sparkes, 2008).

Following parental death, some adolescents used negative aspects of the grief processes to construct a positive self-identity which aided their sense of resilience (Hurd, 2004; Steward, 2008). Young people who are bereaved do indicate personal resilience including the ability to live with sadness and to remember ways in which the dead person enriched their lives. The continuing connection is reflected in comments such as 'Dad would be really pleased about that' or 'Mum would have loved my painting of Hope Valley, we used to go there together before she got ill.'

> Listening to the voices of grieving children, it is important to see their complete pictures by observing their positive moments, happy times, and resilience while attending to their emotions such as sadness and fear. (Eppler, 2008: 6)

'Social capital' factors such as networks of family and friends, participation in clubs and groups and perceived safety in the neighbourhood were strongly linked with emotional well-being' (ONS, 2008: 2). Sociologist Dr Kari Dyregrov and psychologist Dr Atle Dyregrov, based at the Centre for Crisis Psychology in Bergen, Norway, have researched the impact of bereavement over many years (Dyregov, 1996, 2004).Their most recent focus has been on the way in which the bereaved's surrounding network of family, friends and their extended social group offer support (Dyregrov and Dyregrov, 2008).

Some children and young people who have experienced a long-term difficult relationship with a parent who has died may need to be 'coached' to enable them to access positive memories (Stokes, 2009a). They may be encouraged to think about a good time they had together; a place that was special for them and a time they laughed together. It may help to focus on one thing the young person liked about the deceased; one memory that gives comfort and something that was valued about the relationship. This can be accessed by the use of photos too, which can often reveal happier times when the young person was in his early years (Dunn et al., 2005). However, the young person needs to express his ambivalent and negative feelings before he can move to this exploration of positive identification (Batmanghelidjh, 2007).

A personal account

Borsi Cyrulnik's mother and father died in the Holocaust when he was seven. He survived the war, was put into care when it was over and suffered numerous traumas. In his book *Resilience* he argues that 'suffering, however appalling, can be the making of somebody rather than their destruction' (Groskop, 2009: 2). As a psychoanalyst, he has worked in orphanages in Romania, with child soldiers in Colombia and with victims of genocide in Rwanda. 'Resilience is a mesh, not a substance. We are forced to knit ourselves together, using the people and things we meet in our emotional and social environments' (Groskop, 2009: 9).

In conclusion, there are no easy, one-size-fits-all theories that tell us exactly what to do when supporting children and young people. Each unique grieving response takes its own time. As we work with the bereaved our sensitivity, compassion, care and our ability to hold strong emotions and to contain the pain may help the bereaved to travel through their grief. And, though our work is underpinned with theory, it is the relationship we build that is of crucial importance. As psychotherapist Irwin Yalom says, 'Therapy should not be theory-driven but relationship-driven' (Yalom, 2000: 10).

Reflective Exercise 1

The British actor Leslie Phillips spoke of the impact of bereavement on his life:

> It was because of my father dying when I was ten that my life became different. We were just an easy-going Cockney family, but my dad was often ill. But none of us thought he would pop off, and I'll never forget crying all the way to school after he died. We were quickly in financial trouble, so we all found work. Because I did plays at school, my mother answered an advertisement for me to audition at the Italia Conti stage school. By the age of fourteen I was earning more than the lot of them. (Endnotes, *The Guardian*, 14 March 2009, page 8)

- What was the initial impact of bereavement on Leslie Phillips?
- In what way was his mother's actions important to Leslie's future life?
- How does this article reflect his resilience?
- Can you think of any adverse events 'stumbling blocks' in your own life which you have turned into 'stepping stones'? Write a paragraph about what you gained, ultimately, from that adverse experience.
- Phillips says no one expected his father to 'pop off'. What other euphemisms can you think of and what could be the impact of these on children?

Reflective Exercise 2

British author Charlie Higson, now 50 years old, wrote of the long term impact of his mother death when he was 18:

> Losing my Mum early has instilled me with an overdeveloped sense of impermanence of things. I worry about mortality too much. It makes me a workaholic. I write something and I think, 'That might just disappear now, I'd better write something else.' (2008: 12)

- Does writing indicate resilience in Higson's life following the death of his mother? If so, how? If not, can you explain your view?
- What benefit does Higson gain from his 'workaholic' behaviour?
- How do you think young people's view of mortality is changed by the death of a parent?
- Have you created anything that will still be in the world after you die?

The Impact of Bereavement

'Burn the box and let me have my Dad. I'll take him under the duvet and make him warm again.' G., aged eight. Spoken to the undertaker in the chapel of rest.

Introduction

This chapter examines children and young people's physical, emotional, cognitive and behavioural responses to bereavement. It includes the ages and stages of children's understanding of death and bereavement and sections on the death of a parent and the death of a sibling. The significance of family, friends and the wider society in the child's life is explored to show how we can best aid the mourning and grieving child, with particular reference to the most recent research in this area. We will also consider anticipatory grief and differences in gender responses in bereavement.

When a child is bereaved

Children feel the impact of bereavement in physical, social, emotional, cognitive and spiritual ways (Nadeau, 1997). There are many aspects that come into play in children's reactions to bereavement; in fact, it is useful to consider the experience as a process rather than a single act (Felner et al., 1988). Many changes are set in train when death happens, particularly if it is a parent or primary care-giver who has died. The role or function of the person who has died is highly significant since that will impact on the ongoing life of the child. Gender also influences the young person's response to death. Tamm found that boys tended to think of death from a biological point of view as the end of life, whereas girls were interested in exploring the idea of an afterlife and metaphysical meanings in death (Tamm, 1996).

Grief is a family affair (Kissane, 2002). As Nadeau reminds us it is not only the individual who is grieving but the entire family system. The interdependence of the family will influence how the child grieves and reflects his feeling of support or otherwise (Nadeau, 1997). Communication, cohesion and shared grief help children to manage their grief more positively. Each individual within a family grieves differently and at their own pace, and sometimes this means that family members are unable to nurture each other which can lead to relationship difficulties. 'A lack of understanding about the processes of loss and grief can compound difficulties … the provision of information, education and support are vital' (Dowling, 2003: 30).

Physical responses to bereavement

Bereavement affects physical health. Following bereavement children may feel they can't breathe properly, feel fatigue, muscle weakness and stomach aches. They may experience depersonalisation, feeling that they are not really 'in' their body. In addition, severe early stressors such as bereavement can affect the child's physical development as well as susceptibility to disease (Gunnar, 2006).

One study found that bereaved children and young people consult their GPs more often, both before and after the death of a sick parent (Lloyd-Williams et al., 1998). There is a peak of bereaved children's visits to their GP at four months after the death (Lowton, 2002). This may be because people are no longer speaking of the dead person whilst the deceased might still be very present in the child's memory.

The mind and body are inextricably linked (Goleman, 1996; Pert, 1997). What we hold in our minds also manifests in our bodies. We can be sick with worry, worried to death, scared stiff, be a pain in the neck or be too choked to speak. To a large extent, the way we deal with loss defines our health. We know that our thoughts affect our nervous system, which in turn influences our immune system, as the study of psycho-neuroimmunology reveals. Some children somatise their grief in headaches and stomach aches (Worden, 1996). The body's equilibrium can be severely upset by emotional stress. Sir William Osler, the 'father of psychosomatic medicine' said at the beginning of the twentieth century, 'The hurt that does not find its expression through tears may cause other organs to weep.'

The bereaved child or young person may feel empty because of the loss and may try to fill up the 'hole' by eating, excessive physical activity in sports or exercise, playing video games or constantly watching TV. These activities may block out the sense of emptiness. They may physically 'act out' feelings of anger or frustration. Where this happens the young person can be told that their angry feelings are understandable, but that it is not okay to hit out at other people or to injure themselves. These boundaries help the young person to feel safe whilst their intense emotions are understood.

Emotional responses to bereavement

Mental health difficulties may be precipitated by bereavement in childhood (Black, 2002; Meltzer et al., 2000). Children and young people may react to bereavement by denial: 'My dad isn't really dead, he'll come back' or 'It can't be true, it seems like a dream.' Children who are bereaved have a 'significantly increased risk of developing psychiatric disorders and may suffer considerable psychological and social difficulties throughout childhood and even later in adult life' (Black, 1996: 1). Studies have shown an increased incidence of affective disorder (Elizur and Kaffman, 1983; Van Eerdewegh et al., 1985; Weller et al., 1991). A study conducted by Weller and his colleagues found that 37% of the 38 children in their sample who had lost a parent a year previously fitted the criteria for a major depressive condition (Weller et al., 1988). Bereaved children and young people may suffer from panic attacks where their anxiety levels are particularly high. There are specific anxieties linked to fears of abandonment (Stuber and Mesrkhani, 2001), separation and death as well as generalised anxiety (Sanchez et al., 1994).

Bereavement may impact negatively on self-esteem. A research study found that two years after the death, bereaved children had lower self-esteem than their peers and felt less able to bring about change indicating they felt the locus of control was external rather than internal (Worden, 1996). However, the evidence is not clear cut (Baker et al.,1992; Bifulco et al., 1992; Harrington and Harrison, 1999; Harrison and Harrington, 2001). Some research states that it is not only the death that causes difficulties for a child, but what follows on from it. Poor physical care and emotional neglect following a death, particularly, if a child's mother has died, create long-term risks for the bereaved child in subsequent mental health difficulties, such as depression (Harris et al.,1986).

Cognitive responses to bereavement

It can be difficult for young children to comprehend death or make sense of what has happened to the person who has died. Children and young people may repeatedly ask questions about the death. The child goes over the same ground again and again in an attempt to understand the meaning of what has happened.

The experience of bereavement can have a long-term effect on academic performance (Abdelnoor and Hollins, 2004a; Davou and Widdershoven-Zervakis, 2004). Worden (1996) found that one year after the death of a parent, 16% of the bereaved children had concentration problems compared with 6% of non-bereaved children. 'The death of someone close, especially in circumstances where there is already disadvantage, can put children at increased risk of poor social and educational health' (Bird and Gerlach, 2005: 44). We will explore this in greater depth in Chapter 5.

> 'Life carries on, despite the fact that I often have great difficulty concentrating on what I have to do and often have to stop and take a break when I know I shouldn't. But I feel I have to rest between tasks because otherwise it all gets too much.' Rikard, aged thirteen, whose father died. (Sjoqvist, 2007: 23)

Behavioural responses to bereavement

Regressive behaviour following bereavement often reflects feelings of insecurity. The bereaved child may bed wet again, seek to sleep in the parental bed, be unable to complete tasks well within their previous capability or revert to babyish language. Older children and young people may be very challenging. Extreme emotions and acting out behaviour may reveal the inner terror, anger, fear and helplessness. By acting in a challenging or aggressive manner the child or young person is communicating his desire to exert some control over a situation in which he feels powerless. Studies which have explored the lives of bereaved siblings have found a deterioration in behaviour (Hutton and Bradley,1994) and a decrease in social competence (Birenbaum et al., 1989). Feelings of guilt may be part of the reason (Crehan, 2004).

A young child has a limited capacity to sustain extended periods of grieving as the intensity of emotion is too much for the young child to endure, so they grieve in bursts (Silverman, 2000). The Dual Process model of grief described earlier perfectly describes the way in which children grieve. The emotional shock may be interspersed with a seeming lack of feeling. This retreat from the intensity of grief acts as a buffer to protect the child from the pain which may threaten to overwhelm him. Sometimes parents may interpret such turning away from grief as a lack of caring for the deceased and feel upset about this. As the child matures, the capacity to sustain intense emotions increases.

Children and young people need to revisit the loss as they grow and develop (Jewett, 1982). As they reach different developmental levels and when significant milestones arise, they may 'revisit life events and often rework or re-grieve a loss' (Ward-Wimmer and Napoli, 2000: 112).

Children who experience three or more stressful events, such as family bereavement, divorce or serious illness, are significantly more likely to develop emotional and behavioural disorders according to the Office of National Statistics (ONS, 2008: 1), and Box 2.1 gives a list of responses to bereavement. The role of the surviving parent is critical to the well-being of the child post-bereavement, as well as the social environment (Dowdney, 2000; Kwok et al., 2005; Worden, 1996). 'The functioning of the surviving parent therefore seems to be the most powerful predictor of a child's adjustment to the death of a parent' (Lowton and Higginson, 2002: 7).

Box 2.1   Children, Young People and the Impact of Bereavement – Overview

There are overlapping responses here; however, this list will give you an idea of common responses to bereavement.

Emotional responses

- Disbelief – denial, numbness, unreality
- Sadness
- Numbness
- May feel lost and abandoned
- Yearning
- Guilt – may feel that they are to blame for the death
- Confused
- Feels different to other children who have not had the same experience
- Anger
- Grief
- Shock
- Lonely and isolated
- Insecure
- Confusion
- Reduced sense of self-confidence
- Helplessness
- May feel lack of trust in others, in life and in the world around them

- May yearn to follow the person who has died
- Attention seeking/needing
- Sense of presence of the deceased
- Inability to function at previous level of competence
- Burdened
- Regret
- Shame
- Relief
- Agitation
- Anxiety
- Reliving the event again and again, particularly where the death was traumatic, e.g., road traffic collision
- May discover previously unknown emotional strength.

Physical

- Sighing a lot/trouble breathing
- Rapid, shallow breathing
- Pain
- Lethargy/fatigue
- Hyper-activity
- Hair loss
- Appetite changes
- Tremors of hands or lips
- Sleep changes
- Personal neglect
- Tears
- Nausea and/or digestive upsets
- Racing heart/palpitations
- Feeling empty
- Tight throat or chest
- Weakness in muscles
- Feeling cold and shivery
- Rashes, skin problems
- Feeling out of their body – depersonalisation
- Acting out aggression – verbally and physically.

(Continued)

Behaviour

- Difficulty concentrating
- Aggressive
- Resigned and lacking in energy
- Anti-social
- Withdrawn
- Crying
- Mood swings
- Change in eating habit – comfort eating/loss of appetite
- Change in sleeping habits
- Forgetfulness.

Cognitive responses

- Thinking they can visit the place where the loved one is
- Thinking that the person can/will come back
- Thinking death could happen to them
- Development of fears/phobias
- Day-dreaming
- Nightmares/distressing dreams
- Unable to understand/comprehend what has happened
- Unable to concentrate, short attention span
- Over compensating through work or using work as a distraction
- 'Magical Thinking'.

Ages and Stages

> Talking to children about death must be geared to their developmental level, respectful of their cultural norms, and sensitive to their capacity to understand the situation. (NASP, 2003: 1)

Bereavement is a unique experience for each individual, adults and children alike. Children's understanding of death is influenced by their age and stage of development. However, when considering these stages bear in mind that some children mature more quickly than their peers, physically as well as emotionally. In addition, developmental delay, poor mental health and affective disorders such as autism, all influence the child's understanding of death. We will consider in each section the level of understanding of the age group and common reactions to bereavement.

Understanding of death is linked to four components which are
the understanding that physical body of the dead person or cre
back to life; (b) finality: the understanding that life-defining f
death; (c) inevitability or universality: the understanding that a
and (d) causality: understanding the possible causes of death (And

Under Five Years

How children under five perceive death

Children under five have little understanding of time, for example, final or forever may
not be comprehensible (Di Ciacco, 2008). The child does not understand that death is
permanent and believes that death is reversible. At this age children find it hard to understand what is real and what is not real. They are at the 'concrete stage' of thinking, so it is
important to use clear language, for example, to say that the dead person's body stopped
working and they can no longer move, talk or do the other things that a living person can
do (Way, 2008).

Very young children may worry about who will look after the dead person and who will
give them food and they may believe that they are responsible in some way for the fact
that 'Mummy does not come back'. Explanations need to be given in a sensitive way that
does not allow for ambiguity, euphemisms such as 'Your mummy has gone to sleep now'
or 'We've lost your Mummy' only create confusion in the child's mind. It is easy to see
how, for a child, death is sometimes confused with being asleep (Kraus, 2010; Mallon,
1998).

By the age of five though, children are aware that death is important and that it brings
change. Moreover, they are more likely to see death as frightening and connected to
ghosts and skeletons. Children who are very young or who have special educational needs
may find it difficult to say how they feel and will communicate through behaviour rather
than verbally.

Babies and toddlers may not understand what death is but will still react to loss of those
closest to them (Bowlby, 1969). A toddler will react to his parent's distress and he may
respond by crying or becoming agitated. He will pick up feelings of sadness, anxiety and
other emotions of those closest to him. Young children may react to separation by becoming quiet, lethargic, withdrawn, and may lose weight and sleep less well (Christ, 2000).

Characteristic responses

- Inability to distinguish between animate and inanimate – the child may ask, 'Will
  Daddy be playing golf in heaven ?' or 'What will he eat?'
- Fear – the child may ask, 'Will I be the next to die?'
- Curiosity – 'Why did she die?', 'What will happen to the body?'
- Association – to young children everything is linked: if Grandma went to hospital
  then died, a young child may conclude that whenever someone goes to hospital,
  then that person will die.
- Magical thinking – the child believes he may have caused the death or separation
  and/or that if he carries out certain actions the loss will be reversed.

Self-centred – children are self-centred and may respond to death in a way that seems selfish. For example a child may say, 'He's died so who's going to take me swimming now?' By concentrating on the practical issues children seek reassurance that though their world has changed it will continue.

- By the age of six children begin to understand death as irreversible, final and real. This may increase the fear that someone they know will die.

- By six a child may react to death with anger, 'I hate my Dad for dying'. This may be upsetting for the child as well as his family but it is important to recognise that the child is hurting.

A personal account

Paediatric oncologist Lynne Riley's husband died following a road traffic collision. Her son Jack was three and a half and her daughter Alice was sixteen months old. Lynne said, 'Alice … knew something was wrong, she ran round the house shouting "Daddy, Daddy", that was when he had been rushed into hospital.' A year later Lynne returned to work and commented, 'My children were my sanctuary. The useful thing I'd learned from oncology was that you should always be honest with children: if you don't tell them the truth, they will invariably sense that and their imagination will take off. They have as much right to grieve as adults do. Pretending everything is OK is wrong. Jack and Alice had lost their father. The worst thing in the world had happened to them and they had the right to be as sad as I was.'

'Jack came with me to the chapel of rest. He'd painted a picture of heaven and chose some special objects – Richard's best paints and brushes – which he put in the coffin.'

After her husband's death, Lynne read Alan Durant's book *Always and Forever* to Jack. It is a story about a fox who is part of the family and who dies. The last line is, 'The father of the family, always and forever'. She read this to Jack every night for months until he finally chose another book. Lynne said, 'I knew it was helping him.'

Children Aged Seven to Eleven

How children age seven to eleven perceive death

The knowledge that death is permanent is usually well established by seven years of age. They are able to appreciate other people's feelings about loss and are able to empathise. There are also fears of being different where there has been a bereavement in the family or where separation has taken place.

This age group generally have similar reactions to adults: shock, confusion, anger and guilt. There may be regression in terms of bedwetting, lack of concentration, clinging behaviour, increased aggression or withdrawal. These reactions communicate the child's distress. There is a real fear of being abandoned and the bereaved child may ask, 'Who is going to look after me now?' They may worry that the remaining parent may die too.

They also have concerns about their own health fearing they too will die. In some instances they may refuse to go to school seeking to be near the remaining parent or care-giver and have increased generalised anxiety. The child may mask their feelings which may make those around the child think he is unmoved by the death. Children also sometimes have an idea of multiplication; that is, they think if one person dies then another one must, for example, a child whose younger sibling died, asked her mother if it was her turn to die next (Mallon,1998).

Once a child is attending school she has wider access to social groups through her school friends and teachers. Their increased independence and contacts beyond the family allow them to experience diverse situations. Peers at school may share news of a dead pet or the death of a grandparent so they may be introduced to the concept of death. By five to six years of age children understand that life is 'anything that moves'.

Young children question the concept of death. What does death mean? How do people die? Where do people go when they die? Can they come back? They are often curious about death and may ask very direct questions, such as, 'What happens to the person's body when they died?' and 'What happens when they are buried in the ground?' It is important to tell the child that, for example, if their mother dies, that 'Mummy's body stopped working and it was not Mummy's fault, or your fault that she died.' The stage of 'magical thinking', in which children believe that their thoughts or actions were responsible for the death, is prominent at this time (Abrams, 1999; Andrikopoulou, 2004). We need to reassure children that they are not to blame because children may feel shame that they have brought about the death about. However, they sometimes think death only really happens to old people and that the dead can see and hear them, which can be reassuring or unsettling.

Karen Rae's sister Elaine was ten when she died. Karen took it upon herself to protect her parents at the expense of her own feelings: 'The main thing that I've realised now is that I couldn't upset my mum and dad, because every time I looked at them they were crying. I got it into my head – being six – that I couldn't do anything now to upset them … Everything they asked me to do, I did, even if I didn't want to. And I did it with a smile' (Jenkins and Merry, 2005: 112).

Characteristic responses

- Self and others – by this stage the child is usually less egocentric and understands that other people have feelings too. They can show empathy.
- Natural curiosity about the body – how it works and why it stops working. They want facts.
- There may be embarrassment at being different, the odd one out. In the playground, he may be singled out for insensitive taunting.
- They may deny and disguise their own feelings in order to protect those of the adults around them.
- Pockets of grief may overwhelm and distance the child from his or her surroundings.
- By ten years of age, children know that death is part of life, it is unavoidable.
- Thinking about death may lead to spiritual and philosophical questions about mortality.

What do children in this age group need?

Helping children and young people to understand what has happened to a dead person enables them to process the information. It dispels fantasies and myths that may hinder the grieving process. Donna Hastings, senior project worker at Richmond's Hope organisation in Edinburgh says, 'One of the things we say to parents or carers, of bereaved children, is to be as honest as they can be with the child. Children don't need to know every detail but they do need to know how the person died' (Summerhayes, 2007: 5).

Children long to have a whole family and 'after some time, most children of this age requested that the surviving parent found a replacement' (Christ and Christ, 2006: 202). I worked with a seven-year-old boy whose father had died eight months previously. His mother was concerned because he was very angry with her, shouting at her and behaving in a defiant way. What emerged after just one session was that he was angry because she had not got him a new Daddy when he had asked her to. We played a game with some Playmobil figures which included a dog. In the game, at one point the dog figure fell over and I removed it and wondered aloud if the dog had died. He said, 'We could get another one.' We talked about where we could get a new dog. Later, after the dog (pretend new dog) was re-instated, the 'daddy' figure fell over and I took him off the play table. We then explored the idea that it wasn't so easy to get a new daddy because there were no shops to buy one. We talked about his feelings of sadness, but my young client realised that his anger towards his mother was not fair because she couldn't make his wish come true. The clarity helped him to build a much closer relationship with his mother and, after another couple of sessions, he didn't need to see me again.

In this age group, children may say that they wish they could die too. However, this does not mean that they want to kill themselves but that they want to be with the person who has died. This intense yearning is normal and transient; however, if it continues and the child remains preoccupied with this feeling it is important to access professional support for the child. Listening to such feelings can help clarify what the child is yearning for and help them to understand that they still have bonds with the person who has died even though the person is not physically present.

Research indicates that children have quite well-developed ideas relating to death and, with support, recognise that death happens throughout the world, that it is permanent and that the dead cannot come back to life (Lansdown and Benjamin, 1985). Children in this age range know that death is the end of life and that it is irreversible and universal. They understand more readily why death happens through illness and accidents, for example, and they are less likely to blame themselves for the death but may blame others, such as the doctors who cared for the deceased (Jenkins and Merry, 2005). They may also be interested in what happens after death and may ask questions of a spiritual nature. Some children may develop death anxiety and have nightmares that reflect their fear of death.

James (aged ten) spoke of how things had changed with his peers since his brother was killed in a road traffic crash: 'Once, a boy was having a go at me and someone said, "Why are you doing that to him? His brother died." So, people are nicer to me now.' This is not always the case as some young people report being bullied or jeered at because a member of their family has died, as if they are to blame or have somehow been careless.

Adolescence – Eleven Years and Above

How adolescents perceive death

Adolescence is a time of tremendous change and transition. As Hooyman and Kramer state, 'Adolescence is a time of paradox: in order to establish emotional connections with others and to work in collective endeavours, adolescents first must separate themselves emotionally from their loved ones. The teenagers' struggles with parents, teachers, other authority figures, and even peers, represent their efforts to gain a sense of individuality and competence.' (Hooyman and Kramer, 2006: 139). Dr Beverley Raphael, noted Australian researcher into the impact of bereavement, considered that the death of a parent was 'the greatest loss for the adolescent, especially in the earliest years when he or she has not completed the separation process' (Raphael, 1984: 145).

The physical changes at adolescence cause considerable upheaval. Hormones influence mood as well as brain activity. Changes affect the body and influence behaviour, relationships and attachments. The adolescent experiences growing independence during this time of separation from parents or carers as the importance of their peer group increases. At this point in their growth the adolescent is developing an identity which involves awareness of their own sexuality and developing more intimate relationships with others. While the young person may feel more self-conscious and self-centred there may be an increase in impulsive behaviour.

Adolescents are aware of death as final. They can empathise with others and understand the intensity of emotions wrought following a bereavement. By the time adolescents have reached sixth form, most will have experienced the death of a peer from road traffic collisions or through aggressive illness. Most will have seen reports of attacks which brought death such as in media coverage of war, high school shootings and violence within their community. Such events can lead to increased feelings of vulnerability, and a recognition of the fragility of their world (Corr, 2000; Grollman, 1995). However, at the same time, they may tend to think that death happens to other people, not to them and have a misguided idea about the level of their own risk-taking (Di Caccio, 2008).

The teenage years may bring many experiences of loss, for example, loss of childhood, change of school or college, leaving home. Parental relationships may break down or illness may bring about loss. The teenager may experience loss through failure in examinations or not getting a place at university or in the job market. These events impact on the lives of adolescents and their feelings about themselves and others.

Research has shown that those bereaved in adolescence are affected for a long time. The Harvard Bereavement Study found a significant proportion of children and young people experienced more emotional distress two years after the death than immediately following the death (Worden, 1996). Mood swings and feeling low are common. The young person may need more sleep but is not tired at night and may find it very difficult to wake up and function in the morning, and there also may be changes in eating patterns.

Adolescents may express emotions in acting out or in self-harming behaviour as a way of coping with the pain and anxiety of loss. 'Acting out' behaviour may be the expression of feelings that have not been verbally expressed (McFarland and Tollerud, 1999). Alcohol and drug abuse may be a way of 'self-medication', to block out unpleasant emotions. Perhaps unconsciously, adolescents will challenge death by taking part in risky pursuits such as fast driving, increased risky sexual behaviour, drug use or other possibly self-destructive behaviour. They may fantasise about their own death and the subsequent funeral. This can be a way of coming to terms with their loss and recognising their own mortality. Adolescents with a history of poor mental health, such as depression, may be more likely to have suicidal ideation and there is a greater risk of long-term and complicated grief reactions (Christ et al., 2002; Mearns, 2000).

Young people at this age are aware of the finality of death and the emotional consequences of death, They may wrestle with the meaning of life and death and wonder what is the meaning of their own existence. They may find their intense emotions difficult to handle, including angry feelings that may be destructive to others or to themselves. One client, whose mother died of cancer, was furious with her mother because she felt the death, which had not been prepared for, had robbed her of her independence. With four younger siblings and a 'shut down' father she felt responsible for the welfare of everyone else.

School work may be affected as the adolescent student may lack concentration and disengage from academic work seeing school work or academic achievement as pointless. The opposite may also happen, the bereaved student overworks as a means of escape from emotional pain. These reactions are often temporary and after a few months the adolescent reverts to earlier levels of academic performance (Geldard and Geldard, 2000; Lowton, 2002).

The hormonal changes the adolescent undergoes at this stage of development may add to their mood swings after a loss and the young person may feel overwhelmed and confused by their own reactions.

Characteristic responses

- All or any of the responses in the phases described earlier.
- Concern about the well-being of family or friends may lead to the young person masking or hiding feelings.
- Anxiety about their own behaviour prior to bereavement, including self-blame.
- Lack of concentration and motivation.
- May become withdrawn or isolated or, the opposite, involved in frenetic social activity as a means of escape from strong emotions.
- Increased feelings of responsibility for remaining family where a parent has died.
- Increased reflection, questioning the meaning and purpose of life.

Teenagers grieve deeply after the death of a significant person their life, yet may seek to hide these feelings as they increase a sense of vulnerability (Raveis et al., 1999; Silverman, 2000). Many adolescents will grieve in the privacy of their rooms rather than express their feelings in public. They may seem indifferent to the outside observer and to other family members which may cause conflict. A client I worked with expressed anger about her sixteen-year-old daughter who she felt didn't care at all about her father who had been killed following an unprovoked attack in the street. The daughter went out with friends every evening and wouldn't talk about her father. When the men who killed him went to court, the daughter screamed and yelled at them venting her anger and pain. It was at that point that her mother understood the depth of her daughter's anguish and loss.

Many adolescents found that personal growth took place following their bereavement (Ens and Bond, 2005; Hogan and Schmidt, 2002). They felt they 'had grown up faster than their peers, cope better with problems, are more tolerant of themselves and others, and are better able to help others and receive help from others who grieved' (Hogan, 2006: 60). They also believed that they cared more deeply for others. Research has indicated that bereaved teenagers find that there is a transformation in terms of their spiritual, cognitive, emotional and interpersonal development (Balk, 2008).

What do adolescents need following bereavement?

- Clear information that is sensitively given by a caring, trusted adult.
- The opportunity to ask questions and be given honest replies without being overwhelmed by excessive information.
- Reassurance since fear and anxiety often arise after a bereavement.
- Reassurance that they are not to blame for the death. This may be particularly present if the death was by suicide.
- Validation that their feelings are important though each person may express their grief in different ways.
- Inclusion in discussions and preparations for the funeral and in changes that occur because of the death.
- The consistency of routines and familiar activities, including spending time with their friends.
- Opportunities to remember the dead person.

Anticipatory Grief

> The need for truthful information about impending death, knowing the cause, reassurance that the child was in no way to blame (especially when the death is sudden) and that everything possible has been done, seems obvious but is not always appreciated by the adult. (Cranwell, 2007: 31)

Anticipatory grief involves mourning when the terminally ill person and the family is expecting death to happen (Kissane, 2003). The emotions experienced are similar, though not the same as those post-death and include sadness, anxiety, deep concern about the person who is dying as well as hope that some miracle will happen to allow the person to survive. However, anticipatory grief does not replace or decrease the grief of those who have been bereaved.

Grace Christ, director of the Social Worker Department of Memorial Sloan Kettering Cancer Centre, New York, carried out the largest intervention study of childhood bereavement, interviewing 157 children aged 3 to 17, six months before and fourteen months after the death of their parents (Trimble, 2000). Children in the age group six to nine years are more likely to have 'anticipatory anxiety' rather than the 'anticipatory grief' of adolescents (Christ and Christ, 2006). The terminal phase of illness is particularly stressful for young people (Christ and Christ, 2006). She found that the sense of uncertainly during the period of illness prior to the parent's death produced more emotional upheaval for the children than the period immediately after the death. Christ found that the children could not really grasp what would happen in the future. 'Many imagined and feared utter catastrophe' (Trimble, 2000: 2). In the study, she found distinct differences in children's reactions according to their developmental levels, for example, 9–11 year-olds wanted more formal ways to memorialise the death of a parent.

Children and young people who are in the terminal stages of illness show elevated levels of depression and anxiety (Siegel et al., 1992). However, prolonged illness is draining for all family members and at death there may be feelings of relief that death has finally curtailed all the time and effort that have been used to support the dying person. Relief may be accompanied by guilt for having such feelings.

When death is expected it gives the family the opportunity to say their 'Goodbyes'. Children can be prepared by talking to their family and by spending precious time with their loved one (Silva and Cotgrove, 1999; Stokes (2007) 'Mummy Diaries'). Including children in endings helps the child feel involved and valued (Moore, 2009). Julie Stokes, founder of the charity Winston's Wish, delineates four key objectives in supporting children whose parent is dying. These are to give the child a sense of control; to facilitate a meaningful relationship with the dying parent and with the surviving main carer; to help them build a confident life story that they can share with others in whom they trust; and to enable the dying parent to leave a meaningful message for their child that will promote resilience as well as maintain a secure attachment (Stokes, 2009a). We may not be able to persuade parents to be honest with children about impending death but we can encourage and facilitate open communication (Stuber and Mesrkhani, 2001).

Information is important to children and young people (Christ et al., 2005; Raveis et al., 1999). Waskett (1995) points out that when we deny information about an impending death of a parent it can cause an added burden. Later, the bereaved may be angry that the truth was concealed from them whilst other family members were privy to details they had no idea about. They feel excluded and diminished because they were not believed to be capable of handling the news. It also prevents the possibility of final conversations and leave-takings (Cranwell, 2007).

The way in which a family manages an anticipated death, as with reactions post-death, depend on a number of factors (Siegel et al., 1996). These include the nature and quality of the relationships, mental health history, previous experience of loss, support systems available to the family as well as their financial and social status. The way in which the bereaved respond to a terminal illness and death is also influenced by the cultural and religious beliefs (Wood et al., 2006). Where children are supported to understand what is happening to a terminally ill parent, for example, and the questions answered wherever possible, this aids the child's emotional resilience (Christ, 2000). The child 'may be grieving both for the suffering of the parent during the time before the death as well as grieving for the forthcoming death itself' (Holland, 2001: 185). 'However, with adequate family resources, competent substitute care, and emotional support, bereaved children are better able to return to earlier levels of functioning' (Christ and Christ, 2006: 197).

The Death of a Parent

The charity Winston's Wish found that 75% of parental deaths are fathers and 25% are mothers (Stokes, 2004). The death of a parent impacts profoundly on the bereaved child and creates a period of stress in many different ways (Abrams, 1999; Figley et al., 1997; Raveis et al., 1999). The quality of care following the death is of crucial importance: if the surviving parent or care-taker is overwhelmed with their own grief and cannot adequately care for the child or young person, there is a greater risk that complicated grief may emerge (Cournos, 2001).

Hope Edelmen carried out research into women whose mothers had died (Edelman, 1994). She found there was an ongoing impact of mother loss into their adult lives and at different points in the life cycle their loss was revisited. Parental death influences the adult sense of well-being and resilience (Marks et al., 2007).This supports the view that children and young people will return to their loss as they grow and reach different developmental stages. Loss of a father is also a life-long loss (Harris, 1995).

Some responses to the death of a parent

'My dad gets drunk all the time since my mum died. He's never home and I have to do all the shopping and housework.' Alice, aged fourteen.

'My father died of cancer last year. My mother does care but thinks I should be more like my older sister who gets good grades and keeps out of trouble. I feel really angry all the time.' Sophie, aged fifteen.

In the Harvard Child Bereavement Study the researchers asked the children what counsel they would give to other children whose parent had died. Their responses are remarkable. An eight-year-old boy said, 'Don't try and forget him. If you get another father, keep remembering your real father. Don't give up on things. Don't use your father's death as an excuse' (Worden, 1996: 171).

Sibling Bereavement

'It's boring now my brother is dead. It's boring being the only one. I've got no one to play on Playstation with.' Joey, aged eleven.

Each surviving sibling is affected differently following the death of a brother or sister (Davies, 2006; Gibbons, 1992). Many factors come into play: the age of the child, the strength and nature of their relationship, the position of the child within the family; the length or brevity of the deceased child's illness; whether the children were involved with caring for a dying sibling or included in family discussions and rituals, such as planning the funeral (Davies, 2006). Holliday (2002) describes the complexity of sibling relationships in which there is both love and affections woven with rivalry and resentment. Worden and colleagues (1999) compared parent loss with sibling loss and found evidence that suggested that boys suffered more from the death of a parent and girls from the loss of a sibling, especially a sister (Lowton and Higginson, 2002).

Children who live in families where there is open communication, where thoughts and feelings are shown and where there are strong bonds between family members, are less likely to have behavioural problems (Davies, 1999; Raveis et al., 1999). Positive relationships between children and their parent(s) or care-givers are significantly associated with fewer mental health problems following bereavement (Wolchik et al., 2006).

In sibling bereavement the grief of brothers and sisters left behind may be overlooked and they may feel excluded (Giovanola, 2005). This may be physical exclusion in the event that surviving siblings are sent away to stay with relatives until the funeral has taken place. Parents may be so wrapped in the depth of their own grief they may not notice, or cannot respond to, the grief of their children. Siblings may also feel isolated because their parents have each other to console themselves but the remaining sibling may feel that they have no one (DeSpelder and Strickland 2002). '[C]hildren who have a sibling die may have parents who are experiencing more intense levels of grief and for whom the grief continues for a longer time period than children who have a parent die' (Rosen 1996, quoted in Worden, 1996: 116). Surviving siblings may hide their feelings to protect their grieving parents yet parents may perceive this as rejection of support or lack of feeling towards the deceased. As Riches and Dawson point out (2000) 'Many of the children and young people we have worked with express this sense of invisibility' (Riches and Dawson, 2000: 79).

In essence, the siblings of a dead brother or sister will always be siblings, death does not cancel their relationship (Rosenblatt, 2000). For those who believe in life after death, the physical absence of the person does not end their spiritual existence (Bennett and Bennett, 2000; Walter, 2006). Children and young people can be helped by reminding them that 'just because their sibling has died [it] does not mean their sibling was gone from their lives. They do not have to let go of the memories of their deceased sibling' (Linn-Gust, 2006: 2). Siblings have continuing bonds with their deceased sibling (Packman et al., 2006).

Karen's sister died and she commented on the loneliness of being a sibling bereaved only child: 'It was just so lonely because I'd known what it was like to have a sister, whereas if you've always been an only child you've lived with that and life's no different, but I'd had this sister and all of a sudden she was taken away and I was completely on my own' (Jenkins and Merry, 2005: 113).

Surviving children sometimes feel that their parents would have preferred it if they had died, that somehow they are not good enough to make the parent(s) happy again. If parents can express their love and care for the surviving children this will help to validate them and reassure them that they are important. In addition, the death of a sibling may cause the child or young person to confront his own mortality. Such personal death awareness may bring heightened levels of anxiety.

The impact of bereavement of a sibling, especially where this occurs in traumatic circumstances, has the potential to negatively effect later childhood and adulthood. In traumatic loss there is an increased risk of depression (Black, 1996).The cause of death can affect the sibling's reactions. Death by suicide can trigger complicated grief reactions and the shock can be devastating. There is no time for preparation and no chance to say goodbye. (Linn-Gust, 2001). In research undertaken by Nancy Hogan into adolescent sibling bereavement, bereaved young people were asked the to write about what helped or hindered their grieving. The research found: 'Their narratives revealed that spontaneously occurring, painful, intrusive, unwanted, uninvited thoughts, feelings, and images such as blame guilt, and shame related to traumatic circumstances surrounding their brother's or sister's death, made their grief more difficult' (2006: 6).

Studies of the death of a twin indicate that the grief may be even more intense than a child bereaved of a parent or a parent bereaved of a child (Bryan, 1995; Woodward, 2006). In her research into the experience of bereaved twins, psychotherapist Joan Woodward, founder of the Lone Twins network, carried out research into how a surviving twin is affected by the death of her twin. The clearest finding was that the loss of one's twin is a very profound, one which creates severe distress and had a marked effect on the remainder of their lives. When the death of a twin happens in childhood, the surviving twin may be overprotected leaving the child feeling oppressed, or the opposite may be experienced where the surviving twin is rejected by the parents.

Reflective Exercise

What follows is part of an article entitled: 'Mummy, why did God take Daddy to heaven? It's not fair is it?' ('Femail' in the *Mail on Sunday*, 4 May 2008, pages 44–45).

Barbara Want, the widow of BBC Radio 4 presenter Nick Clarke, described the reaction of her four-year-old twin boys, Benedict and Joel, to the death of their father, who died following extensive treatment for cancer. She said, 'When I told them their Daddy had died, they asked if they could watch television' (p. 44). At school one son became aggressive but regressed to babyish behaviour at home. Joel became more withdrawn and was highly anxious if he could not locate his mother in the house or if his teacher was out of sight. Barbara recognised that children jump in and out of grief. People suggested to her that her children had 'got over it', 'But,' she said, 'children never "get over" a loss of this magnitude. And that is why it matters that they get help and support in their grief, in the way that adults can and do' (p. 44).

Barbara Want highlights the difficulty facing the bereaved parent in trying to support their children immediately following death: 'After Nick died I treated my children abominably. I screamed at them and – I find this hard to admit – I hated them for being a burden as I sank deeper and deeper into incapacitating grief' (p. 44). Her son Joel, told his teacher, 'I'm scared that when I'm at school the angels will take Mummy too.'

A year and a half after Nick Clarke's death, Barbara said, 'The "work" continues. Children revisit their grief throughout their childhood, particularly at significant moments such the start of the New Year or a first football match where there is only one parent watching from the sidelines. It is "work" because it is hard and painful at times. But something that Benedict told me last week gave me hope that we are on the right track. He said, "Mummy, there are tears that are sad but there are also tears that mean you are happy, aren't there?" That has to be progress' (p. 45).

Your thoughts

- What differing grief responses do you see in Benedict and Joel?
- What is your response to the fact that the boys wanted to watch television when told of their father's death?
- Can you identify key events when children may re-visit their grief?
- Why was Joel anxious when he could not locate his mother or his teacher?
- Do you think children 'get over' grief?

Core Skills for Bereavement Counselling

'Time doesn't heal, grieving does.' Anon.

Not all bereaved children and young people need the support of outside agencies. Rosemary Wells, author of *Helping Children Cope with Grief* (1988), was widowed when her children were eleven, fourteen and seventeen. She did not believe that her children needed a bereavement counsellor, rather they needed 'love, security and a listening heart. To be there if they want to talk; to be honest; to show them you care' (Watts, 1988: 36). However, one in five children whose parent has died are likely to require specialist support (Dowdney, 2000). For these children and young people we have evidence-based research which demonstrates that we have strategies and skills to make successful interventions (Coyne and Ryan, 2007; Jordan and Neimeyer, 2003; Sandler et al., 2008). In general, counselling in schools is associated with large improvements in mental health (Cooper, 2009; Peel, 2009). It is important to remember that many children can be helped by professionals already known to them, for example, teachers and pastoral staff in their schools. The counsellor's task may be to help front-line staff who work face-to-face with children and young people and support them to assist bereaved children.

The aim of the counsellor is to offer independent psychological support to the child or young person and to ease some of the burdens they are carrying (Lendrum and Syme, 1992). However, adults who are not trained counsellors can offer significant aid by supportive listening and empathic care (Dyregrov and Dyregrov, 2008; Graves, 2008). Grieving is not a problem to be solved, but a process to be experienced. As people who wish to play a part in the process supporting distressed children and young people, we have to accept that while we can validate the young person's feelings we cannot stop his pain.

The Aims of Grief Counselling/Support

- To enable the bereaved to accept the loss.
- To provide support and safety.
- To help the bereaved to recognise the grief process and to reassure them that their feelings are 'normal'.

- To enable the bereaved to explore the loss and the feelings evoked.
- To help the bereaved live without the physical presence of the deceased.
- To help the bereaved identify positive strategies in coping.
- To help the bereaved access positive support from others in their lives.
- To help establish a continuing relationship with the person who has died where appropriate.

'Counsellors need to respond to each bereaved client in the light of their individual characteristics, and to be aware of not only the context of the current bereavement but also the unique development of the client's own attachment history, the pains they may have suffered and the defences they have had to build to protect themselves.' (Harris, 2009: 28)

Whenever we are working with a bereaved person it is important to be aware of their culture, ethnicity, belief systems and world-views (Wolfe, 2008). As Paul Rosenblatt wrote, 'Differences are present even in American culture. We should not assume that somebody who speaks our own language and comes from the same part of the world has the same beliefs and understandings and will express feelings in a familiar way. It pays to treat everyone as though he or she were from a different culture. To help effectively, we must overcome our presuppositions and struggle to understand people on their own terms' (quoted in Wolfe, 2008: 11).

In the Beginning: Core Counselling/ Support Skills

Any counselling service or organisation supporting children must work within child protection guidelines to ensure every child is safe. It is also important for the person supporting the child to feel safe and to take realistic safeguarding procedures for instance if home-visiting or working in isolation. When working with a child ensure that you have appropriate permissions from parents and others, and ensure that the child understands your role.

When working with a bereaved child find out what the child knows about the death. What has he been told and what does he understand? Has the information he has been given enabled him to understand what happened? What are his fears and feelings? It is important not to assume we know what the child is feeling and ask about the whole range of feelings not just about being sad or angry. In addition, try to discover what strengths are helping him now. Previous losses as well as concurrent losses, such as divorce, death, a sibling moving away and so on, all add to the impact of loss on the child. It is important to find out how previous and concurrent losses have been dealt with. How did the child respond to previous losses? Can you recognise resilient qualities in the child?

There are many factors which play a part in building trust and empathy. Below are a selection of core skills based on the work of American psychologist Carl Rogers, who developed Client Centred Therapy. These core skills adapt well in working with young people in a safe and supportive way. For students with special educational needs they are particularly valuable since they enable us to reflect the feelings of young people who may be distressed and confused about their life and their difference to others (Mallon 1987; Read, 1996).

Empathy

As someone who 'tunes in' to the world of the child, by developing the skill of empathy you show the child that his feelings and story are valued. Neuroscientists say this skill is developed through 'mirror neurons'; regardless of culture, race or class, facial expressions are universal: sadness, disgust, happiness fear and surprise show in faces all over the world (Ekman and Rosenberg, 2005). Mirror neurons were discovered by Iaccomo Rizzolati in 1995. Later research expanded by neuroscientist V.S. Ramachandran stated that the development of sophisticated mirror neuron systems in early man set the stage for the development of empathy and the ability to adopt another's point of view (Ramachandran, 2006). When we look at another person we grasp their intentions,

Empathy involves trying to see the world through the eyes of the young person you are supporting. From an adult perspective you may recognise that her anxieties are unfounded, however to the young person they are real. By being empathetic you will gain insight which will in turn help her through tough times.

Active listening

As we listen we help the child to explore and express grief by telling the story, to celebrate the life of the deceased, and to discover the legacy that remains and strategies for coping (Graves, 2008). Active listening involves your whole attention (see Box 3.1). It is about not just the words, but the music behind the words and involves listening to the tone of voice as well as observing body language. The Dyregrovs remind us that 'everything you do is communication' (2008: 11). How we respond to the bereaved, our body language, our presence or absence, our words or lack of them are all forms of communication whether we are friends or in a more professional role.

Box 3.1   Active Listening Guidelines

- Do keep an open mind.
- Do listen to *how* things are said.
- Do observe non-verbal communication.
- Do ensure that your verbal contributions are clear and relevant.
- Do ask for clarification if your haven't understood.
- Do be honest when feeding back feelings.
- Do be prepared to work hard at listening.

Some Pitfalls to Avoid

- Don't interrupt.
- Don't react emotionally to personal 'red flag' words.

- Don't think about what you are going to say next whilst the other person is talking.
- Don't make assumptions about what people are going to say.
- Don't finish people's sentences for them – you could be wrong.
- Don't prematurely evaluate the situation.

Positive, unconditional regard

Young people in distress need to feel that you care for them, warts and all. To show positive regard for him, you need to put aside your prejudices and preferences, and avoid being judgemental. Listen and don't condemn or show disapproval if their feelings are not ones that you would have expected. Young people, like adults, need the best possible support, especially when they feel out of their depth as many young people do following a bereavement.

Respect

Young people react with heightened sensitivity when they are upset or feel that they are different from their peers, for instance when they have been bereaved. They imagine injury in harmless remarks and feel undermined by minor criticism so sensitivity is of paramount importance. Be aware of the young person's personal attitude towards death and any cultural or religious beliefs she may have. Respect the importance of these. Disaffected young people have often been criticised and condemned for their differences and it is essential in building up rapport that we recognise any hurt that has been experienced.

Encourage the young person to ask for what he wants rather than leaving it to others to guess from his behaviour. It is helpful to make the hidden agenda visible, for example, to a young person who is repeatedly complaining of stomach ache, you might say, 'Some young people, when they've had a nasty shock like you've had, sometimes have stomach pains because they are upset. Are you feeling a bit upset now?' This reassures the young person that his feelings are being taken seriously. Respect for the young person helps maintain his feelings of self-worth.

Genuine acceptance

As a person supporting a young person you need to show by your balanced, compassionate attitude that you can accept the young person's feelings whatever they are. Students with special educational needs may feel rejected by the wider society and some of their peers. Differences may elicit bullying or turn an angry or distressed young person into a bully. We can accept the person and his difficulties without condoning aggressive and unkind behaviour.

As you work with the young person you may find yourself as the object of hostility as well as a source of support at the same time. The young person sees your help perhaps, as something that reveals his vulnerability and this can cause conflict as he wants people to see his 'I can cope' self. Working through this conflict is an essential part of the healing process.

Be truthful

Lying to young people causes all sorts of difficulties, not least because the young person may find it impossible to trust in future if they are let down by someone they believed and trusted. Don't promise what you can't deliver, for example saying 'Everything will be all right' when it may not be. Answer questions truthfully without overloading the young person with additional information.

Non-possessive support

Most children who have experienced some form of loss may go through a period of dependency. This need not be problematic, however you need to ensure that you do not encourage the young person to become solely dependent on you. Possessiveness discourages personal autonomy and will not help the young person in the longer term.

Helping the young person develop independence and self-confidence is a key factor in overcoming loss of any kind. If the young person feels positive about himself he can usually seek help from other trusted adults outside the home – grandparents, neighbours, teachers or friends – when he is distressed or when that customary support stops. Fear and self-blame may cause a young person's self-belief to be undermined so she will need affirmation to build and keep up self-esteem.

Reflection

By reflecting what you have heard back to the child or young person you show that you have really listened. This builds trust and shows that you value what they are saying. In a way it is like acting as a mirror, for example the young person says, 'I was so upset when they told me my brother John had died but I couldn't say anything. I think my Mum thought I didn't care.' You might reflect this by saying, 'So you were really upset when you found out John died but somehow you weren't able to show that. And, you thought that your Mum didn't realise you were upset and that you were not bothered about his death.' You may use the same words or slightly alter them but the point is to show that you are really attentive and attuned to the young person's words and emotions.

Confidentiality

One hundred per cent confidentiality cannot be guaranteed when working with children and young people and their families. Where there are signs of abuse, neglect or fear that the child may be harmed in some way, we need to involve Child Protection officers. Clearly, the counsellor, or bereavement support worker, needs to explain at the first meeting what the confidentiality contract will be, as dictated by the organisation in which they work. Moreover, ethical guidelines of the support workers professional body need to be taken into consideration (BACP, 2010).

Closing the counselling session

It is important to end the session sensitively and effectively. At the onset, ensure that the young person knows how long the session will be. About ten minutes before the end move towards terminating the session: 'We have ten minutes left before we finish, so it might be helpful to bring together what we have covered today.' You can ask the young person what he feels has been important or useful or you might summarise and point out what seemed significant to you. It may be helpful to point out what strengths or resilience you have noticed which can reinforce feelings of self-esteem.

Brian Cranwell explored bereaved children's responses to counsellors. One girl explained how counselling helped her: 'All these little worries you have that you want to say to mum, that I'm keeping in a bottle. I just kind of undid the screw and they all came out, and it's quite nice actually' (2007: 32).

Gender Differences

Gender differences in grieving have been identified in grieving adults (Attig, 1996; Filak and Abel, 2004; McLaren, 2004; Stroebe et al., 2007). Less research has been done with children and young people. Research by Dr Shelly Taylor (2004) indicates a physiological basis for these differences. She found the 'fight or flight' response to stress was largely true for men whereas, women 'tend and befriend'. She argues that hormones influence each sex differently. In responses to the hormone 'oxytocin', nicknamed the 'cuddle' hormone, women when stressed move to nurture those around them (tend) and move towards people with whom they will feel safe (befriend). In men, testosterone limits the effect of oxytocin. These reactions may well be reflected in the grieving responses of boys and girls.

Men and women, boys and girls, may use different coping patterns. Females may adopt an 'intuitive' response to grief, while males have an 'instrumental' response (Martin, 2000). The former relates to the way grief is expressed in an affective way, while 'instrumental' responses are experienced in a more physical way, in restlessness and physical and mental activity. There are many ways of responding to grief which are influenced by family, culture and society (Biddulph, 1997; Brewer and Sparkes, 2008). Gender differences in responses are marked, and traditional talking cures that are better attuned to girls' needs must be supplemented by treatment options for boys that combine activities (doing things together) with talking' (Dyregrov, 2004: 81). Julie Stokes, founder and clinical director of Winston's Wish, has found that interventions with 'hard to reach' boys which included an outward bound weekend – adventurous and physically challenging – were important in engaging the young people and in building a resilient mindset (Brewer and Sparkes, 2008; Stokes, 2009b).

The Child Bereavement study found that children who lost a parent of the same gender were more likely to stay connected to that parent and '[t]he most attached children were those who lost mothers rather than fathers, and were more likely to be girls than boys' (Worden, 1996: 31). Perhaps it is no surprise that adolescent boys were least likely to stay attached as they are in a process of transition and in a cultural milieu which would expect them to 'move on' in their grief. In a longitudinal study, 1987–1993, Nadine and colleagues found that a father's death leads to more negative affects on sons and a mother's death leads to more negative affects on daughters. Parental loss is also reflected in men's health more negatively than women's health (Melhem et al., 2007). The importance of male role models for boys has been well documented (Biddulph, 1997; Neal, 2007) and the death of a father has a significant impact on the identity formation of young men. A study by Dowdney found that parentally bereaved children show high levels of psychological disturbance, with boys being more vulnerable than girls (Dowdney et al., 1999).

Bereavement Support Groups

Bereavement support groups are an appropriate and effective way to help bereaved people (Corr, 1996; Klass, 2000; McCarthy with Jessop, 2005; Wolfelt, 1994). They offer the bereaved child a sense of understanding, acceptance and support. Bereavement support groups are especially helpful in combating feelings of isolation and enhancing self-esteem. They provide a safe place to explore their bereavement and to share their experiences with others who have been bereaved (Hindmarch, 2000; Ross and Hayes, 2004). Therapeutic support groups can be very effective in minimising complicated grief reactions, easing feelings of grief and enhancing resilience (Pfeffer et al., 2002; Schut et al., 2001). In addition, where it is an open group, the bereaved young person values a service that offers a 'revolving door' where they can re-visit the group as need arises (Firth, 2005).

The Foulke's model (1984) of helping each other is useful in group work. In it the leaders try to create a safe space, with clear boundaries and a contract so that all members know what the group work is about and the expectations that all participants share. This is important for the facilitators too as the dynamics between the facilitators will influence the atmosphere and function in the group. Working one-to-one with a bereaved child is quite different to working with a group where the dynamics of all involved play a part in the therapeutic process (Stokes, 2004). In such group work it is important to recognise the importance of endings in all sessions not only at the end of the whole course (Gilbert, 2008).

There is evidence that adolescents prefer working on grief issues in a group setting rather than a one-to-one setting (Mearns, 2000). Where parents are unable to manage their loss effectively, support groups may provide an alternative family (Zambelli and De Rosa, 1992). They can obtain information or clarify thinking about what they have experienced, meet others and gain support from their peers. Support groups give the bereaved the opportunity to express their emotions and to have their experience validated in a non-judgemental setting (McKissock, 2004). Peer relationships may flourish as the participants explore their shared experience of bereavement and as they realise they are not alone or isolated in their grief (Bacon, 1996).

It is imperative that there is sufficient time to adequately pre-plan any group work you do with children and young people (Murthy and Smith, 2009). There are key issues you need to address and these are listed below to help you:

- Who is the target population of the group?
- What are the criteria for participation in the group?
- What age groups will you include?
- Will the group meet the differing cultural and religious needs of the participants?

All children and families need to have preliminary meetings to explain what the group is about and to assess suitability for inclusion. Not all children will gain from being in a bereavement support group especially if their experience has been traumatic and is very different from the other participants, for example, if the bereavement is through death by suicide. In selecting members, sensitivity to cultural diversity and norms are important in order that each member feels comfortable and accepted. Activities within the group also need to reflect different cultural or religious values. Clearly the child's emotional maturity level has to be taken into account Developmental needs and emotional needs vary widely so these need to be taken into account when deciding if a child is suitable to join the group. The main carer of the child or young person should also be involved so that they understand what the group is for and can support the child between sessions (Ross and Hayes, 2004).

Identify a safe, discreet place where the group can meet. This should be a private space where there will not be interrupted. A cosy, warm atmosphere is helpful in setting the scene so that children and young people feel welcomed.

All adult members supporting the children in the group must have a current criminal record check to ensure they are safe to work with children and young people. It is important to have at least two adult facilitators in the group. This way, activities can be shared and if a child becomes particularly upset the person who is not leading at that time can offer one-to-one support. In addition, all group leaders and volunteers should have ongoing support, de-briefing and the opportunity to reflect on the group process and the role within the group.

Open group

New members may come at any time. It means that introductions will be made often but if it is an ongoing group with no specific time limits it allows members to continue to be present for as long as they need the support of the group.

Closed time-limited group

Once the young people have agreed to the group they continue with the same members until the end of the group. This may be decided by the group facilitators, for example, eight weekly, two-hour sessions. New members are not allowed to join once the group has started. This allows members to build up trust and knowledge of other participants and allows for strong bonds to be made. Young people may feel more comfortable knowing that there is a fixed ending point.

First meeting

The first meeting should include:

- Greetings and ice breaker exercise to help the group feel at ease.
- Explanation to reinforce the purpose of the group.
- Setting the ground rules.

Basic rules involve confidentiality, listening as each person speaks, respecting people's feelings and inviting the participants to choose ground rules they see as important.

In a programme devised by St Helena Hospice, at the first meeting each member is invited to make a photo frame for a photo of the loved person who has died. This provides an enjoyable activity using paints, glitter, beads and various art materials and at the end the photo of the deceased is placed in the frame using blue tack. This activity gives a focus to the group and helps the child or young person speak about their lost loved ones. At each subsequent meeting, the photos are placed on the wall and taken home at the end of each meeting.

Group activities can be designed to recognise strengths. Participants could produce a visual poster with a head with big ears for being a good listener; a huge heart for giving and receiving love; and a helping hand to hold on to in times of feeling alone. The group can share ideas about what helps them in their mourning. Such positive sharing allows the members to support each other and develop their skills of empathy.

As well as looking at emotions such as sadness and fear, children in groups can also look at the positive emotions that sustain them (American School Counsellor Association, 2005). The young person could look at what has helped them deal with their grief. Who in their family they can talk to? What happy times can they remember prior to the bereavement and since the bereavement?

Family interventions, where the counsellor, listener or befriender interacts with all the family, or those willing to participate, can provide extended support for bereaved children and young people. As each member tells their story, from their perspective the other members can understand how the death has affected each person in a unique way. This leads to increased understanding of how each person grieves and what each person needs to help them through the difficult times (Hooyman and Kramer, 2006). It is important that we understand how the family makes meaning of the death because this will influence they way in which they grieve, and that we are aware of any cultural influences which are significant to the family (Nadeau, 2001). Family therapists have adapted Worden's tasks of mourning into four goals: these are '(1) Share acknowledgements about the loss, (2) share the experience of loss and put it into context, (3) reorganize the family system and (4) reinvest in other relationships and life pursuits' (Hooyman and Kramer, 2006: 220–1). Family interventions may be particularly helpful where there are young children and adolescents (Black and Urbanovicz, 1987; Carr, 2000).

Group Activities

When working with groups it is important to create a safe, contained space for children to speak. It is also essential that no child feels pressurised to speak when they do not want to. Lynne Ami DeSpelder (DeSpelder, 2009) instructs the children who take part in her bereavement groups to use the technique of 'I pass'. Any student who does not want to share an experience says 'I pass' and their privacy is respected. She also has a very helpful opening activity. Each person is given a card. On one side is written, 'What brings you here?' and on the reverse is the question, 'What would you like to take away from this course when it is over?' These cards bring out similarities and differences. They also show the composition of the group in terms of experience, curiosity and personal needs.

It is useful to have some activities to fall back on if the group is silent and finds it difficult to talk. Many of these are given in Chapter 6 which discusses creative strategies; however, some of these below may help:

- Write or draw spontaneously on large sheets of paper pinned to the wall or plain wallpaper lining rolled out on a hard surface. Draw anything that comes to mind, no rights or wrongs. Or draw anything that expresses feeling you've had since the death of your loved one.
- Create a collage using images from magazines.
- Make a joint book of memories.
- Release helium balloons with messages attached (using biodegradable balloons and a short thread/string for environmental reasons).

Helen Fitzgerald (2000) advocates a starter with 'My Story' which group members complete. What follows is an adaptation from her original version:

My Story

The person who died in my life was …

The cause of death was …

I first found out about the death when …

People who were with me at the time were …

At first I felt …

Now, I feel …

I felt angry because …

Now, I worry about …

My friends are …

The adults in my life …

What helps me is …

What doesn't help me is …

After death, I believe my loved one …

Since the death I am more …

What I hope this group will do is …

Self-awareness and the Impact of Grief Counselling on the Support Worker

It is vital that you are aware of your own feelings about loss and death in general. Your attitude, behaviour and comfort level are just as important as any words you use, perhaps even more so. Acknowledge and allow the child or young person to feel their pain, you will not help by trying to rush them through it or 'fix it'.

It has been suggested that working with child bereavement can cause adults to react more strongly because it touches their own vulnerabilities (Hogwood, 2007). It is, therefore, vitally important that counsellors and volunteers consider what mechanisms are in place to maximise self-care and what support networks are readily available and ongoing.

Supporting bereaved children and young people is demanding as well as rewarding so it is important that you take care of your own physical and emotional well-being. Your personal resilience is enhanced by factors noted by Valerie Maasdorp, hospice manager in Zimbabwe. In the face of working with adversity, she advocates, 'Being well-trained for one's work; having a well-balanced personal life; maintaining a high degree of optimism; the ability to think creatively and being able to "stay with the pain" and not withdraw'(Schuurman, 2008: 9).

Supervision is essential for the bereavement counsellor (Shohet, 2008). In addition to taking care of yourself, to ensure you do not experience compassion 'burn out', supervision enables those you work with to be more secure. A supervisor will help you analyse your responses, guide you through complicated and demanding case-work and give you the opportunity to reflect on your practice (Henderson, 2009).

Reflective Exercise 1

- How does your experience of loss affect your feelings about working with bereaved children?
- What do you fear most when working with a child or young person who has been bereaved?
- What strengths do you bring to helping bereaved children and young people?
- Can you access support should you need it? Who is available to offer you support?
- Who would you refer a child to if she or he needed more specialist help?
- Can you identify any personal development or training needs?

Reflective Exercise 2

Ben was sixteen when his father died:

> 'My first thought was, "I can get a tattoo now". He was really strict and would never agree to me having one. Now, I felt I could be like my mates, but then I felt awful! Imagine thinking about a tattoo when your Dad's just died. I did feel really sorry for my Mum. She'd lost the man she loved and she was in bits. She couldn't stop crying. I tried to do the stuff he did at home and helped out. I never cried, not even at the funeral but I still feel bad about how I reacted.'

- How might Ben's reaction to his father's death be influenced by his gender?
- How did you feel when you read of Ben's initial responses to his father's death?
- What factors might impact on a person of this age when a parent dies?
- Can you recall any loss you had at this age, not necessarily bereavement? What was your response? Does it still have an impact on how you live your life?

4

Understanding Death: Mental Health Issues in Vulnerable Children – AHHD, Autism and Children with Special Educational Needs

'They put me in care because my Mum's new husband didn't like me. I thought I was going mad in there and started to cut myself, especially after my friend died. I wasn't there to see it happen but I kept thinking about him all the time. I just wish I could wind the clock back to when I was little and my granddad was still here.' K., aged fourteen.

Children and young people with learning disabilities, children who are in the care of the local authority because of family breakdown, children who are in secure accommodation because of criminal activity and young people who have physical or mental health conditions that set them apart from the wider society, are still faced with loss and bereavement. Sadly, these groups have often have been disenfranchised and excluded from taking part in events surrounding dying and death (Read, 2003). It is imperative that their needs are recognised and that they are included in these family and social rituals (Mitchels, 2009; McDougall, 2008; Stokes, 2009a; Oswin, 1991).

Mental health is of vital importance in child development. The NHS Advisory Service (2002) defined healthy mental health as, 'The ability to develop psychologically, emotionally, intellectually and spiritually. The ability to initiate, develop and sustain mutually satisfying personal relationships. The ability to become aware of others and empathise with them. The ability to use psychological distress as a developmental process. So that it does not hinder or impair further development.' Bereavement can adversely affect healthy mental health.

Between 50% and 66% of children and young people who are bereaved of a parent show distress and symptoms of depression which may persist over time (Ribbens McCarthy, 2006). One study found that the range of mental health difficulties were more prevalent among those who were bereaved a parent or sibling than those who had not (Green et al., 2005). The Common Assessment Framework for Children and Young People (DfES, 2005b), the standardised approach to assessing children's needs across all services, provides guidance following bereavement. It advises that where significant changes have been observed in a child or young person who has been bereaved it may be appropriate to initiate a common assessment. Such a process may be particularly helpful for those vulnerable children and young people who may be at greater risk of impairment following a bereavement.

Safeguarding Vulnerable Children

We all have a responsibility to safeguard vulnerable children. Children with developmental delays or disabilities have limitations due to insufficient development of their intellectual, physical or emotional capacities. Such disabilities may include physical disorders such as cerebral palsy, limited vision as well as language and speech disorders, reduced mental capacity and developmental disorders such as autism (Gurian et al., 2009). Children who have such disabilities need increased support when faced with traumatic events. 'The rates of identified mental health problems in children with special educational needs are higher than the general population' (Meltzer et al., 2003) reported by Everatt and Gale, and it is reasonable to conclude that they will be more vulnerable to the impact of bereavement than those young people without special educational needs. Valuing People (Department of Health, 2001), the national learning disability strategy, recognises the needs of this group and emphasises the importance of social inclusion, civil rights, choice and independence. The report explicitly states that children and young people with a disability are entitled to the same support that other children are offered.

A child with hearing impairment may not pick up cues and a child with visual impairment may not be able to read facial expressions. When giving information the individual disability has to be taken into account and support offered in an appropriate way. Warning signs of distress may not be verbalised which may be part of the reason for the erroneous view that children with disabilities did not feel grief (Hollins and Esrehuyzen, 1997). Their grief can be observed in facial expressions, nervous tics, sweating, feeling sick, changes in language patterns, acting-out behaviour and withdrawal. Research indicates that people with learning difficulties experience bereavement in the same way as the general population (Oswin, 1991; Summers and Witts, 2003). A study by Hollins and Esterhuyzen (1997) found that the loss of a parent in the previous two years led to higher rates of irritability, lethargy, inappropriate speech and hyperactivity as compared to a control group.

Children and young people with learning disabilities are often reliant on others to facilitate the grieving process (Read, 2003). The locus of control for children with learning disabilities is usually external, largely, they rely on others to anticipate and meet their needs. Parents and care-takers may, by being overprotective, prevent them from playing their role in the rituals following death and so disempower the young person. Marginalised groups often experience disenfranchised grief and disenfranchised death (Todd and Read, 2009). Disenfranchised grief happens where the loss cannot be openly acknowledged, publicly mourned or expressed in the social setting of the bereaved (Doka, 2002; Mallon, 2008). In this situation the bereaved may not be socially sanctioned or recognised as having the 'right' to grieve because of their learning difficulties or disability (Walter, 1999).

Those who have communication difficulties may need creative resources to explain about death. The use of photographs and life story work can place the death in the context of the family (Jackson and Jackson, 1999). A 'Life Story' book can explore the past, acknowledge what is happening in the here and now and make plans for the future. Photographs can also help the bereaved child to retain the memory of the deceased in a concrete way. 'Feeling Faces', laminated faces that express feelings of happiness, sadness, anger and confusion can be used with children who have impaired language. These can help them communicate their feelings (Towers, 2008).

There has been discussion in the past about the benefits of counselling for people with learning difficulties (Dodd and Guerin, 2009). However, the essential aim of working with children and young people is to help them understand what death means, what has happened and how this effects those who were part of the life of the one who died. It may be more helpful to offer counselling and support to bereaved adults who are caring for the child or young person and to help them develop care giving skills.

When the parent or carer of a child with intellectual disabilities dies, it is not only the loss of a loved one that the child has to deal with, he also loses the person who is most familiar with his special needs, his likes and dislikes and the person with whom, they have the most trusting relationship. Forewarning children what to expect where death is anticipated, for instance where a parent has an advanced terminal illness, can help prepare them for the bereavement (Black, 1996). Dora Black also recommends 'the importance of a child becoming attached to whomever is going to be their major caretaker when their parent dies' and that this may make the death of a parent less traumatic (Everatt and Gale, 2004: 32). Obviously, this must be done with great sensitivity and with the agreement of the dying parent, since otherwise, it could damage the parent–child bond at a critical point.

Children and young people with intellectual disabilities may be excluded from the rituals and rites that happen after death, such as viewing the body, attending the funeral and visiting the grave. This is sometimes described as 'benevolent exclusion' (Downey, 2002). Those seeking to protect the intellectually disabled person from the pain of bereavement in effect isolate them in their grief. Such 'disenfranchised grief '(Doka, 1989) prevents those with special needs the opportunity to express their grief and leads to feelings of isolation. This can also prolong the mourning process (Bonell-Pascual et al., 1999). However, research shows that people with intellectual disabilities react to loss and bereavement in much the same way as the rest of the population (Dowling, 2002; Hollins and Esterhuyzen, 1997; Oswin, 1981).Using counselling skills in a flexible and creative way that reflects the individual needs and capabilities of the person with intellectual disabilities, can make a significant difference in the grieving process.

Attending the funeral is an important part of recognising the finality of death. For a child or young person with disabilities, it helps 'place' the person and 'can reduce repetitive questions about where the dead person is, and also the frequency and intensity of 'difficult behaviour' (Bonnell-Pascual et al., 1999; Everratt and Gale, 2004: 34; Sheldon, 1998). Reports from funeral directors indicate that people with learning disabilities are frequently excluded from any discussions about the funeral either by relatives or funeral directors themselves (Raji et al., 2003). Religious and cultural factors also influence whether children with disabilities are included in funeral rites, in a number of instances, death is expected to be met with composure, with no outbursts of emotion. A belief that those with disabilities may not act in a socially acceptable manner may lead to exclusion so they are discouraged from taking part in the funeral (Raji et al., 2003).

Offering Support to Children and Young People with Learning Disabilities

When offering support, as with any grieving child or young person, it is important to take into account the child's cognitive and developmental level (Blackman, 2003). Language needs to be concrete and consistent so that all involved in supporting the child with learning disabilities use the word 'dead' rather than confusing euphemisms. Try to respond to the child's needs, be led by them and respect the fact that they may not want to talk or communicate with you at that time. Try to give the child choices in activities while still maintaining the security of safe routines and clear boundaries (Hand-in-Hand, 2007). If you need extra support or information you can contact your local Social and Health Care Disability Team.

Creative approaches in exploring death and bereavement have been found to be effective in helping young people deal with loss (Read, 1999). Painting, drawing, making music and colouring in picture books, such as *When Someone Very Special Dies* by Heegard (1991), can give the opportunity to express feeling and release tension (Barber, 1999). Children with learning disabilities may feel more comfortable sitting next to the support worker rather than opposite (Hand-in-Hand, 2007).

As some children find it hard to identify with pictures in books about bereavement it is helpful to make up their own life story book using photographs and drawings. This personalised account will be easier for them to grasp rather than becoming stuck because they cannot identify with the boy with blonde hair when they have dark hair. Sue Read states, '[L]ife stories can be a powerful way of identifying with an individual and can be cathartic in bringing back memories, good and bad, of issues and people that could be forgotten. They can also be a concrete record of work undertaken to review at appropriate times through the process of bereavement support' (Read, 1999:12). This can also be done as a 'story board', pictorially demonstrating the process prior to the death of the person and subsequent events; this will help the young person express their feelings and tell their story.

Autistic Spectrum Disorder (ASD)

A child or young person with autism needs clarity and preparation for loss, including illness and bereavement, especially if a significant carer or family member becomes ill and may die. As with other children, they will understand and adjust better if they are involved and prepared as much as possible which enables them to cope more effectively with a major bereavement (Allison, 2001). It is the unexplained and unknown that frightens young people with ASD so wherever possible they need to be prepared for changes. It may be helpful to make a timeline or calendar that plots any hospital appointments or treatments that a significant person with an illness has. This could also include any changes that might occur, such as a different person picking them up from school or staying overnight with someone else. To help the child deal with changes it is helpful to tell him what will stay the same, giving areas of stability to reassure and reduce anxiety (NAS, 2003).

Explaining death as part of the life cycle, using visual material that explains the life cycles of plants or insects, can help the child with autism understand the concept of death. They need to know why a person looks different, for example, if they are losing weight because of an illness, as the unknown and unexplained changes cause anxiety. Such anxiety may produce challenging behaviour (NAS, 2003). There is a series, 'Books Beyond Words' which explain burial, cremation and bereavement to people with intellectual disabilities. These are illustrated but have no text and could be used with children and young people with autism or with other learning difficulties.

Differences in behaviour following death may indicate grief reactions though these may not be recognised by those who care for the child or young person with ASD

(Howlin, 1997). Sometimes, children may become obsessed with death. Obsessions are quite common with children with ASD and the Autism Helpline has an information sheet, 'Obsessions, Rituals and Routines' which offers strategies to help.

Looked After Children

Around one in twenty-five school-age children and young people in the general population have experienced a bereavement through the death of a parent or sibling; in the population of looked after children, this figure is much higher (Ribbens McCarthy, 2006). Many children in the care of the local authority come from backgrounds where there has been abuse, neglect and cumulative loss, including death of parents (DfES 2007). A Report from Social Services Inspectorate *When Leaving Home is also Leaving Care* (1997) found a dismal picture. More that 75% of care leavers have no academic qualifications; more than 50% of young people leaving care after the age of 16 have no employment; 17% of young women leaving care are pregnant or already have a child, 38% of young prisoners have been in care and 30% of young people who are homeless have been in care. There has not been a significant change in these percentages in the intervening years.

Children and young people in the care of the local authority may have experienced many losses, including being separated from their birth family (Penny, 2007). Many children who are in the care of the local authority have experienced insecure attachments. Some children are taken into the care of the local authority because of the death of a parent. They may be placed in care voluntarily under Section 20 of the Children Act, where parents retain parental authority or are the subject of a Care Order, where parental authority is shared with the local authority. One study found that 30% of looked after children under five had been bereaved of a close relative (Cousins et al., 2003). Children and young people in care may see themselves as unlovable and set for failure and this sense of aloneness and fear is often expressed in their narratives and play (Cattanach, 2007).

> I entered the madhouse called care as an escape from bad parents, but in the home I was introduced to glue-sniffing, burglary and flick-knives. I also gained instant respect as a hardcase among my peers at school – all the tough kids were supposed to come from care. (Benjamin Perks, 'Home where the Heart Aches', *The Guardian*, 11 July,1990)

Bereaved Young People and Crime

Young people who have experienced cumulative loss are more likely to become involved in anti-social and criminal behaviour. Youth offending teams were set up in 2000 with the aim of preventing and reducing offending by children and young people. A study of youth offending in the North West of England shows that 'feelings of loss and rejection have a larger than expected influence on the lives of clients' (Kerr, 2004: 44). The case files of 1027 children and young people were studied and the results show what an impact loss has: 68% had experienced family disruption which resulted in permanent loss of contact with one parent; 42% had experienced rejection by parents or carers; 18% had experienced homes that were impermanent; 13% had experienced bereavement; and 7%

had experienced loss because a parent or carer had become disabled and could no longer care adequately for their child. In all, 92% of children and young people had experience of one or more of these situations. In considering the records, no evidence of bereavement counselling for any of these young people had been offered.

Bereavement is one of the five most common health problems encountered by a youth offending team (Youth Justice Trust, 2001). Fifty-seven per cent of Section 53 offenders, those who commit the gravest crimes such as murder, in one study, had experienced a significant bereavement or lost contact with a significant figure (Boswell, 1995; Higgins, 2001).

Children in Secure Accommodation

Every year 8000 children go through custodial settings (Lewis and Heer, 2008). Children in custody are a vulnerable group (McDougall, 2008). A study which explored the impact of bereavement among young offenders found that 'those with a history of loss and bereavement in childhood or adolescence were particularly emotionally vulnerable' (Vaswani 2008: 2). In a review of the use of secure accommodation in Northern Ireland, the authors found that the offenders 'have extensive experience of bereavement, many have difficult relationships with their families, as well as high levels of special educational needs or disabling conditions, including emotional and mental health problems (Sinclair and Geraghty, 2002: 4).

Young people in custody suffer intimidation and bullying and there are extensive examples self-harm, high rates of suicide and mental health disorders, including raised levels of anxiety (Lambert, 2005). In addition, between 20% and 30% of young people in custody have learning disabilities and difficulties (Talbot, 2008). Because of these difficulties they may be excluded from certain activities and support and may not benefit from courses offered to reduce the rate of re-offending because of their inability to read or write. They may also find it difficult to stay in touch with family and friends because of communication difficulties, such as completing the visiting order forms. 'I had my visiting form sent back because I didn't know their last name. I had to wait six weeks for the officer to phone and find out their last name. Nobody knows everyone's last name, especially if they can't read' (Member of Working for Justice Group, cited in Talbot 2008: 14).

Staff who work in secure accommodation are likely to come across many bereaved young people in their work. They may have a legacy of bereavement in their history or may be bereaved whilst they are in the custodial setting. A study in 2008 by (Vaswani) found that those young people who were persistent offenders were six times more likely to have been bereaved of a parent than the general population. Others, not included in this figure, had experienced the death of a friend or relative in traumatic circumstances including suicide, drug overdose and murder (Penny, 2009a: 3). The lack of support for young people following bereavement may cause some to turn to drugs and become involved in criminal activity, particularly where there are other factors of deprivation in their lives (Finlay and Jones, 2000).

In addition to bereavement issues, young people are anxious about being away from home and feel guilty about the person who has died and worry about surviving family members. In some cases they will not be allowed to attend the funeral or may be escorted by prison officers in handcuffs. They may not have the opportunity to say 'Goodbye' or share in family rites and rituals. Alison Penny of the Child Bereavement Network in her research with young people and staff in secure accommodation identified a number of factors that might help someone who has been bereaved while in custody (2009a: 4). These include, making something to put in the coffin, writing something to be read at the funeral or grave side, listening to the person's favourite music, keeping a momento, and to have a service or prayers in the chapel in the secure setting at the same time as the funeral. This way young offenders will not feel so isolated in their grief. The CBN 'Healthier Inside' programme delineates strategies that can be used by staff (2008).

Some young people who are in secure accommodation may have belonged to a gang. Tom Sackville wrote of Jon, whose father was a member of a gang and who expected his son to do the same. Now 18, Jon has experienced eleven deaths and four attempts on his life by rival gangs. The power of the gangs and the trauma experienced by belonging is all-pervading. As Jon says, 'The only way you can leave a gang is in a coffin … I realised if I didn't do something, my son would become part of the gang too and it would never stop.' He took part in a project to help him break free of gang culture (Sackville, 2008: 14). For many young people in secure settings their experience of bereavement and fear of future losses may cause severe emotional distress.

In 2009, the National Children's Bureau's 'Healthier Inside' programme provided a 'Toolkit' to help deliver the government's 'Every Child Matters' policy in secure settings (Lewis and Heer, 2008). It consolidates key elements to help staff deliver health and well-being entitlements for young people as well as the needs of staff working with young people in custody (Fitzpatrick 2006; National Children's Bureau, 2008).

Referring Children on to Specialist Care

There are some children and young people who do not manage to grieve in a way which sustains them, rather they become 'stuck', trapped in chronic sorrow or unable to re-invest in life without the dead person. Some indicators that the child needs professional help may be seen in:

- Prolonged depression.
- Inability to relax.
- Decreased interest in their personal appearance; self-neglect.
- Deterioration in physical health.
- Inability to enjoy activities which gave pleasure prior to the bereavement.
- Changes in sleep pattern.
- Behavioural problems and difficulty in concentration at school.
- Listlessness.
- Feelings of worthlessness.

Specialist help may be accessed through the child's GP and the local CAMS (Child and Adolescent Mental Health Services). The specialist support could involve psychotherapeutic work on a one-to-one basis or in a group, play therapy, family therapy or specific bereavement counselling through organisations such as Cruse or Winston's Wish. When you need to refer a child, the organisation will usually undertake some form of assessment to ascertain what the child or young person needs (Machin, 2009; Webb, 2002). All of us who work with children and young people have a duty of care towards them and if you feel out of your depth in working with a child it is vital that you refer on to more specialist agencies.

In conclusion, working with vulnerable groups includes the use of all core support skills and great sensitivity to appreciate the myriad losses which have been experienced throughout their lives.

Reflexive Exercise 1

In 1980 Ben Gunn was 14 when he killed a friend. On the way home from school they had an argument. Ben attacked his friend and fatally wounded him. Ben phoned the police and waited until they arrived and he confessed immediately. Both boys were looked after children and had had difficult childhoods. Ben had gone into care at the age of 11, two years after his mother died. He began running away from home and his father had him taken into care. After the shock of the crime and arrest wore off, in a matter of days, he was appalled by what he had done, Today he still has visual flash backs to the events and more recently, the flashbacks have become auditory – 'a perpetual replay of all the sounds' (Allison, 2009: 2).

- What aspects of loss can you identify in Ben's early life?
- How might being placed in care have affected him?
- In what ways has the death of his friend affected him?
- What are some of the difficulties young people in secure accommodation face?

Reflective Exercise 2

Vulnerable children and young people may be excluded from taking part in mourning practices following bereavement and thus their grief is disenfranchised.

- Why might vulnerable young people be excluded from events such as attending the funeral?
- What steps could be taken to help them take part?
- Have you had experience of being marginalised following a loss or bereavement? If not, can you think of another person who has?
- What impact did it have on you or the other person?

5

The Role of the School: A Whole School Approach to Bereavement and Loss

'I was so tired when I first knew. I was scared to do anything at first – going out, going back to school. When I went back, they asked me how he died. At first I didn't tell them, then when I got used to it, I told them.' H., aged ten. Her father died by suicide.

The Role of the School

The British government recognises that bereavement impacts on children in most aspects of their life. The PSHE and citizen framework and Healthy Schools initiative includes health-related matters including bereavement (Child Bereavement Network, 2004: 55), SEAL (Social and Emotional Aspects of Learning) and PSHE (Personal Social and Health Education) programmes also link to education around grief and bereavement (Penny, 2009b). As set out in the Department for Education and Skills (2005a) Common Core of Skills and Knowledge for the Children's Workforce under 'Supporting Transitions', anyone working closely with children needs to know how to support children where there is family illness or bereavement and to know about local resources where they can obtain further help for the child. The training of the whole school staff in issues concerning childhood bereavement is of vital importance. In order to help all children deal with bereavement and loss it needs to be embedded in the broader scheme of developing emotional literacy throughout the child's school career (McCaffrey, 2004).

Front-line teaching and support staff can help students acknowledge their loss by giving them permission to express their emotions. It is useful to bear in mind the words of Elisabeth Kubler-Ross, 'There are thousands of children who know death far beyond the knowledge adults have … those little children [are] the wisest of teachers' (quoted in Rogers, 2007: 31). Children and young people do have a depth of wisdom that can help staff respond appropriately; what we need to do is give them the opportunity to be listened to.

School staff can provide care, continuity and compassion in the security of a place that the young person knows well. Bereavement is a natural part of life: it is not a medical condition, it is not a pathology, it is not a mental illness and it needs to be acknowledged by the school staff (Servaty-Seib et al., 2003). It is important that staff support bereaved students whilst still treating them normally so that they are not treated differently to their peers. Schools in which there are students who are asylum-seekers or refugees will also have cumulative losses as well as experience of bereavement (Price and Iszatt, 1996; Rutter, 2003).

> 'At school there is a welfare officer who is kind. She says that I can come and talk to her if I want to. I don't want to. But it's good that she says it.'
> Armin, aged thirteen. (Sjoqvist, 2007: 61)

Shipman et al. (2001) found less than 10% of schools had a bereavement policy which might be one reason school staff feel uncomfortable or uncertain when dealing with bereavement and loss. More than half of teachers said they felt inadequate in handling bereavement issues (Shipman et al., 2001). Teachers, and other staff who work in the front line, in direct face-to-face contact with children may be very uncomfortable with discussing bereavement with children (Lowton, 2002), which is why training in the area of grief and bereavement is so crucial (Hare et al., 1986). School staff are role models for students (Dogra et al., 2002), therefore it is important that staff are emotionally available to students. Educators are in a position to provide a safe environment where children and young people can explore the concepts of death and bereavement. They can make a significant difference to the child's sense of security as they experience the turbulence of emotions surrounding grief (Shipman et al., 2001).

When a child or young person has been bereaved, school may the one constant in their lives (Lowton, 2002). The same peer group awaits them, the same staff as well as the familiar routines. In a study of young people who experienced bereavement whilst at school, all commented on the fact that friendships changed and that '[b]ereavement was a "label" worn with reluctance' (Abdelnoor and Hollins, 2004b: 88). For many students school is a safe haven where they can choose to talk or not to talk. However, they may worry about returning to school because they wonder what the reactions of others will be. It is helpful to contact the bereaved family and the student to ask what preparations they would like prior to the young person's return.

The grieving child may need to contact a remaining parent in order to reassure herself that he or she is still safe so allowing phone calls home or text messages can be helpful. Some children express their distress by refusing to attend school; they become school phobic. This often indicates feelings of anxiety or depression. Separation anxiety may be misinterpreted as school phobia. The young person enjoy school but cannot bear to leave his home in case another member of his family dies. This is often an unconscious process but it is useful to understand that it may be a motivating factor in the child's refusal to come to school. A child who experiences the death of a parent is likely to be disorganised for a considerable period of time. Teachers often underestimate the length of time grieving takes; it usually lasts well beyond the first anniversary of the death.

> As the family may be unavailable to facilitate the child's grief process due to its own grief, the bereaved child often expresses his or her sense of loss at school. (Eppler, 2008: 191)

How many children and young people are affected by bereavement?

In research published in 2001, Shipman et al. found that 79% of schools have children on roll who have been bereaved within the previous two years. Another study found that

63% of a group of 15–16 year-olds outside mainstream schooling had been bereaved by someone close to them (Cooper, 2002). In the USA, research by Kathryn Markell found that '30% of college students had been bereaved in the previous twelve months and 39% in the previous two years' (Markell, 2008: 12). Such losses impact on student academic performance and willingness to engage in study. The closer the relationship between the deceased and the bereaved, the greater the student distress.

Those children living in lower socio-economic groups are more likely to experience bereavement as mortality rates are greater for this group and falling more slowly than in other groups (Acheson, 1998). We also know that income usually falls after the death of a parent (ONS, 2002). Families living in tied accommodation, such as military service personnel, are at risk of secondary losses following the death of a parent, since they must leave their homes and relocate. This has a domino effect in that the bereaved child or young person may have to move school, leave friends behind, lose connection to their known community and start all over again in a new location. In these transitions, teachers have an important role to play.

Claire was 15 when her sister aged 18, died by suicide: 'As for school and exams, it all seems so pointless most of the time. I feel I have a huge stone in my heart and a heavy coat on my back.'

Bereavement and academic performance

The experience of bereavement can have a long-term effect on academic performance (Abdelnoor and Hollins, 2004a; Davou and Widdershoven-Zervakis, 2004; Dowdney, 2000). One study into the effect of parental death involved 105 two to seventeen year-old children. Interviews were recorded at one month and thirteen months after the event in a structured interview with the surviving parent. They showed a significant degree of impairment in school performance (Van Eerdewerg et al., 1985). Increased rates of anxiety, withdrawal from engagement with peers and teachers, lack of motivation and low mood all interfere with the learning process. When helping children and young people to achieve their full potential we need to listen to what is helpful to them (Downey, 2002).

In some situations a bereaved young person may be pressured by school staff or parents to concentrate on academic work and examinations, however this is not always possible when the young person is preoccupied with the death. Young adults who had been bereaved four years prior to a study on the impact of death in the family said that their concentration and motivation were disrupted (Abdelnoor and Hollins, 2004b). The following examples describe how the young people felt:

Ceri was a 16-year-old girl whose best friend killed himself on New Year's Eve. She should have met up with him earlier that evening but hadn't. Her mother in particular, tells her to put it out of her mind and concentrate on her GCSEs.

Lizzie's sister was stillborn and she was more disorganised in the months following her death. She said, six months after her death, 'I was told off for losing a book. I started crying and thinking about Chloe and the teacher goes, "Oh, you don't have to be that sad just because you've lost someone".'

'Exams can be taken again, life can't.'

Sudden or traumatic death in the school community

Disasters impact on school communities. After the cruise ship, *Jupiter*, sank there was a decline in academic performance which was reflected in poorer than expected GCSE results the following year (Yule and Gold, 1993). In a discotheque fire in Goteborg, Sweden, 400 young people were present. Sixty-three young people died while 213 were injured. Two years later Broberg and colleagues conducted research to ascertain the impact the disaster had had on the survivors. There was significant decrease in school performance. 'In all, 23% indicated that they had either dropped out of school because of the fire or that they had to repeat a class' (Dyregrov, 2004: 78). Earlier research (Dyregrov et al., 1999) showed that after the sudden death of a student in an accident, one in five of the classmates continued to experience a high level of distress nine months after the loss.

The impact of traumatic loss can cause anxiety disorders, depression and Post Traumatic Stress Disorder (PTSD). This may affect an individual, the school community as a whole or specific peer groups within a school. Whatever the event, the experience affects academic attainment and absence (Yule, 1998). Memory and concentration are negatively affected especially in those subject areas that require high concentration such as mathematics, sciences and grammar (Streeck-Fisher and van der Kolk, 2000). 'We have studied two cases of children who experienced a serious difficulty in learning to read after witnessing a parent's violent death' (Pynoos et al., 1996: 344).

There are a number of reasons why trauma affects school performance (Dyregrov, 2004). Recurring intrusive thoughts make it hard for the student to concentrate (Yule and Gold, 1993); PTSD affects cognitive functioning; mood states may lead to disruptive behaviour, which has academic and social implications in school life (Schwartz and Gorman 2003); stress interferes with the sifting process so the student is unclear about what educational priorities are; and 'PTSD leads to a change in information processing where there is a sense of continuous threat tying up attentional resource, a hyperactive nervous system' (Dyregrov, 2004: 80).

Students who have been traumatically bereaved find school follow-up rituals to be helpful, particularly where there were opportunities to take part in communal rituals to mark the life and death of the person who died (Dyregrov et al., 1999; Hogan and DeSantis, 1994). In addition, bereaved young people want staff to recognise that they have been bereaved – they do not want the loss to be ignored. Schools do have a key role in ensuring that educational progress is maintained and may find that their role could 'include encouraging a restorative orientation at appropriate times, and doing what they can to ensure that the loss can be expressed, in safe and supported surroundings' (Abdelnoor and Hollins, 2004a).

Critical Incidents

Each school community has its own unique ethos which influences how critical incidents such as the death of a student or staff member are managed. Headteachers and teachers in schools, as well as support staff, may find themselves anxious when faced with loss so it is important to consider what strategies can be put in place should a critical incident occur. The following information, ideas and strategies will add to the human dynamic of care and compassion that lies at the heart of every good school.

Schools are advised to have a critical incident policy so that staff know what procedures to activate when such an incident happens (Klicker, 2000; McCaffrey, 2004). This includes details of how to inform a student of a death also known as death notification (Servaty-Seib et al., 2003). The way a person is informed influences their reactions, both immediately and over the longer term. 'Although the content of a death notice (that one or more persons have died) undeniably presents numerous challenges to adjustment, the process of death notification (the way in which it is performed) can significantly affect the extent to which survivors cope with these challenges' (Stewart, 1999: 302–3).

Where a parent is not available to break the news, then a significant figure of authority within the school, such as the headteacher, should inform the student that the death has happened. This should be done in a quiet, private, comfortable room, using direct language not euphemisms. There may be a wide variety of reactions and the student needs to be reassured that her responses are acceptable and she should be encouraged to express her feelings – empathic listening is very important at this point. It is helpful to ask what she wants to happen, who she wants to be informed in the school and someone close to the student should stay with her until relatives arrive or she is taken home. Close involvement and liaison with the student's family will assist the process and increase the student's sense of security.

In informing a student of a death, you can preface the news with 'I'm sorry, I have some sad news.' Do not begin with small talk because the student will sense that something out of the ordinary has happened and may feel anxious and confused. The nature of the student's relationship to the deceased will influence the extent and depth of their reaction (Servaty-Seib and Pistole, 2006–2007; Worden, 2002). The student may have questions, such as what caused the death, where the deceased is now, where the rest of her family is. These should be answered in an honest, direct way without giving unnecessary additional information and bearing in mind any parental wishes which have been passed to the person who is the death notifier.

On receiving bad news the child may feel numb, devastated, shocked, hurt, disbelief – any range of emotions. Ensure you accept the child's response in an open, compassionate way. Children and young people are often inhibited and anxious about expressing feelings that are different, and may express only those which are 'allowed'. If you are present when the news is delivered make sure the child knows that you are really there to help. Actually say, 'I am here, you aren't alone.' Safe touch can reassure and comfort; however, do respect any cultural or gender boundaries which may make this inadvisable. The child who feels isolated and abandoned will be reassured by your physical presence, you act as an anchor when he feels tossed about by the sudden change.

Critical Incident Planning Considerations

- Identify those members of staff who have experience in this area, for example critical incident training, and who can act as a resource for other staff.
- Clarify the role of staff; they are not counsellors but trusted adults who are known to pupils and parents.
- Recognise that some members of staff may not be able to offer support because of their own experiences and needs.
- Discuss such issues as breaking news to pupils and parents; anticipate questions from pupils, parents and outside agencies including media.

- Make a list of other agencies which can be drafted in to offer support where appropriate.
- Consider what support staff may need as they offer support to students and who will de-brief them.
- Complete a plan which is practical and which can be implemented immediately there is a critical incident.
- Have a central resource which includes details of ages and stages of children and young people's grief to which school staff can refer.

Box 5.1 Lists the key tasks to be carried out following a critical incident.

Box 5.1   Key Tasks Following Critical Incidents

- Dispel myths and rumours.
- Use assemblies to do this if a school trip or community event has brought death or trauma. Media mis-reports may lead to distortion of the facts.
- Make sure all staff know the systems put in place to support the child/children.
- Establish guidelines as to counselling, caring and guiding the child to ensure she or he is not overwhelmed by too much 'help'.
- Keep pupils to the security of the normal school routine whilst still being sensitive to personal needs.
- Prepare an information sheet for parents so they can understand children's response to loss.
- Wherever possible allow pupil to choose their key Pupil Support Worker.

The Role of the Headteacher

The main role of the headteacher when a pupil or school staff member dies is to support staff and pupils. Initially you will need to:

- Check the accuracy of the information.
- Clarify when and where the death occurred and any relevant details. It is important to be fully informed so that rumours can be quashed.
- Find out what arrangements have been made for the funeral.
- Contact parents/relatives, if not already done so at this point, to offer condolences and to find out how they want you to respond, for example, do they want you or other staff to attend the funeral?

Not all this information may be available straight away, however keep yourself informed and then inform other staff.

Informing staff

Some staff may need to be told individually, for instance the pupil's class teacher, whereas others may be informed in a group. Include administrative and support staff and inform absent staff members as soon as possible. The closer the relationship the more likely it is that the person will be upset. This is an emotional time so be prepared for it. Core support skills described in Chapter 3 may help you handle the situation more sensitively and effectively.

As soon as possible after you have talked to the child's class teacher, gather the rest of the staff together and inform them. Where people are told as a group there is less likelihood of misinformation or misinterpretation of facts as they are passed from person to person. Discuss how the pupils should be informed of the death.

Pupil Support Worker (PSW)

Where a child has been bereaved you and your staff may decide to identify one person who will be the key worker with the child. This designated Pupil Support Worker (PSW) can co-ordinate information within the school and with outside agencies, if they are involved, and act as the chief provider of emotional support to the child. Pupils may be asked who they would prefer to have as their PSW.

Informing the pupils

The pupils who are closest to the dead person may need to be informed individually or in a small group by the staff member who is closest to them. This may be the class teacher alone or with the headteacher or another member of staff. Clear language is vital to ensure confusion is minimised.

Tell other pupils in small groups or as a class. Once again the class teacher should tell her own class; however, where this causes anxiety, the headteacher can tell the pupils with the teacher present. In some instances, the school assembly may be the most appropriate place to inform pupils.

How? Where? When?

- Prepare the pupils for sad news.
- Gently tell them what has happened – simply and with no euphemisms.
- Explain what the school is doing and that all pupils will receive a letter to take home to tell their parents what has happened.
- Be prepared for questions.
- Give time to respond to the children and give time for them to talk.

Ensure that any child who seems unduly upset is comforted and keep a watchful eye on their progress over the following days. The peer group of the children can also provide ongoing support and solace to a grieving child.

Informing parents and others

Write to parents of other pupils in the child's class, or all the parents if yours is a small school. The primary school is an important part of the community and the parents are a central part of the partnership. As well as expressing your sympathy about the event, give basic details of the circumstances of the death, ensuring you do not disclose any confidential information and explain how children in school were informed of the death. It may be helpful to include some details about how children may respond to bereavement and to give a contact telephone number should they want someone to talk to or if they are in need of support.

The Chair of Governors should be told. A letter of condolence may be written as a mark of respect. The Chief Education Officer, will on receipt of the information, send a letter of condolence.

'A safe haven'

Immediately following a death create a safe haven. We all have a basic need for safety, and when we experience loss it touches our deepest fear of abandonment and annihilation. To provide stability zones that familiar faces and places bring, pupils need:

- Safe places.
- Safe people.
- Safe situations.

Safe places

- Identify a place in school where the child can go if she feels especially upset or anxious. Hopefully, the classroom will feel safe anyway but where else can you designate a safe space? It could be the headteacher's room or a corner of the library or reception class which has a comfortable chair or couch and soft cushions. Identifying a designated 'safe space' is important for any school as a priority.

Safe people

- Designate a Pupil Support Worker (PSW) to whom the child can go knowing that the person is fully informed of the loss that he has experienced.
- All staff, including caretakers, lunchtime assistants and administrative staff, who know of the loss can be prepared to support the pupil if he wishes it.
- School staff should acknowledge that a child has been bereaved, to offer condolences for instance, without pressurising him to talk.

Safe situations

- As far as possible the pupil should be protected from any situations which exacerbate his feelings of loss. It requires sensitivity and insight to be on the alert for possibly painful reminders of the loss.

  'When I went back to school after my dad died, I didn't want to be popular just because he died. Girls came up to me and said, "Do you want to play with us now?" But, I said I wanted to play with Kate and Esme who I always play with. I didn't want to be popular just because of that.' Renee, aged nine.

Staff Supporting Each Other

When supporting staff, as with children and young people, it is important to recognise individual differences. Some people wish to talk about their feelings and experiences while others prefer to cope by getting involved in activities or focusing on the needs of students. Staff meetings can be used to raise issues about the impact of the death and how staff feel they are being supported or what needs they have identified.

Traumatic events connected with a school can seriously effect everyone involved and school counsellors and support staff can come under considerable pressure. Donnelly and Rowling, studying Australian schools, found that leadership was of paramount importance as was good management working from a management plan. The clear communication between all involved was of critical importance (Donnelly and Rowling 2007).

Overview – What can we do to help?

- Listen, listen and listen some more.
- Stay with the questions that have no answers.
- Be there.
- Allow the pain, confusion, grief and anger.
- Reassure that feelings are normal and will eventually pass.
- Be non-judgemental. Children need to have their feelings received without judgement or criticism.
- Continue to be available, not just immediately afterwards but for as long as it takes.
- Recognise that grieving doesn't have time boundaries; it takes as long as it takes.
- Ask the pupil to tell you if they feel alone or upset and agree some form of support, for example, quiet time in the library or reading corner.

Caring for Staff in Schools

Staff in schools have time constraints, targets to meet, other children to teach and many diverse responsibilities. However, there are simple things that you can do which value the child and help him through a time of enormous impact and, whilst doing that, cherish yourself:

- Recognise your own experiences of loss may be re-awakened.
- Seek support from colleagues if you are unsure about what to do.
- Understand that at times you will feel inadequate or hopeless but remember you're not a magician who can make things better with the flick of a wand. You are a human being who can be there to offer whatever you can of your own humane self.

Teachers and other school staff cannot protect children and young people from loss through bereavement, but they can help them to respond to and recover from loss so that they do not have to face it alone. You can make a difference.

One Moment

A 14-year-old pupil was stabbed in school in Lincolnshire in 2003. Speaking of the incident the headteacher said, 'You cannot appreciate how utterly sad and distraught you are. It was one moment. One moment' (Ward, 2003: 3).

The school arranged for a book of condolence which was later given to the murdered boy's parents. Following the incident the pupils were sent home without being told about the murder so that they would not be on the premises when the press arrived. In addition, the headteacher felt it was of paramount importance that the staff get together in order to support each other and the pupils. They met the following day and arranged two fellowship days for pupils and parents and teachers to meet to give mutual support. The timetable was suspended for those days and a Methodist minister and counsellors were present in case any person wanted their support. The headteacher said, 'Our experience as staff was that the strongest support was from our colleagues. We thought children would get the strongest support from their peers and that turned out to be right' (Ward, 2003: 3).

> [M]ost of a child's education is for life which leaves him helpless in dealing with death. (Budmen, 1969: 11)

Holding a Memorial

When a student or member of staff has died, a memorial will help students and staff to feel they are 'doing something' as there is a strong urge to mark the passing of those who have been significant in their lives. Holding a memorial does not have to be an elaborate event, though it may be. Below are some ideas of what you can do. They can be used on their own or combined, the important thing is that they are relevant for those who are involved.

- Light a special candle and offer the opportunity to reflect – on the person who died, on the relationship, on the qualities of the dead person, on the positive memories that remain, etc.
- Listen to a piece of music that reflects the person or a piece he enjoyed.
- Write a Memory Book. Children and staff can write some comments or a positive memory that can then be collected together in a special Memory Book. This can be kept in school or given to the family of the deceased.
- Plant a tree or garden in memory of the person.
- Create a wall display to mark their contributions.
- Gather helium balloons to be released by staff and students.
- Set up a group to raise funds to support the person's favourite charity or to donate funds to organisations.

Organisations such as Winston's Wish and the Child Bereavement Charity provide excellent resources and material that can be used in schools.

Reflective Exercise 1

Lindsay Nicholson's husband died of a rare form of leukaemia. Four years later the elder of her two daughters was also diagnosed with a rare cancer. The impact on the younger daughter Hope, aged four, was profound. She was sent to live with her grandparents as Lindsay spent most of her time with Ellie who was critically ill in hospital. She wrote: 'It was agony for the three of us to be apart. And I felt impossibly torn between the differing needs of my children. One so dangerously ill, the other so little and homesick. Hope stopped growing and stopped learning to read. And I believe it is only now – she is 13 – that she is back on track academically. As you struggle on, people say you are being brave, but bravery implies choice and actually you don't have choice at all' (First person, *The Guardian*, 23 February, 2008, page 3).

- What multiples losses occurred in four-year-old Hope's life?
- How did this affect her school work?
- How might bereavement affect a child's ability to learn?

Reflexive Exercise 2

- What strategies does your school have to support students and staff?
- Do you have a critical incident policy?
- If you have had a bereavement in school, consider how people were informed, what their responses were and how the bereaved were supported.
- What changes would you like to implement to ensure bereaved students are well cared for?
- How could you feel more supported when working with bereaved students?

6 Creative Approaches in Working with Grief and Mourning

'I painted one side blue for the sadness and painted yellow on the other side because you can't be sad all the time.' C., aged six. His father died suddenly in a sports accident.

Creative strategies in working with grief and in palliative care are receiving increased interest as their therapeutic value is recognised and as we learn that creative activities help to promote healthy grieving (Bertman, 1999; Bolton, 2007; Hieb, 2005; Wood, 2008). As psychoanalyst Anthony Storr says, 'The creative process can be a way of protecting the individual against being overwhelmed by depression; a means of gaining a sense of mastery in those who have lost it, and, to a varying extent, a way of repairing the self damaged by bereavement' (Storr, 1989: 143). And, 'after all the theoretical foundation and experience of working with children and young people it is useful to feel free to use your intuition' (Stokes, 2009a: 16).

Using creative techniques can allow you the freedom to use your imagination and intuition. However, there are two very important aspects to consider in using creative techniques in grief work. The first is that you need to feel comfortable using them so try these techniques before you use them with children and young people. Secondly, creative work is very powerful and can evoke intense emotional responses so be prepared for strong expressions of feeling, whether it be sorrow or joy.

Creative activities include making and remembering using a range of different materials which need to reflect cultural diversity using artefacts, pictures, dolls from different ethnic backgrounds, stories which are culturally diverse, music from around the world, or maps and globes that embrace different ethnicities (Hooyman and Kramer, 2006). They include making memory boxes, collages, photo murals and making masks, stories, biography, poetry, drawing and artwork, puppets, dolls and strategies using natural objects and toys and lantern ceremonies (McWhorter, 2003).

Whatever the creative media, the aim is to give children and young people the opportunity to express their feelings in ways other than verbalisation which for some children is too direct. Instead, through symbols and metaphors they can express their feelings (Bannister, 2003; Mallon, 2007). Art is a way for grieving children to gain an inner sense of security and safety at a time in their life which is filled with uncertainty and change (Rogers, 2007). Art making is often a two way process which involves the activity and then reflection on what has been made (Mallon et al., 2005; Thompson 2003). 'The creative response to loss is only one example of the use of the imagination' (Storr, 1989: 144).

Healing through creative expression is central to the work of Linda Goldman who describes four stages of a child's path through grief. These are Understanding, Grieving, Commemorating and Going On. Understanding helps the child make sense of the death according to their developmental level. Grieving is shown by the emotions which come and go as we respond to loss: these include shock and anger, searching and yearning, despair and disorganisation and rebuilding. In Commemoration, the child learns to value the life of someone who has died and shows that all lives have value, which helps the child make meaning of the death. The final goal, is to help children to 'Go on', to re-invest in life and develop skills of recovery and the ability to find joy in life and to gain confidence to carry on (Goldman, 2002b).

What follows are a series of creative activities which you can adapt for working with individuals or with groups.

Writing

> Writing is a form of therapy; sometimes I wonder how all those who do not write, compose or paint can manage to escape the madness, the melancholia, the panic and fear which is inherent in the human situation.
> (Graham Greene, quoted in Storr, 1989: 123)

Writing comes in many forms which all have a potential part to play in working with grieving children and young people, for the process of writing has healing and cathartic qualities (Marner, 2000). In a writing workshop for children and adolescents with cancer, children expressed their intense feelings including fear of injections, fear of not being cured, revolt, hope and raised the question of why they had cancer. They were able to communicate feelings to family and physicians that had previously not been expressed or understood (Oppenheim et al., 2008).

Julie Cameron in her book *The Artist's Way* (1995) advocates the writing of three morning pages a day to set the creative spirit free. J. Earl Rogers, based his creative writing work with bereaved children's groups on this idea but calls them 'mourning pages' (Rogers, 2007). Members are encouraged to write for ten minutes about whatever comes into their heads without censoring their thoughts, worrying about spelling or handwriting. The essential part is to write whatever is there. Where children have difficulties with this he provides 'jumping off lines' that may start a train of thought. Some jumping off lines might be:

- The last time I saw …
- I remember when …
- What I miss most is …
- What I'm glad about is …
- I felt angry when …
- What I'm confused about is …

Writing includes lists and letters, diaries, journals and acrostics. Memorials and memory books can include all types of writing which can be kept for the rest of the child's life. Such writing can bring forth expression about the child's loss and yearning (Gersie, 1991).

Prompts for writing could include some of the following:

- Feelings about life now.
- Facts about the person's death and what followed.
- New experiences that have happened since the death.
- Life before the person died and life now.
- What I liked about the person who died.
- What I sometimes didn't like about the person who died.
- Fears about my life now.
- What helps me in my life now.
- Feelings about what makes me strong to deal with difficult things.

A young person might find solace in writing a letter to the person who has died. Where there is ongoing, regular support they could write a letter to the dead person and choose a photograph or drawing to accompany it. Then both can be pasted in a Memory Book.

Diaries and Journals

The word diary comes from the Latin 'dies' which means 'day'. A child can be encouraged to record events on a daily basis so they can express their feelings and look back on them when they are grown up. This helps the child to recognise that in bereavement they are going through an important transition in their life. You might say to a child or young person:

- A diary is a place where you can write down thoughts and feelings you may not want to tell anyone at the time. You can keep it completely private or share it with others – the choice is yours.
- It's a place to express yourself when you are angry or upset.
- It's a place to explore inner feelings and ideas.

The following extracts from diaries show how writing a diary can be a real support to children and young people at critical points in their lives. They can also be used to show to children which may inspire them. The following extracts are from two girls who were caught up in war. For two years Anne Frank and her family hid from the Nazi's in an attic and it was there that she began her diary on her thirteenth birthday. Zlata Filipovic, eleven-years-old, was caught up in the siege of Sarajevo.

> 'The nicest part is being able to write down all my thoughts and feelings, otherwise I'd suffocate.' Anne Frank, March 16, 1944.

> 'Not being able to go outside upsets me more than I can say, and I'm terrified our hiding place will be discovered and that we will be shot.' Anne Frank

'Mommy and daddy won't let me watch T.V. when the news is on. But you can't hide all the bad things that are happening from us children.' Zlata, p. 28–9, March 24, 1992

'Is it possible I'll never see Nina again? Nina, an innocent eleven-year-old girl the victim of a stupid war. I feel sad. I cry and I wonder why? She didn't do anything. A disgusting war has destroyed a young child's life.' Zlata, p. 45, May 7, 1992

Biography or Life Book

Children and young people can explore the life of the person who died by writing the story of his life, which helps them keep the memory of the person alive. They can extend their knowledge by asking family members about incidents from the person's life, their interests and hobbies, special times they shared and so on. In telling the story the child makes meaning of the person's life which is a crucial aspect of the journey through grief (Neimeyer, 2005). Healing includes the 'storying and re-storying' of lives (Tomm, 1990).

The opportunity for the child to tell their story from their point of view is of paramount importance (Gilbert, 2008). We can help by enabling them to reflect on their experiences, help them fill in the gaps, make sense of some of the confusions and provide facts where rumour has left distortions. Children learn about themselves in the stories that others tell them and from stories they make up themselves (Cattanach, 2007).

There are some other suggestions for writing:

- Make lists.
- Choose a best part of the day and a difficult part of the day to record each night before you go to bed.
- Record three good things that have happened each day. This can be your 'Good Feelings' journal.

In *Ways To Live Forever* (Nicholls, 2008), a fictional account of a boy who is very ill, Sam writes about his life. He begins with a list:

List No. 1 Five Facts About Me

1. My name is Sam.
2. I am eleven years old.
3. I collect stories and fantastic facts.
4. I have leukaemia.
5. By the time you read this I will probably be dead.

Poetry

Poems written by poets can be used as starting points to inspire bereaved children and young people. They can also write their own. Here are two examples on the theme of bereavement:

Dad

Dad was someone who had everything
In the right place –
Including his heart.
He never called us little terrors.
He always called us the little ones or the kids.
He never hit us, but told us reasons why
(when we weren't reasonable).
He wore smart shoes, comfortable trousers.
When you tried his shoes on
they were warm.
But when the time came for him to leave us
there was no warm feeling in his shoes.
No warmth or familiar smell in the clothing –
Nothing.
And he left a gap in the word comfort able.
Julia (11)

When I Am Lonely

When I am lonely
and my brother will not play with me,
I feel like the last petal
left on a flower
and the other petals
are floating away.
Victoria (6)

Stories

'If our stories are stronger than our biology, then narrative themes and plots can play forth whether we are present or not' (Hedtke, 2001: 6). Story telling is an important element in therapeutic work (Freeman et al., 1997; Ross and Hayes, 2004). 'If children are not able to tell their story to interested others, they may well "act out" and present difficulties at home or school' (McIntyre and Hogwood, 2006). Smith and Pennells (1995) describe a technique called 'the Story Wheel'. Group members sit with their backs to each other in a circle and each person contributes a sentence to an improvised story about loss. This allows a story to emerge in a non-threatening way since no member of the group has to reveal their experiences and feelings and ideas can be explored without personal risk-taking.

Narrative counselling is founded on the idea that we make meaning of events in our lives by building them into stories. These stories can adapt and change as our lives alter, so they are an ever-developing narrative (Eppler et al., 2009; Eron and Lund, 2007) As play therapist and psychotherapist Ann Cattanach says, 'From childhood we learn about ourselves from the stories people tell us and the stories we tell about ourselves. From these stories we begin to form our identity and a sense of self' (Cattanach, 2007: 7). By

telling and re-telling their stories children and young people can begir
aspects of successful actions, hope and resilience.

The student can be given prompts to help them write the story.
before…? When did you first find out about…? The style of writing car
suit individual needs, for example, in comic strip layout where captions
with drawings.

J.M. Barrie (1860–1937), the author of *Peter Pan*, experienced a tragic childhood. He was the ninth of ten children, three brothers and seven sisters. When he was aged six or seven, his brother died in a skating accident. His mother became depressed after her son's death as the boy was regarded as her favourite child. Barrie dressed in his brother's clothes to try to please her and to gain her affection. An obsessive relationship between mother and son seems to have begun there. He never grew taller than five foot (1.5 metres). Like Peter Pan, in one way he never 'grew up'. Peter Pan remains as a child and in the story lives in Neverland with the Lost Boys. Barrie turned personal tragedy into this everlasting story.

Bibliotherapy

Books can be a useful addition to the creative tool kit of the counsellor or those working with children and young people (Cook et al., 2006; Gladding, 1997). Through a structured, thoughtful approach to using books or extracts, you can focus on the specific needs of the child. Reading can influence the child's mood, her understanding and behaviour. (Jones, 2008). As the child reads or listens to the story he can find a common bond to his own life and, as their fictional difficulties are resolved, the child can identify with book characters. Psychologist Bruno Bettleheim highlights the importance of fairy tales (Bettelheim, 1978). Through these children can make sense of the puzzling world around them. Through contrasting good and evil, threat and protection and so on, the child can project their feelings on to the characters. They also help children and young people see the universality of their struggles and their experience. Vicarious success can engender hope, which is so important in the healing process.

Bibliotherapy can help the child recognise emotions, give the opportunity to think and talk about death, give insight into how difficult situations can be managed and help relieve feelings of isolation (Berns, 2003–2004; Bowman, 2003). There are many examples of children's books that deal with bereavement and express both the pain and anguish, as well as the resilience to adjust to the loss (Jones, 2008). Judy Pascoe's book *Our Father Who Art in A Tree* (2002), tells the story of a ten-year-old girl whose father has died. She senses his presence and hears his voice. It is a sad, funny and humorous book and explores the conflicting emotions bereaved children feel.

Fictional characters can help children and young people understand how others deal with death, grief and mourning (Markell and Markell, 2008). They used books such as the *Harry Potter* series by J.K. Rowling, *The Secret Garden* by Frances Hodgson Burnett and *Charlotte's Web* by E. B. White to narrate the stories of characters who have been faced with the death of those they love. There are many others which show how meaning can be made from the loss. However, not all children and young people will engage with the characters or the story may be too close to home (Cook et al., 2006). The literature chosen should reflect the age, social and emotional developmental evel of the children or group and be of the appropriate reading level if the child is to read the story.

Creating Film Strip Stories

Brendan McIntrye and Jemma Hogwood, of the charity Winston's Wish, introduced a method to help bereaved young people make a narrative of their experiences (McIntyre and Hogwood, 2006). The technique allows the children to externalise their story so they can see what happened in a way that helps them to separate it from themselves. When events are externalised, children can begin to feel more in control of their emotions and behaviour and see other ways of managing these feelings (Eppler et al., 2009; Freeman et al., 1997). Drawing can often allow the child to express feelings that they cannot put into words. They need to tell their story as they understand it at the time. This may alter as they gain more insight and information about the death and events prior to it and subsequent to it. This is done by drawing incidents as a 'film strip': recording what happened at the death, who was involved, where it happened; what happened leading up to the death; and what has happened since the death. This technique enables the child to see that there is a past, a present and a future. The film script enables the young person to have a narrative structure to contain their experience. (White and Epston, 1990)

Narrative Play

Narrative play is a form of communication with children using stories, myths, tales and narratives with the aim of sharing and making sense of life events. 'It is a collaborative approach where the adult helps the child to order their experiences through the use of imaginative play processes' (Cattanach, 2007). The stories do not have to be factual, based on 'true' events – they can be imaginary tales but they still express what is felt and understood by the child or young person. They will be influenced by the culture in which the child lives, his family and his wider relationships (White and Epston, 1990). 'Through play children can project thoughts, feelings and conflicts on to the play characters' (Dwivedi, 1993: 11). Virginia Axline's book *Dibs in Search of Self* emphasised the importance of play as a form of communication and children's play tells us the story they want us to hear (Axline, 1964).

Drawing and Painting

Drawing and painting give direct access to emotions without the need for words (Edwards, 2004; McNiff, 1992). Drawing a picture of the person who died or a special family time can help the child talk about the person and happy and sad memories (Goldman, 2000).

You could have a series of suggestions on cards which can be offered to the child to help explore their response to their bereavement. These could include:

Draw something that frightens you.

Draw a dream you have had recently.

Draw something that makes you feel happy.

Draw something that makes you feel safe.

Draw a sad time in your life.

Draw your family before … died.

Draw your family now.

Draw something that makes you angry.

Draw something that makes you laugh.

Draw a place that you like to go to.

Draw a person you like to spend time with.

As with all the other creative activities described, the idea is not to complete a polished piece of art but rather to experience the process. As art therapist Shaun MacNiff says, 'Trust the process' (1992). It is in the act of creation that healing can take place. However, you do not have to be a therapist to use drawings. Approach the drawing with curiosity and sensitivity and let the child or young person express what it means to them, if they choose to talk about it (DeSpelder and Strickland, 2002). Drawings provide a form of communication of children's anxieties and feelings generally (Massimo and Zarri, 2006).

Photographs and Videos

Photographs, videos and memorabilia can be used as sensory triggers to allow connection to emotions. Annette Kuhn (2002) states that family photographs are about memory and memories, about our stories which are shared with others. They encourage recall of earlier memories that have been forgotten for some time (Gough, 2003) 'Photographs can be particularly useful with people who have expressive language difficulties and have been used in a number of contexts'. In looking at photographs, one is honouring the memories. Photographs, as do other objects connected to the deceased, create a concrete focus for sharing.

> Photographs are footprints of our minds, mirrors of our lives, reflections from our hearts, frozen memories that we can hold in silent stillness in our hands – forever if we wish. They document not only where we have been, but also point the way to where we might perhaps be going, whether we know it yet or not. (Judy Weiser, www.photo-therapy-centre. com Entry page)

Creating a Safe Space

This activity can help a child build resilience in identifying safe places which bring comfort and security. First he can create a safe place on paper. Encourage the child or young person to draw or write words to symbolise what comes to mind when he thinks of any of the following:

- Warmth.
- A cuddly blanket.
- A teddy bear or other stuffed toy.
- Someone you trust.
- Something that you trust.
- A comforting colour a soothing scent.
- Moments from the past that were safe.
- A very safe place.

The child can also bring their own associations. To extend this you could ask the child if they want to visit the safe place they have identified. In vivo work may involve revisiting the place where the death occurred, for example, the hospital, the cemetery, or other places of importance (Hindmarch, 2000).

Scrapbooks

The scrapbook can be made by the child and include writing, letters, photographs, sympathy cards; in fact whatever the child wants to include. It is a useful activity at times of transition when the child can include items from the past and others that refer to the future. It gives purposeful activity, within the young person's control, when many aspects of life are beyond their control (Sori and Hecker, 2003).

Claywork

Clay can be used to model places, people and feelings. The manipulation of the clay can be soothing and the impermanent nature of the finished object may allow the young person to be more adventurous in their exploration (Edwards, 2004; Mallon et al., 2005).

Masks

Mask-making or mask decoration can be done with children of any age. Begin by helping the child to think about people's faces and the expressions they use to show how they feel. The child decorates a ready-made white face mask or paper plates to show how they feel. They can decorate the mask with wool, shredded paper, glitter or any other appropriate materials.

They can use one mask to show how they look to the outside world and another one to show how they feel on the outside. *Michael Rosen's Sad Book* illustrates this in a powerful way and could be a helpful stimulus for mask-making with young people (Rosen, 2004). They may relate this to how other people 'mask' their feelings in public. Masks can be then shared with others if the child is doing this in a group setting.

Memory Boxes

A child may want to make or use a box to contain special articles of the dead person (Smith and Pennells, 1995; Stokes, 2004). A shoebox covered with plain paper that can be decorated by the child or you can buy memory boxes from specialist bereavement organisations such as Winston's Wish. The child may include photos, DVDs, CDs and anything that holds special memories of the person who died.

Sometimes memory boxes are made by parents for their child prior to their death (Neville, 1995). The box may include letters to the child to be opened at specific points such as when the child changes school, gets married or has their own child. Sometimes special family stories or aspects of the family history are included so that the child has a sense of continuity.

Memory Garden

'Memory Garden: Bereavement card deck' is an illustrated card deck which shows an individual flower on each card with a caption such as, 'A scent that reminds me of the person who died ...' or 'I will always remember...' These deal with many aspects of loss and bereavement and may be particularly useful when working with children with special educational needs. They are designed by Lisa-Marie Arnason and are available in the UK from www.winslow-cat.com; however, these could be made with children themselves who, in the process, decide what categories/memories to include.

Children can be encouraged to plant a memory garden. In a way this reflects the words of Rabbi Grollman (2008): 'Grief is like weeding a flowerbed in the summer. You have to do it over and over again until the seasons change.' The children can choose the plants and flowers and in caring for them see how seasons change and how the cycle of life develops.

Memory Stones

This is an exercise I first saw on Winston's Wish website and I have used in many ways with bereaved young people. Children quickly grasp the idea that the stones can represent feelings and memories. Three stones are used to symbolise feelings:

1 One stone is sharp and jagged. It may represent the rough, hard, difficult to manage feelings the young person has. In holding the stone tightly, the child may feel that sharp edges hurt. You can point out that the child may have some memories or feelings which hurt too.

2 One is a smooth, ordinary stone. This can represent the ordinary, everyday day memories that the young person has about the person who died and the times they shared. The fact they liked to watch a DVD together at the weekend or that the person liked chocolate biscuits.

3 Finally, there is a shiny, sparkling gem stone such as rose quartz. It looks special and precious, this can be associated with very significant memories the child has or qualities of the deceased person. It may be a particular holiday or a great birthday party.

The stones can be held together in one hand which can enable the child to recognise that differing feelings can exist side by side in our minds and hearts just the way they can in our hand.

Shells

In much the same way as stones, buttons and rocks you can use shells to help the young person express their feelings. A box with a variety of different colours, shapes, textures and size can provide a choice as the person chooses a shell for each important person in their life. Jackie Burke, a counsellor at Treloar School and College, a specialist setting for pupils with complex physical disabilities, describes how powerful this technique was when used with a young person who was stuck as she, Jackie, was also stuck. She said, 'Some of her choices took me by surprise and opened up her world for me on a level that was unseen and not felt before. For her, it relieved the stuckness … it also enabled her to make sense for the first time of where she thought her place in the world was' (Burke in Towers, 2008: 29)

Box of Buttons

Buttons can be used to represent feelings, ideas, people and situations. The child chooses one button that fits with how she is feeling today. Then chooses another that represents her when she is feeling angry, sad, annoyed, peaceful and so on. You can photograph the resulting collection and build up a record of the sessions.

Roadside Memorials

Roadside memorials are to be found throughout the world and have become a rit-ualised way of mourning those killed in road traffic crashes, some are spontane-ous, made soon after the event and some are permanent (Klaassens et al., 2009). Memorials are sometimes made at the site of a traffic collision in which someone has died. Children may contribute to and subsequently visit such memorials. The creation of the memorial, usually with photographs, messages and flowers, is connected to the sense of presence of the deceased at the place where he died (Clark and Franzmann, 2006).

Body Mapping

This is a way to explore feelings and to enable the young person to reconnect with her emotions (Hemmings, 1995). You can either use a ready-made template of a body outline or, if the child feels secure enough, ask the child to lie down on a large piece of paper, wallpaper lining paper is good and inexpensive, then you draw round the child making an outline of his body. A thick felt tip marker is ideal. Next the child colours in within the outline placing feelings and words in various places in the body.

They may write words such as confused, worried, frightened. You could also ask the child to make a code for colours, for example, red = anger, blue = sadness, and put the colours in the place they feel the emotion. This activity can open a discussion on when they have the feelings, what they do when they happen and who helps. This can help the child build up their strengths and resilience (Mallon et al., 2005).

Feelings Faces

Gather a selection of images of faces with different emotions. You can label these and laminate them. The child then picks out one which reflects how he is feeling and this acts as a springboard to talk about their emotions. You could ask the child to choose images for other members of their family or friendship group.

Alternatively, you could draw stylised faces which demonstrate different emotions. Possible words to illustrate are: worried, sad, angry, unhappy, bored, guilty, happy, shocked, disappointed, abandoned, relieved, puzzled, hurt, miserable, lonely, sick, scared and happy.

Puppets

Puppets allow the child to project their emotions and explore feelings in an active way. The child can gain sufficient distance from his personal experience in order to explore distressing emotions and can engage puppets in dialogue that might be difficult to express as themselves. Puppets are available from www.puppet.co.uk but it is worth exploring the idea of making your own or helping children to make them.

Collage

Using magazines, fabric, paper, snippets from newspapers, maps, photographs and any objects that feel appropriate, the child puts the images together to make a collage, The child can enter the world of art-making without being able to draw or paint, which may be less intimidating for some (Rogers, 2007).

Treasure Box of Textiles

Gather together all types of textiles from cotton to corduroy, satins to suede and in all colours of the rainbow. Invite children to choose the colours and textiles that tell their story. Textiles can also be made into a patchwork memory quilt.

Balloons

Balloons can be used in a symbolic way. The young person can write a message to the person who has died, attach it to the balloon and then release it. This activity can be repeated each year on the anniversary of the person's death. A creative approach to releasing guilt is to write the things that the young person feels guilty about on to a biodegradable helium balloon and release it (Rothman, 1996).

Transitional Objects

Most children and young people keep something that belonged to the dead parent (Worden, 1996). This is sometimes a gift they received from the dead person or given by a surviving parent. Sometimes, the child takes something which reminds them of the deceased. When Cheryl was eight her grandmother died. Ten years later, when she was packing to go to university, she showed her mother a bar of soap she had taken from her Gran's. She said, 'I just wanted to have it with me to remind me of her. For a long time I could still smell her when I sniffed the soap but gradually it faded.' Volkan (1972) gave the term 'linking object' to describe objects that keep the mourned linked to the dead person.

At the end of her Treasure Weekends, residential support weekends for bereaved children, Shirley Potts gives a hand mirror to each child to remind them of their own uniqueness and individuality (Lansdown, 1999).

Pebble Technique

This was devised by Holly van Gulden and Lisa M. Bartels-Rabb. 'Pebbles are one-liners, not conversations, that raise an issue and are then allowed to ripple until the child is ready to pick up on it' (van Gulden and Bartels-Rabb, 1999: 200). The one-liner might be used when a child is drawing for instance, 'I wonder if you inherited your ability to draw from you Mum. You are really good at drawing.' The child may at some point pick up on what they had in common with the deceased family remember or talk about how that are different. The 'pebble' provides the opportunity for further communication. It can relate to any emotions and it is up to the caring adult to find ways of incorporating them in the support work (Di Ciaccio, 2008).

Dolls

Dolls in all shapes and sizes, home made or bought, are very helpful in working with children and young people. Through dolls they can play out events that have happened, use them as dialogue and express how the dolls might feel if someone she loved dies and simply be a comfort, to hold close.

Home-made dolls with blank faces, that is with no details, can be customised by the young person, as Ana describes (see below). Ana sent me a letter in response to a request I made in a therapeutic journal for innovative ways of working with children who had experienced loss. I have shortened it a little but I have included it at length because she so eloquently describes how she uses her home-made, cloth dolls:

> I volunteered as a reader at a primary school and there was a little girl whose mother had just died and she would not talk to the teachers. I was asked to read with her, as they felt that I may be able to help. It was difficult at first as she seemed to be lost. Then one day I was carrying one of the dolls that I had made for my daughter, her eyes showed interest for the first time and I used it as an opening to talk.
>
> I asked her if she would like one and she nodded, for me that was a breakthrough. The next week when I brought [the doll] in she opened up to me

and started to talk about what was worrying her. We had, what I have come to realise are usual conversations with children who are suffering, 'disjointed sentences', which are 'thrown' into a conversation, they are not related to the topic in hand but very clearly tell you what they are feeling at that moment in time. Some time later her father thanked me for the doll and said that it had made a difference to his daughter.

More recently I have been working with secondary school age students. I began a craft class for some students who had found the transition from primary to secondary school difficult. At first we began by making mixed media cards and the students could make them for whomever they wanted to. One of the students wanted to make one for his mother who was dying from cancer.

These students would come to my office during the week and noticed the dolls on my window sill. The boy whose mother had cancer came in one day and started a conversation about my dolls – this was just an opening – and as the weeks went by he used the dolls as an introduction to how he was feeling. I asked him if he would like one. I told him that I had some 'blank' dolls, ones without features or clothes that I could bring in. He liked this idea he said that he wanted to be able to draw on his doll and write words that were important to him.

He brought the doll in to show me once, it was a true representation of his own feelings at that time. After that he kept it private, his own special symbol of what he was feeling. I removed the dolls one day and another student came in and asked me where they were as she liked seeing them and had brought a friend in to see them. Again this student lost a close relative and she used the doll as an excuse to talk. Interestingly enough she did not want one of her own, she just liked coming in to talk about them. The dolls names changed as often as the students came into my room.

I had not intended for the dolls to be used, I had only brought them in to brighten up my room and would never have dreamt of the impact they made. Dolls are significant for me, in that I find them comforting and am always surprised at how they affect different people. I know that some people are afraid of them. I am also aware of the impact of having a doll to turn to in a time of crisis, something to hold onto, something familiar, something that will just allow you to be yourself without having to answer questions. The students who liked my dolls said that they liked being in my room because they were not asked probing questions and could just be themselves and it was ok to cry, laugh, be sad or happy. (Ana)

Miscellany

There are many other creative techniques which you can use with bereaved children and young people; however, I do not have enough space here to explore them in depth.

Some you might like to consider are music and song (Heath, 2009) and drama (Casdagli, 1995). Physical activity such as dancing, running, jumping and more discipline forms, such as Tai Chi, yoga and martial arts, can release frustration, anger and tension. At the Richmond's Hope Centre in Edinburgh they have a 'Volcano room' with a punch bag for younger children that plays nursery rhymes when it is hit. They also have a wrestling dummy and padded walls to help children express grief and vent feelings of anger.

And the last word to Thomas (aged eight), 'If you had a tree you could put some things on it, like wind chimes. I put one on my tree and when it spins round it reminds me of my daddy.'

Creative Writing Reflexive Exercise 1

Find your Reflective Notebook and a pen. Think about a bereaved child or young person you are working with or have worked with in the past.

- Write the 'Jump off' heading 'When … died I felt …'
- Write in the voice of the young person.
- Set a timer for seven minutes.

Write down your response. Don't stop to analyse what you are writing or to censor it. Stop when the seven minutes are up.

Creative Writing Reflexive Exercise 2

On reading what you have written about the bereaved young person, reflect on how this impacted on you.

- Set the time for seven minutes.
- 'Jump off' heading: 'When I read what I had written I …'

7 Interactive Support On-line

'When my sister was killed by a car, it was on the news and the internet. It upset me that that other kids were going on the internet but my brother liked it because his name was there too.' Clare, aged eleven.

The internet has become a major factor in the lives of children and young people. Bereaved children access it to share feelings about friends and family who have died, to place messages of condolence and to seek help at times of distress (Oliveri, 2003; Salter, 2004). This chapter will consider what is available for children and young people on websites with message boards and chat rooms, which are properly monitored. The UK Council for Child Internet safety, set up in 2008, monitors the content of websites that children and young people visit (News, *Therapy Today*, 2009: 4). Whilst, these websites offer instant access for young people they may still require more help than is available from an internet site.

There has been a huge increase in the use of online social networking by adolescents. A study by Williams and Merten (2009) found that the activities included adolescent internet users directing comments to the deceased, posting memorial messages, current events and previous shared times, ways of coping with the loss, discussion of the cause of death, religious beliefs and thoughts on attending the funeral. Some teenage site users regularly visit the profiles of dead friends, immediately after the death they may visit on a daily basis (Aitken, 2009). This unlimited freedom to comment and share views enables the adolescents to feel less isolated and maintain continuing bonds with the deceased.

Road for you

Internet sites often include Frequently Asked Questions (FAQs), stories, poems and narratives of young people's journey through grief. Cruse Bereavement Care provides a site, The Road For You, RD4U, which was created by young people themselves and suggests helpful activities for young people following a bereavement, and has a gallery where photographs can be exhibited (Salter, 2004). They are updating the site to ensure that children and young people with sensory disabilities and special educational needs will have easier access to the site.

The Road for You is part of Cruse Bereavement Care's Youth Involvement Project and young people can email for support. The requests are forwarded to trained volunteers who then respond. They can read the experiences of other bereaved young people and send their own stories for others to read. The site has general advice as well as animations, games and there is a dedicated 'Lads Only' section. Young people are involved in the ongoing development of the site and some are trained to work as volunteer supporters for their peers. The feedback from users is that the site helps them to feel less isolated and helps them to recognise that others have coped and that they can too. www.rd4u.org.uk

Brave Kids

Brave kids is a website for children and young people with chronic, life threatening illness or disabilities. It is American-based and provides information, a message board for young people to post questions and comments and share feeling and thoughts about their conditions. www.bravekids.org

British Institute of Learning Disabilities

BILD produces a series of books that explain death and bereavement to children with learning disabilities. www.bild.org.uk

The Child Bereavement Charity

The charity has a site for young people which includes articles and leaflets covering such subjects as 'Going back to school or college', 'Seeing the body or not' and 'Adjusting to changes'. There are forum postings as well as suggested reading and recommended DVDs. These can be purchased on line from the CBC shop. They also provide links to valuable UK websites. The charity provides specialised support, information and training to those bereaved by the death of a baby or young child.

There is a young person's advisory group which talks about how the person might feel and how to remember the special person who has died, and going back to school or college after the death. There are forum postings on a variety of topics. It includes 'Ten things to do on special days', 'Ten things to do on Father's day', 'Ten things to do on Mother's day', and 'Fifteen ways to remember people at Christmas'. It is a very brightly coloured site, with lots of engaging activities and multi-cultural images. www.childbereavement.org.uk

The Childhood Bereavement Network

There are many useful resources on this site including a downloadable letter a bereaved young person can send to a friend explaining what support they might need. There are videos which may be helpful for young people. They include 'You'll Always Remember Them, Even When You're Old', which has children ages 6–12 talking about their experience of bereavement and one called 'It Will Be OK', developed by bereaved young people aged 13–18. www.childhoodbereavementnetwork.org.uk

Childline

Childline is a free and confidential information and advice service for children and young people. The website has information on a range of issues. There is a message board, 'Hot Topics', and plenty of information on a wide range of issues. If the young person prefers to write the address is Chlidline, Freepost NATN1111. No stamp required. www.child-line.org.uk

Compassion Books

This American site is useful for anyone searching for books dealing with grief and bereavement. All the items have been chosen and reviewed by professionals or those who have experienced loss. As well as books it has relevant videos, CDs and other resources which can be bought. www.compassionatebooks.com

Connexions Direct

Offers information and advice for young people aged between 13–19. It has information on relationships, rights and bereavement. www.connexions-direct.com

Dougy Centre

The Dougy Center was the first in the USA to provide peer support groups for grieving children. It offers information and support and acts as a referral point for other services. A fire in June 2009 destroyed the centre but the interactive site is still in operation. www.dougy.org

The Grief Encounter

The Grief Encounter charity has an interactive website with Teen Zone, Kids Zone and games as well as more general information. Bad Time Rhymes is a section devoted to poetry written by bereaved young people. www.griefencounter.org.uk

GriefNet

GriefNet is an internet community of persons dealing with grief, death and major loss. It is directed by clinical psychologist and traumatologist, Dr Cendra Lynn. GriefNet operates 24 hours a day, every day of the year. It has space for children and young people to post poetry, writing about their experience as well as a gallery for artwork. There is also a memorial site for 'Kids and Animals', a loss children experience but which is frequently overlooked as being unimportant. It also has a comprehensive book list suitable for bereaved children and young people.

A companion site, Kidsaid.com is specially for children and young people. Kids-to-kids is for those aged 12 and under; and k2k-teens is for those aged between 13–18. In order to ensure young people using the service are kept safe, each child or young person has to obtain the permission of a parent or guardian to join the online community and moderators contact the parent to ensure permission has been given. www.kidsaid.com/k2k-support

Healing Place

The Healing Place, a centre for loss and change, offers grief support for children and teens, families and guardians. Though it is not an interactive site it provides useful information. www.thehealingplaceinfo.org

kooth

This is an online counselling service for 11 to 25 year olds. It has a message board, a blog and has a moderated site which offers peer support and counselling. Eighty-nine per cent of kooth users prefer online counselling to telephone support. www.kooth.com

Muslim Youth Helpline

This offers faith and culturally sensitive counselling services to Muslim youth in the UK. Outreach workers can also visit young Muslims who are in custody. www.myh.org.uk

Papyrus – Prevention of Young Suicide

A voluntary organisation whose aim is to prevent young suicide and to promote positive mental health and well-being in young people. It provides information and support for those affected by suicide in young people. It provides advice and offers information on how to communicate with young people who have contemplated suicide or are considering it. It provides resources for parents and carers, professionals and young people. www.papyrus-uk.org

Partnership for Children

The charity's aim is to help children and young people throughout the world to develop skills which will enhance their present and future emotional well-being. It includes material on bereavement for parents, teachers and children. www.partnershipforchildren.org.uk

Richmond's Hope

Richmond's Hope is a charity that supports children who have been bereaved or suffered significant loss. 'Not all children will need the support of a project such as this, but we are here to help those who do.' www.richmondshope.org.uk

Riprap

Riprap provides online support for children and young people when a parent has cancer through forums where they can share experiences or discuss a topic related the death and bereavement. There is an A–Z glossary of terms related to cancer with explanations about palliative care and anticipatory grief. It has site house rules to ensure user safety. www.riprap.org.uk

Samaritans

Confidential, non-judgemental support, 24 hours a day for anyone suffering distress or despair, including anyone who is feeling suicidal. It also responds to emails and letters. The website offers information on emotional health, links to local branches where the young person can speak to someone face-to-face. www.samaritans.org.uk

Sibling Survivors

This is a supportive community of people whose sibling has died by suicide. Based in the USA it contains articles, information and support. www.siblingsurvivors.com

Skylight

This New Zealand site (Skylight, 2007) offers suggestions to help children and adolescents stressed by bereavement. Here are some:

- Eat good food.
- Sleep well and have rests when you need to.
- Ask for what you need.
- Take time to do nothing – maybe stay with a relative or friend for a break.
- Do something physical.
- Give yourself permission to feel whatever you feel.
- Praise yourself.
- Don't expect too much of yourself – forgive yourself.
- Laugh – and don't feel guilty if you are having a good day!
- Listen to your favourite music.
- Read the stuff you like.
- Hang out with good friends – keep connected – talk with others.
- Spend time with people who care about you.
- Spend time alone when you need some space to think.
- Keep safe – don't do dumb stuff.

www.skylight.org.nz

Starbright World

In their own words, 'This is a virtual hangout where you can build on existing friendships or create new ones, from home or from the hospital. Starbright World is an online social network where teens (ages 13 to 20) who have serious medical conditions, and siblings of seriously ill teens, can connect with each other via moderated chat rooms, games, bulletin boards, videos and more.' www.starbright.org

Virtual Memorial

There are a number of sites on the internet where the bereaved child or young person can create a memorial. GriefNet.org has a three-step process which is completed in a matter of minutes which allows the bereaved person to create a memorial which may later be elaborated with photographs, poetry, a blog and music.

Memorial websites allow people to grieve for their friends, family, pets and celebrity figures and those whose death is the subject of media coverage. In the public shared space, photos can be uploaded, videos and music added and comments and condolences offered. There are a number of public sites including Friends at Rest, Gone Too Soon, Much Loved and Lasting Tribute. Jonathan Davies, who set up Much Loved, commented on this phenomena, 'The death of [Princess] Diana brought about a change in how we grieve publicly, and then the internet connected people and provided a place for it' (Saner, 2009: 10). Today his site has 12,000 memorials. These sites give a forum to express feelings and come to terms with what has happened.

>   www.muchloved.com – charity memorial website
>   www.rememberedforever.org – charity memorial website.

Voice

Voice offers advocacy and support to children and young people in public care. The website provides information on young people's rights, leaflets and posters and can help with any problems or questions about being in care or in a secure setting. www.voiceyp.org

Winston's Wish

Winston's Wish is a leading authority on childhood bereavement and the largest provider of services for bereaved families in the UK. The charity offers support and resources to parents and professionals and children.

The site for children and young people is engaging, well designed and represents ethnic diversity. It has a number of areas to explore which includes Frequently Asked Questions, including medical questions for 'Dr Doug'. There is a Graffiti Wall, where a message can be sprayed or printed; a Skyscape, where stars in the night sky can be chosen and the bereaved can write thoughts that be read by others; a Talk section, where messages can be left for other young people and forums to discuss particular topics. The IntEract section includes DVDs and podcasts to download, all relating to children's experiences of bereavement.

There is also a valuable section called 'Do'. This gives ideas to help young people on days that are likely to evoke memories of the those loved ones who have died. In addition, there is a calendar to record important dates. There are downloadable materials for children and young people to use.

The site also includes guidelines on site safety and users who want to access the Feelings and Talk sections have to register and state the name of their Internet Provider (IP). Addresses are recorded and checked to ensure user protection. www.winstonswish.org.uk

Young Minds

This charity is committed to improving emotional well-being and supporting mental health of all children and young people. It has many sections including one for children and another for young people. It covers feelings, fears and information on specific mental health issues. It also offers videos, podcasts, a twitter and a newsroom. www.young-minds.org.uk

8 Traumatic Death and its Impact

> Although individual responses to traumatic events differ from child to child … the consistency of core response is clear: heightened anxiety, generalized fears, and loss of self esteem. (Garbarino, 1992: 69)

Sudden death which occurs in traumatic circumstances affects the bereaved child profoundly; it may be in witnessing a death in a road traffic collision or witnessing a sudden death from natural causes, such as cardiac arrest. Such experiences have both short-and long-term implications for the child who may well be affected for the rest of his life (Black, 1996; Perry and Szalavitz, 2006). Death because of murder, suicide, and in other devastating circumstances may cause Post Traumatic Stress Disorder in children (Trickey, 2005; van der Kolk et al., 2006). At the present time much trauma is connected to gangs, gun crime and suicide in young people's lives (Batmanghelidjh, 2007). As a result of criminal activity many young people find themselves in custodial settings or, because of other reasons, in the care of the local authority (CBN, 2008). These children and young people are ones who may be among the most disadvantaged in society and offer significant challenges to those who offer bereavement support (Penny, 2009a).

Death in Traumatic Circumstances

> 'The one word that best describes grief is sadness: the one word that best describes trauma is terror.' Anon. (National Institute for Trauma and Loss)

Trauma is defined as 'an experience that threatens life or physical integrity and that overwhelms an individual's capacity to cope' (National Child Traumatic Stress Network, USA). It leads to intense fear and feelings of helplessness. Some traumatic incidents may be short lived, for example, a sudden road traffic collision, or continue over a longer period, such as in repeated sexual abuse or continuous intimidation because of gang culture.

The work of Janoff-Bulman highlights the impact of traumatic events. She says that it is not fear that makes traumatic events psychologically harmful, but the way they undermine our basic assumptions about the world as a safe, ordered, just, caring and ultimately, meaningful place. This is similar to the view of Colin Murray Parkes, who writes of the way in which our 'Assumptive World' is destroyed by sudden death. Our assumption that life will carry on as normal is shattered by the traumatic death of someone we love. For children this is likely to be more intense because they are dependent on those around them to stabilise their world (Black and Trickey, 2005). 'Ultimately, what determines how children survive trauma, physically, emotionally, or psychologically, is whether the people around them – particularly the adults they should be able to trust and rely upon – stand by them with love, support and encouragement' (Perry and Szalavitz, 2006: 5).

When the 'fight' or 'flight' response, triggered by trauma occurs, it releases chemicals into the body. 'An interplay between adrenaline and nordrenalin (the flight–fright hormones) as well as cortisol (the stress hormone) creates a complex chemistry, both battling with and generating stress' (Batmanghelidjh, 2007: 57). Continued nervousness after the event can drain the body of resources which in turn may compromise the child's immune system and make them more vulnerable to illness or infection (Pfeffer, 2007). When an infant suffers traumatic loss it can alter the way the brain organises and internalises new information. In addition, there 'may be a permanent change in neuropsychological function and emotional development mediated by the right orbito-frontal cortex' (Perry et al., 1995). Early trauma can also bring about critical changes in the limbic system of the brain (Di Ciacco, 2008). This area is connected to the regulation of emotions. Where the child is unsupported and has no significant carer to aid the grieving process, the developmental process may cease. The child may miss the critical point in their early years on which to build a healthy emotional foundation (Chrouso et al., 2003; Cozolino, 2002; Siegel, 1999). Box 8.1 lists common reactions following traumatic bereavement.

Box 8.1 Common Reactions Following Traumatic Bereavement

Cognitive

Confused thinking

Nightmares/distressing dreams

Poor concentration

Lack of interest in things that previously were important to the child

Ruminating about what has happened

Thinking they cannot cope

Recurring thoughts or images of the event

(Continued)

Emotional

Anxiety

Guilty

Fear

Easily upset

Irritability

Anger

Feeling overwhelmed

Feeling disorientated

Panicky and panic attacks

Resentful

Burdened

Behavioural

Change in eating habits

Change in sleep patterns

Hyperactivity

Hyperarousal

Argumentative

Withdrawn

Aggressive

Increased dependency

Restlessness

Physical

Feeling tired/fatigued

Restless

Cold and shivery

Feeling nauseous

Tenseness in muscles

Stomach aches

Self-harm

Dissociation

Children bereaved by traumatic events

Not all children who experience trauma have traumatic grief, many experience normal grief reactions or uncomplicated bereavement. However, there are considerable numbers who do require support. In working with traumatised children and young people the aim is to facilitate the safe release of feelings, to regain a sense of control, to clarify what happened and reduce/eliminate self-blame, to gain a sense of trust in the future and to put the event in perspective. The child may fear that something similar will happen again, that the bereaved child or young person will be left alone, that she won't be able to cope, that while she is at school something awful will happen to her remaining parent and that it will be her turn next. Often children and young people need concrete reassurance that they are safe. While the scar of the trauma will remain it need not be the raw wound it is immediately following the traumatic event.

Where traumatic death has occurred the bereaved may be offered help by police, victim support and social services. This may add to the disorientation felt by children and young people since the routine of their world may be severely disrupted. Children are often afraid of what is strange, particularly where children have a learning disability. The affect of trauma may affect the child's thinking ability and they may become distracted and feel confused, seemingly having lost the compass of their life.

Children also become fatigued by feelings of fear (Stokes, 2004). Unsettling feelings following trauma may be triggered by loud noises, smells, or objects associated with the trauma. The young person may be unaware of these triggers and in working with them it may be helpful to see if there is a pattern in their responses and help them to understand the cause of their distress.

Children reflect their trauma through their behaviour, their drawings and artwork and in play. It is, therefore, important to provide a wide variety of opportunities for children to express their concerns through non-verbal means, as was described in Chapter 6. These are unconscious attempts to regain mastery over what has happened to them, particularly when they cannot verbally explain or express their feeling about what has happened to them. 'Language, a function of declarative memory, is generally not readily accessible to trauma survivors of any age after a traumatic event. In particular, Broca's area, a section of the brain that controls language, is affected, making it difficult to relate the trauma narrative. In fact, when a trauma survivor attempts to speak, PET scans, actually show the Broca's area tends to shut down' (Malchiodi, 2008: 2).

Disasters

Disasters happen in different contexts: disasters may be worldwide, impacting on many countries and many continents; they may be localised, affecting the immediate locality or community or they may be personal, affecting an individual and his family. The traumatic murder of a parent, the suicide of a sibling or the death in an horrific road traffic collision has immediate impact on the individual yet, because traumatic death attracts attention, the personal tragedy often becomes public property. Whatever the nature of the disaster, interest from the media may further complicate the young person's response to the death and delay the grieving process (Christ and Christ, 2006). Unexpected images that appear on the news or in the local press traumatise the bereaved even further, it causes unanticipated re-exposure to the trauma (Libow, 1992). Previous traumatisation, can pre-dispose children to subsequent re-traumatisation (Kosminsky, 2008). Secondary adversities such as upheaval through police involvement, delayed funerals until coronary reports have been completed and legal procedures which affect the family all increase the burden of the bereavement. In her work with fire fighters and their families after 9/11, Grace Christ emphasises the role of the media in delaying grief as the bereaved are repeatedly exposed to images of the disaster (Christ and Christ, 2006).

A child or young person may be caught up in a disaster through events that happen in the school community. At such a time it is important that the school has a Critical Incidence Plan that can be put into immediate action (Harrison, 2002). Meanwhile, a child may at some point need professional help. Dora Black, child psychiatrist and an expert on the impact of trauma on children says that, when working with children, 'The goals in treating children … are to help them to anticipate, understand, and manage everyday reminders so that the intensity of reminders and their ability to disrupt daily functioning gradually lessen' (Harris-Hendriks et al., 2000: 49). When traumatic loss has occurred it is helpful to ascertain if the child has a history of previous trauma so that appropriate interventions can be put in place. Re-activated trauma increases the child's vulnerability to complicated grief.

Following a disaster it is important to regain some sense of control. Children and young people can be helped to recognise what areas of their life they have control over and to understand that there are adults who will help to keep them safe. We can reassure them that the event is over and that we will do all we can to keep them safe. Regular routines, regular meal-times, relaxation and play all help in the healing process (Goldman, 2000). However, these reassuring routines are frequently disrupted. In fact, 'recent disaster studies have documented increases in domestic violence, child abuse, and delinquency during the post-disaster period' (Goenjian, quoted in van der Kolk et al., 2006: 346).

The experience of disaster as well as other traumatic events, may cause dissociative symptoms in the child or young person (Laor et al., 2002; Silberg, 2003). These may be seen in trance states or 'black outs', long periods of non-responsiveness or lack of attention, depersonalisation, as well amnesia for traumatic events (Carrion and Steiner, 2000). These can be triggered by images in the media, so if the bereaved can be protected from seeing too much material by a reduction in watching news items related to the disaster, it will help reduce fresh exposure to the cause of their distress.

People who experience traumatic bereavement face issues that are often beyond the comprehension and experience of others. For example, the bushfires in Australia in 2008, as well as bringing death and destruction, cut off those affected from their normal sources of support. This increased sense of isolation adds to the distress of those caught up in disasters. Children and young people who experience traumatic loss may feel isolated from their peers which may cause them to become withdrawn and unavailable to participate in activities engaged in by others. In addition, those who work with traumatised children and young people may experience secondary trauma as they listen to stories that are told and witness the extreme emotions that are expressed.

The child's adaptation to loss is ongoing and at different points in their development, different issues will arise (Kosminsky, 2008). We can help children and young people become more resilient by encouraging them to build positive relationships, promoting a sense of optimism and hope and helping them to learn problem-solving skills. Hope is one of the strongest predictors of getting better after a disaster (Raphael, 2005)

Suicide

'He's gone but he's not gone because I think of him everyday.' Hannah, aged ten, whose father died by suicide.

In the UK, death by suicide is the fourth most common cause of death among 15–19 year olds (Silva and Cotgrove, 1999). This means that many young people may be faced with the suicide of a peer. Nearly 74% of all deaths of American adolescents are caused by accidents, murder or suicide (Corr et al., 2003). Such deaths arouse strong emotions since '[t]he person who takes their own life implicitly rejects life but in so doing rejects family and friends too' (Eke, 2009: 31). Yet, in many instances grief in surviving peers may be disenfranchised, as others consider that they have no cause to grieve, particularly where criminal activity was involved (Oltjenbruns, 1996). Others believe that, as the death was not of a family member, it has less importance, not appreciating that the friendship network is of key importance in this age group (Hooyman and Kramer, 2006).

There is still a great deal of stigma around the subject of suicide, although in the UK it is no longer a criminal act as it was until the Suicide Act of 1961. Many people regard it as an act of madness or selfishness, with little compassion for the person who took his own life. Children who are not told that the death was by suicide, or where secrets are held about the cause of death, may feel excluded and confused (Lukas and Seiden, 2007). The bereavement process may be complicated because of feelings of shame and humiliation (Heikes, 1997; Lowton and Higginson, 2002). This may cause children and young people to deny that the deceased died by suicide. The family, including the children, may feel 'blamed and shamed' by the suicide (Ratnarajah and Schofield, 2008: 625). The death of a parent by suicide is reported to provoke anxiety in children immediately following the death, anger after six months and shame a year later (Cerel et al., 1999). It may be one of the most difficult things to say to a child or young person that a parent had died by suicide but it is important to find the words to tell the truth (Winston's Wish, 2008). Adults may avoid talking about the traumatic death but such avoidance maintains traumatisation (Black and Trickey, 2005).

Those bereaved by suicide have great difficulty making meaning out of the death (Beautrais, 2004; Jordan, 2001). Studies have shown that a child bereaved by parental suicide show a significant increase in psychiatric symptoms, behaviour problems and social difficulties (Cerel et al., 1999; Pfeffer et al., 2000) and children may experience an ongoing, unending void in their lives following a parental suicide (Stimming and Stimming, 1999).

Critical incidents, such as suicide, happen suddenly and attack the person's sense of control over their life and their surroundings (Mitchell et al., 2009). The loss may also trigger secondary losses such as moving house and school, increased likelihood of financial difficulties in the family, and emotional withdrawal by the surviving parent (Ratnarajah and Schofield, 2007). Survivors of suicide, where a family member or peer has died, may feel judged, that somehow it was their fault and they should have prevented the death (Martin, 2000).

Young people may also worry that the mental health difficulties their parent suffered from may be passed on and fear that they may inherit the difficulties. Suicide in a family puts other family members at a greater risk of suicidal behaviour (Brent et al., 1988; Ellenbogen and Gratton, 2001; Jordan, 2001). Children may fear that when they reach the age of the deceased sibling or parent who died by suicide, they may do the same (Linn-Gust, 2006). This fear is not often voiced but it is important to recognise that this shadow may be carried for many years (Sethi and Bhargava, 2003; Simone, 2008).

Eckersley and Dear describe suicide as 'the tip of the iceberg in a sea of suffering' (2002: 1900). When working with children and young people it is important to recognise the context of the family prior to the suicide. In assessing the needs of a child or young person who is bereaved by suicide we need to look at the life story prior to the suicide and the quality and intensity of the relationship with the deceased (Silverman et al., 1994–95). Studies have shown that a child bereaved by suicide may have been living with a parent or other family member with mental ill health for months if not years (Cerel et al., 2002). The strain of living in such circumstances impacts on all the family and the suicide may be the culmination of a distressing and unstable period. The suicide may bring forth ambivalent feelings including relief that the strain or psychological turmoil is finally over (Wertheimer, 2001). A key aspect of being bereaved by suicide is the sense of abandonment (Ratnarajah and Schofield, 2008). A child or young person may feel that they were abandoned before the suicide occurred, for example, where a parent was addicted to drugs or alcohol or where there had been a history of mental illness or depression. Suicide survivors feel isolated from the world around them (Rubey, 1999). Wright and Partridge (1999) express the view that where the person who died by suicide knew that their child would find the body, it is a form of child abuse.

'One significant, recurring finding suggests that there was often no shared expression of grief within the family at the time of the suicide' (Simone, 2008: 44). This lack of communication can cause the child or young person to feel rejected because 'closed' communication does not foster positive grieving. Research by Barlow and Coleman (2003) indicates that families who communicate directly and openly are able to join forces to process their grief. They become companions on their journey through grief and act as mutual supports (Schoka et al., 2003). Where children hide their grief for fear of upsetting another family member the process of grieving is inhibited (Holland, 2001). Children need to be able to talk about the suicide if they want to (Campbell, 1997; Hammer, 1991; Stimming and Stimming, 1999).

Alison Wertheimer (2001) describes those who are bereaved by suicide as 'survivors' and those who work with the suicidally bereaved may become secondary survivors. The impact of the work may evoke feelings of anxiety and disempowerment particularly where the bereaved may want to 'join' the person who has died or who struggle with survivor guilt. Supervision is vital for anyone who is counselling or supporting those young people bereaved by suicide (Eke, 2009)

What do children and young people need following a death by suicide?

Children and young people need age appropriate information given as honestly as possible (Baugher and Jordan, 2004). By telling the truth we may prevent the child imagining a gruesome scenario as often the child's fantasies are even worse than the actual event. In answering the child's questions and being open to their exploration of the whys and whats of the situation we allow them space to think about what has happened and avoid the child blaming himself in silent despair. The child and young person will take in as much information as he needs at the time but may well return to the subject again and again as he matures and reaches different levels of comprehension and different developmental points. Children who live through terrifying ordeals can endure such hardship where there are competent adults who care for them (Masten et al., 1990).

Knowledge about common reactions to traumatic events can be very helpful to children and young people. Understanding that their reactions to traumatic, sudden death are normal reactions to an abnormal situation can free them from the sense that they are falling apart or going mad. For example, they may be plagued by disturbing dreams but may feel less threatened when they know that disturbing dreams are one of the classic reactions to a traumatic event.

In *Dying to Be Free* by Beverly Cobain and Jean Larch (2006), one of the authors talks of her own near suicide attempt. Her account reveals how any thoughts or consideration of those who would be left behind were totally eclipsed by the freedom that death offered her. This may be a hard concept for anyone, let alone a child, to understand or accept; however, the idea that the person who chose to die by suicide believed it was the best way forward, despite having loving relationships with those left behind, may offer some consolation.

Self-harm following bereavement

Suicide and self-harm are significant causes of ill health and death in adolescents (Silva and Cotgrove, 1999). For adolescent males, death by hanging is the most common method, whilst females generally choose self-poisoning. In the USA guns are used by over 50% of adolescents who die by suicide. Losing a parent through bereavement or separation and divorce in early life has been shown to be a risk for both suicide and self-harm in young people (Adams, 1982; Gutierrez, 1999). Survivor guilt, whether because of actions taken or not taken, may result in self-harm, suicidal ideation and substance abuse. 'Bereavement in early childhood is certainly one of the predisposing factors that has been associated with suicide in later life, along with a host of others that seem to have chaos as a common theme' (Silva and Cotgrove, 1999: 7). Silva and Cotgrove provide a list of pointers towards a risk of self-harm in recently bereaved adolescents. They include:

- Depressed mood
- Recent change in behaviour
- History of self-harm
- History of mental illness
- Threats of self-harm
- Substance abuse
- Impulsivity
- Hostility/help-rejecting attitude
- Deteriorating support
- Legal problems.

Children with special needs or circumstances have normal responses to traumatic bereavement. Their response is influenced by their level of understanding and the level of support available to them. What all children and young people need is simple explanations about death and trauma and care which harnesses their strengths and addresses their fears. Their individual character traits and inherent nature influence how they respond to loss by suicide (Mandleco and Peery, 2000).

As those who work with traumatised children it is useful to remember the signs that might alert us to the need for immediate intervention:

- Behaviour that is a danger to themselves or others.
- Talking of suicide or of the wish to be dead or wanting to join the person who has died.
- Losing the line between fantasy and reality.
- Where there is little or no room for the child's needs to be met because of a parent's poor mental health, depression or acute grief.

A personal account

'My husband died by suicide when my son was just a few months old. Now he's four and he keeps asking me questions. I find it hard at times but you just have to go with the flow and answer what you can, as honestly as you possibly can. I was a bit teary the other day at the nursery, on the anniversary of his death, and though the nursery have been wonderful, this person said, "Well, just think of the positives at least there is no one to argue with". In a way I was grateful that she has never had the experience so she doesn't know what it means to be bereaved like that' (Participant, Glasgow conference, May, 2009).

Death by Road Traffic Crashes

According to the Brake, the road safety charity, every 30 seconds someone is killed on roads. There are 1.2 million deaths and 50 million injuries every year worldwide on roads (Brake Conference, 2009). Such sudden deaths leave families reeling. Though each family is unique, a common response is the need to know the truth of what has happened to their dead loved one. As in other traumatic losses, the bereaved child or young person may find that their life is never the same again.

A personal account

When four-year-old Rachel's father and her brother's best friend died after their car was hit by four-by-four, driven by a driver who was over the legal alcohol limit and using a mobile phone at the point of collision, the impact on the remaining family was devastating. Rachel wore her father's fleece for four days and asked if her father would be coming back on Easter Sunday. She was really upset that he wouldn't be returning like Jesus. Her eight-year-old brother, who was in the car when the tragedy happened, tried to kill himself the day before his ninth birthday because he couldn't bear the idea of being older than his best friend who had died. He survived when his friend perished and felt survivor guilt especially since they had swapped places not long before the crash occurred. (Ruth, mother)

Murder and Manslaughter

All children who witness a murder or have a loved one who was murdered will be affected – in a sense they are co-victims. When a member of a family is killed, there is more than one victim: the whole family may feel they have been destroyed (Morrison, 2001). Grief in these situations is severe and chronic. However children and young people bereaved by homicide may be given less attention than the spouse or parents of the victim.

The work of psychiatrist Dora Black has made a significant contribution to our awareness of the impact of uxoricide, spousal killing, on children. She writes, 'We saw over 500 children where one parent killed the other and in two-thirds of the cases there had been previous domestic violence. When we saw the children after the death of their mother (90% of our sample), they told us that they felt the killing was their fault, because they had provoked dissension between their parents. Sometimes they had been told, "we never quarrelled until you were born"' (Black, 2007). Where children had witnessed the murder of a parent there was a greater incidence of Post Traumatic Stress Disorder (Black and Trickey, 2005).

Murder may be the tragic culmination of years of family strife. In a follow-up study in which one parent had killed the other at least two-thirds of the children had experienced long-standing conflict between parents, about half were present when the killing took place, about half were discouraged from talking about it and in one-third of cases there was active hostility from the extended family (Black and Trickey, 2005). Subsequent disruptions may mean that the child is placed in local authority care or placed in a foster home after the imprisonment of the perpetrator. When the prison term ends the child may then return to live with the parent who committed the murder. This can often be extremely disturbing for the child and '[o]ur clinical experience is that children who return to the surviving parent's care on the whole do badly' (Harris-Henricks et al., 2000: 212).

A study of ten families in which a family member had died through homicide considered the Bowlby phases of grief responses including protest, despair and detachment. It found that during the protest phase homicide survivors experienced the characteristic reactions Bowlby described but, additionally, they experienced overwhelming rage which often overshadowed feelings of sadness. There was also a strong urge to seek revenge. Children in this phase demonstrated similar feelings along with regression and severe school problems (Poussaint, 1984).

'Children and adults who are bereaved by catastrophic events are particularly at risk of psychiatric disorder' (Black, 1996: 1). This view is supported by much research (Goodyer, 1990; Pynoos et al., 1993). Children and young people may fear for their own safety and may be troubled by thoughts that they may be the next victim. 'Children exposed to a violent occurrence require the opportunity individually to thoroughly explore their traumatic experience at the earliest possible occasion' (Pynoos and Nader, 1990).

War, Terrorism and Civil Conflict

The effect of war on children is devastating. At present there are 30 wars worldwide, at least two million children have died in the last ten years, five million have been disabled, twelve million are homeless, approximately 90% of casualties in armed conflict are civilians and over 50% are children (Tufnell, 2005). Children fleeing war as refugees and asylum seekers may have experienced or witnessed violence, rape, murder and torture. This may lead to anxiety and depression, psychic numbing, Post Traumatic Stress Disorder as well as sustained feelings of anger resulting in violent outbursts (Barenbaum et al., 2004; Yule, 2000). We cannot afford to ignore the needs of these young people who have been bereaved of so much in their lives (Black, 1996).

Children need extra support at times which are highly stressful, such as during war or where there is a threat of terrorist activity (Goldman, 2002a). Children who are closest to a significantly traumatic event will be the most affected by intense feelings of anxiety, fear and powerlessness. This happened in the USA when, on September 11, 2001, two planes crashed into the World Trade Center twin towers. As well as direct exposure to the event, millions witnessed the attacks on television.

Dr Leila M. Gupta of UNICEF has completed extensive research into traumatic bereavement in families in conflict settings (Noppe, 2008). Her research in Rwanda, Sierra Leone and Afghanistan includes narratives from children hiding under dead bodies, children witnessing the torture and murder of their family and friends and witnessing the amputations of limbs as punishment by 'soldiers'. According to Dr Gupta 'in the past few decades more than three million children have been killed in wars and approximately 143 million children were parentally bereaved' (Noppe, 2008: 1). Despite the horrific nature of the children's experiences, intervention programmes designed to address their trauma has proved therapeutic (Gupta and Zimmer, 2008). These include story telling, group sharing, drawing pictures, writing activities, role-playing, drama and singing traditional songs. Even short-term interventions 'led children to report that they felt better, had fewer bad dreams and experienced a sense of relief for being able to give expression to their horrible experiences' (Noppe, 2008: 2).

In recent years the wars in Iraq and Afghanistan, among other places, have claimed the lives of both civilian and military personnel. Children and young people whose relatives died are profoundly affected and grieve in their own unique way. Jodie was 17 when her brother's vehicle was blown up. She visits his grave and said, 'I talk to him in the cemetery. Sometimes I stand, other times I kneel down and talk to him like he is there. Sometimes I cry; other days I just pass the time of day. I feel silly and self-conscious speaking to a grave, but whenever I look round, nobody is paying the slightest bit of attention. There are other people there at the gravesides, crying and mourning in their own way, talking to their loved ones and praying. It is definitely therapeutic' (McDougall, 2008). She also said that having a brother who died as a 'war hero' makes others view you as someone to admire as well as to feel sorry for you. However, we know that soldiers returning from war zones may have been profoundly affected by their experiences. 'In consultations in regions of war, we have noted cases in which soldiers returning from war, often traumatized or depressed, have used military weapons to commit suicide and the aftermath has been witnessed by their children' (Pynoos et al., 1996: 346). Children and young people may be directly affected by war, whether they were physically present or not.

Violent Death and Living with Violence

Some young people live in a world of gang violence, school shootings, random acts of terrorism and street crime (Batmanghelidjh, 2007). Whether these are personally experienced or viewed via the media they can cause severe distress to the young person who must live with a heightened sense of vigilance (Goldman, 2002b; Nader et al., 1999). 'Even adolescents who are not directly exposed to violence are surrounded by images of violent death in the media, the Internet, advertising, video games and their communities' (Hooyman and Kramer, 2006: 155). Where a young person witnesses community violence such a gang-related shootings, the trauma may be ongoing rather than a one-off. Such events keep the young person in a heightened state of vigilance which damages emotional and physical well-being (van der Kolk et al., 2006). In some cities children and young people feel as if they are living in 'war zones' (Corr et al., 2003). As we see the increase in street violence more teenagers are at risk of violent death (Doka, 2003). Students may be exposed to violence in their colleges or in the immediate vicinity of the college as they go to and from the educational institutions (Williams, 2009).

On April 20 1999, two students went into Columbine High School, Colorado, USA and with pipe bombs and semi-automatic weapons proceeded to kill 12 students and one teacher and maimed many others. It was one of the worst massacres in American history and, ten years later, survivors continue to live with the horror of their experience. Valeen Schnurr was there when it happened: 'I'll never be normal. I really struggled with survivor guilt, with why my friend had to die. I've forgiven them for what they did but an event as traumatic as that changes you, it moulds you into a different person' (Day, 2009).

The school performance of children and young people exposed to community violence is negatively affected (Saltzman et al., 2001; Schwartz and Gorman, 2003). '[T]raumatised young people may experience breakdowns in key attentional and task-related skills that can jeopardise academic performance' (Dyregrov, 2004: 79). In addition, they found that 'around one in five of the classmates that experienced a student's sudden death in an accident experienced a high level of distress nine months following the loss' (Dyregov, 2004: 80).

Where children and young people experience cumulative trauma though witnessing domestic violence, community gang culture, bullying, maltreatment and so on, there are negative implications for their learning capabilities (Juvonen et al., 2000). Research from Streeck-Fisher and van der Kolk (2000) states that it causes problems with attention, difficulties with sensory perception, reduced capacity to learn from experience, problems with understanding visual and spatial stimuli, and poor retention of information because of the way in which the trauma has impacted on specific areas of the brain. In addition, loss through bereavement impacts on both the young person's motivation and their capacity to take in new information, as is explored in Chapter 5.

Reflexive Exercise

'When I was fifteen my sister was killed. She went to a friend's house and just never came home. She'd rung at 8.45 to say she was setting off home but she never arrived. That same night, a woman walking her dog, found her. She'd been strangled. My Dad came home and said "She's not coming home" and he broke down. The next months were a blur. I remember the funeral; there were reporters all over the place. I broke down completely. I kept thinking she'd come back and say it was all a joke.

'After that we moved house, across the country. I had to drop back a year because I couldn't think straight. Part of me hoped they'd never find her murderer because it would drag it all up again. I felt guilty because she died when she was two years younger than me and I felt selfish because I wanted to get on with my life.

'I had terrible dreams; dreams where someone was stabbing me. Now, I'm twenty and I'm still scared of going out on my own. I don't think I'll ever get over it, I don't think you ever can.' Shelley.

- In what ways did Shelley's traumatic bereavement experience change her life?
- How did feelings of guilt affect her?
- In what way was her school career affected?
- Do you think being an adolescent had any particular significance on the way she reacted?
- How could you support someone like Shelley five years after the murder of her sister?

9 Working with Dreams to Ease the Grieving Process

'I dreamt I was watching TV. It went off and then it was my Dad. All angels came round him and me.' G., aged 10, following the death of her father.

Dreams follow the grieving process and we can harness their power when working with bereaved children and young people (Cooper, 1999; Mallon, 2002). We find dreams in which the dreamer feels numb, angry, guilty or devastated. We find visitation dreams in which the dead live on and communicate with their loved ones. There are universal themes in dreams following bereavement which appear across cultures (Bulkeley, 1995). There are also dreams in which continuing bonds link the dead and living together, especially at special times such as anniversaries.

Grief reactions such as anger, guilt, sadness, helplessness and abandonment are found in the dreams of the bereaved (Adams et al., 2008; Davidson et al., 2005). Dreaming is generally responsive to experiences that precede it during the day (Punamaki, 1999) so it is not surprising that someone who is with a dying person or who has been bereaved should have dreams that reflect this event. Emotional arousal affects the intensity of dreams rather than their length or specific content of the dream (Hartmann and Basile, 2003), thus people anticipating bereavement, those who have been bereaved and those who are dying may well experience heightened intensity in their dreams. The content and atmosphere of a dream can trouble the child or young person for days, as lingering fear or anxiety colours their mood. In learning to work with dreams we can empower children and young people to face their fears and gain resilience (Barrett, 1992; Garfield, 1997; Schredl, 2000).

Everyone in the world dreams and children dream because dreaming is part of the cognitive process where learning is laid down in the brain and memories are classified and stored (Evans, 1983; Mallon, 2002). As we sleep the brain sifts through our waking experiences and continues to problem solve. Where there has been a traumatic event in the life of a child, the unconscious continues trying to make sense of the events, for as human beings we try to make meaning from our experiences (Neimeyer, 2001). Dreams of the deceased are part of this meaning-making process as we try to understand and come to some reconciliation with what has happened: dreams facilitate the grieving process (Knudson et al., 2006; LoConto, 1988; Mallon, 2006a). Dreams following bereavement may reflect the stages or progress of the grieving process (Garfield, 1996).

We know that at a certain point in childhood, as early as three years of age, children have specific dreams, which they can usually relate (Bulkeley et al., 2005). Early theorists saw dreams in different ways. Sigmund Freud (1965) [1900] saw children's dreams as mainly concerned with wish-fulfilment. His contemporary Carl Jung (1965) claimed that early childhood dreams are archetypal, 'big dreams' which often stay with the person for her whole life. More recently, Revonsuo (2000), pointed to the prevalence of chase themes in children's dreams, as support for his 'threat simulation theory'. Indeed, there is a prevalence of dreams of threat, fear, danger, anxiety and helplessness in the dreams of children and young people (Mallon, 1998; Punamaki, 1999).

I have found in my work with children and young people and in my research that following a bereavement, or in anticipating death, there is often a heightened intensity in their dreams (Goelitz, 2007; Grubbs, 2004; Mallon, 2000a). Bulkeley and Bulkeley (2005) report in great detail how people who are dying have dreams which have a great impact on them because they help reduce their fear or engage them in facing their concerns about living and dying. The dreams provide a springboard for discussion with those who provide care at this ultimate transition point. Some people who are terminally ill dream of a deceased relative coming to accompany them on the next stage of their journey. These dreams usually bring great comfort as connection is made once more (Mallon, 2000b).

Dreams and nightmares are one of the most significant indicators of stress in a child or young person's life and many bereaved young people recall bad dreams (Abdelnoor and Hollins, 2004b). Children dream of being shot, stabbed, strangled, kidnapped and poisoned. Recent research shows that '[c]hildren … felt more physically vulnerable in their dreams than did adults. This seems an accurate reflection of most children's emotional experience in the waking world' (Bulkeley et al., 2005) – a view that is supported by the work of Camila Batmanghelidjh (2007).

Universal Dream Themes

There follows a number of typical themes or 'motifs' which appear in children's dreams which Kelly Bulkeley and his colleagues found in their research into earliest childhood dreams (2005). Each is followed by an example from a child or young person with whom I have worked:

1 **Threat simulation**: the dreamer is threatened by a person, animal, or some other creature.

> 'I was on holiday and I went for a walk and this man climbed up the hills and was chasing after me with a knife and I ran to a house and he murdered me in there.' Tara, aged thirteen.

2 **Misfortune**: The dreamer has some kind of unhappy incident such as an accident, injury or an unexpected difficulty.

> 'Once I dreamt about a man who was a member of an army, who got blew up right in front of my eyes. Then I got shot three times in the eyes so I couldn't identify the person who blew the soldier up.' Emma, aged ten.

3 **Family**: The dreamer is a witness to, is part of, or is a threat to a member of his family.

> 'This man came in and then he argued with my mum, then he got hold of my little brother and took him and chucked him on the floor. Then he got hold of him and strangled him and all his neck was like a thin line.' Ian, aged ten.

4 **Void landscape**: The dreamer is in a strange, limitless, elemental landscape.

> 'I dreamt that I was running up a hill with a boulder rolling up after me. There was no one there and the whole place was barren and really weird.' Tom, aged fourteen.

5 **Wish-fulfilment**: The dreamer has something pleasing and desirable.

> 'I can change into anything I want and do anything I want. I changed into the strongest person in the world and went to help people in fires.' Kezia, aged six.

6 **Mystical**: The dreamer comes across a supernatural or spiritual figure who has special powers.

> 'I dreamt Jesus chose me as his first angel, I was so proud.' Pattie, aged seven.

7 **Flying**: The dreamer or another dream character flies and rises above the earth.

> 'I flew away to a desert island with my two sisters and the king of the sea came and lifted the island and brought us to heaven. There were angels flying and at the gate of heaven, I saw angels welcoming me in.' Sean, aged eleven.

The threat motif is apparent in many dreams of children and young people, particularly where there anxieties about their family, themselves and fear about the community in which they live (Barrett, 1996; Revonsuo, 2000).

Children and Adolescent Dreams of Their Own Death

> An uninterpreted dream is like an unopened letter. (The Talmud)

Children and young people think about and dream about death (Adams et al., 2008; Mallon, 1989). Adolescence, in particular, is a time of increased concern about mortality. This stage of development, known as the period of storm and stress, is a time of rapid biological, psychological and social change.

> At no other phase of the life cycle are the pressures of finding oneself and the threat of losing oneself so closely allied. (Erikson, 1968)

The process of relinquishing close ties of dependency on parents in order to develop closer bonds with peers causes upheaval and stress (Mallon, 1989). Uncertainty about personal capabilities, sexuality and the future are hard enough to handle but even harder when bereavement occurs. Dreams are important in 'revealing what the subconscious is preoccupied with' (Batmanghelidjh, 2007: 33).

> 'I thought the house was on fire. I was at the window coughing and my mum and dad and sister all got out of the house and I didn't and I was burnt. Then the fireman came and that's when I woke up. I thought I was dead. I dreamed I was dead.' Maddie, aged eleven.

Adolescents may also have suicidal ideation as was seen in Chapter 8 so it is not surprising that they should dream of their own death as the following examples show:

> 'It's dark. There are two versions of me – one standing in a kind of lake and the other "me" standing on my shoulders. The water is rising quickly but I can't move. As the water reaches my chin the "me" standing on my shoulders starts talking then, a knife appears in that "me"'s hands. I reach down and slice the throat of the me standing on the floor. Both versions of me fall into the water. The first me is bleeding profusely and the second me is drowning. I wake up.' Esme, aged sixteen.

This powerful dream narrative which involves self-murder, demonstrates the split some adolescents feel. The versions of 'me' are both in danger, one from the rising water the other from the knife. Either is a great threat and the dreamer cannot survive other than by waking up. Such overpowering dreams are frequently experienced following trauma (Barrett, 2001). When she had this dream Esme was going through a period of severe anxiety and low mood.

Dreams can alert those who support and work with young people of depressed mood. Listening to dreams can provide the opportunity to explore feelings which could lead to self-harm. If you are concerned and feel unable to offer the appropriate level of support then help the young person to understand the need for a referral on to a mental health professional.

> 'I had a dream that I was going to my own funeral. I had been very upset that day so maybe that made me have that dream.' Fiona, aged thirteen.

> 'My nightmares are like drowning or falling off the top of a multi-story building and I can feel what it is like; water all around me and the wind whistling past my ears.' Lee, aged twelve.

Dreams may re-enact traumatic incidents in the young person's life. Sam, aged 14, said, 'I usually dream about accidents. About being run over by a car and falling on to a spike. Both these really happened to me and I dream about them again and again.'

Dreams of the Death of Other People

Children and young people dream of others dying. These may reflect waking fears about the well-being of people they care about or may represent deep-seated anxiety about being abandoned.

'I had two separate dreams where my mother died.' Alice, aged fifteen.

'In my dream my dad has grown very old and is really ill. He later dies. I feel as though it is my fault and get really upset.' Tom, aged thirteen.

'I was being chased by my brother on a rocky mountain. At the end I fell and while I was falling all I was doing was praying this important prayer from the Qu'ran so I would go to heaven.' Mina, aged fifteen.

'I dream of people passing away and leaving me to sort out things behind them. My most frightening dream was that everyone in the world had died and I was the only person alive.' Philip, aged twelve.

Dreams in fictional characters also reflect waking worries:

I hated thinking of him underground. I'd dreamt one night he pulled a rope and a light turned on in his dark coffin. The dream was a cross section of earth. There was a thin green line of grass, then a weight of brown earth, then my father lying in the coffin with a bare bulb by his head illuminating the box. (Judy Pascoe, *My Father Who Art In A Tree*, 2002: 2)

Illness

Often illness, their own or other people's, will influence the types of dreams children have. Some are influenced by the child's fears as it was for Nadia, aged 12: 'When I am ill I dream that the medicine is poison and will kill me.'

Ricky, aged six, has many bad dreams. In one he dreamt that he was picked up by a stranger who stabbed him. Some months prior to the dream his brother had 'nearly been kidnapped' but had managed to run away from the man who tried to abduct him. In another he 'dreamt I had cancer and I died.' Such dreams are influenced by life events. Rick's maternal grandmother had cancer and he was frightened by the physical changes in her and picked up the fear in his mother. The dreams express his vulnerability, both about his brother's safety, and therefore his own. If his big brother so narrowly escaped the 'bad man', how could he escape such an attack?

Jon, aged 11, dreams about his grandmother dying. She suffers from a chronic incurable illness.

In some instances a young person will dream of attending their own funeral (Mallon, 1989) as Janette, aged 13, describes:

'When I had the measles I dreamt that I died and I came to my funeral. I saw myself laying in the coffin. It was blue marble and I was laying on a light blue silk sheet and I had my hands crossed on my chest. And while I was in the coffin dead, I was also at my own funeral, crying and leaving flowers down by the coffin. Then I woke up and looked at myself in the mirror to make sure I was there.'

Moira, aged 15, had the following recurring dream:

> 'I'm walking along in a graveyard when I suddenly see my grave in the distance. I'm shocked that I'm there and I'm not sure what to do and my Mum and Dad have already died and I can see their graves as well. I just don't know what to do and it becomes a nightmare. I just well, I just feel my life's falling apart.'

Moira manages to keep her feeling of anxiety out of the public eye. She told me, 'I cry a lot because I don't know what it will be like when my Mum and Dad die. I don't know what it's going to like without them. It worries me' (Mallon, 1998: 54). Children and young people often keep their anxieties secret from parents particularly where this involves the illness or death of the parent. To raise the subject may feel like making it more concrete and make it more likely to happen and children are loathe to do this so they do not share their worries. Such dreams may be triggered by fear of the illness and fear that they might die. In other instances, the dreams may reflect a feeling that they will only be truly appreciated when they have died.

Visitation Dreams

Many bereaved young people feel that the deceased have visited them in dreams. Such dreams have been researched over many years and they are not uncommon (Adams et al., 2008; Bulkeley, 2000; Mallon, 2008; Moody, 1993; Vickio, 1998). Dreams in which the deceased person visits the dreamer can indicate that the dreamer has moved from disbelief to acceptance that the person has died though continuing bonds remain (Mallon, 2006).

'Visitation dreams' in which the deceased comes back in a dream may bring comfort:

> 'There was a knock on the door. I answered it and it was my Dad. He looked really well and he had a suitcase. He said, "I've just come to say, I'm OK and I'm going off on holiday now. I just wanted you to know I'm alright."' Billy, aged thirteen.

This dream brought Billy a great deal of comfort. Though this is not always the case, some children who wake up from such a dream feel bereft as they are reminded the person is no longer in their physical world.

> 'My happiest dream was when my granddad came back to life so that I could see him.' Milly, aged twelve.

Novelist Jeremy Gavron's mother died by suicide when he was four years old. As an adult he dreamt of her: 'I had the only dream I can remember having of her. As a child I had often fantasised that she wasn't really dead, that one day she would come back, and in my dream she did come back. She was a middle-aged woman, plump, grey-haired and motherly. I can no longer remember the details of the dream, only the intense feelings of happiness with which I woke up, and which stayed with me for days, undimmed by the knowledge that it was only a dream.' She'd left a suicide note which included the words 'P.S. tell the boys I loved them' (Gavron, 2009: 2).

Reassurance may be found in dreams, for example, in explaining the reason for the death (Barrett, 1992). Donna Schuurman, executive Director of the Dougy Center in the USA, recounts an interview she had with a teenaged boy: 'Philip described a meeting he had had with his deceased mother in a dream. In the dream he asked her why she'd killed herself and she told him that she knew she'd never be well, that she wanted him to have a life free of her antics and unpredictable behaviour. Philip looked at me and said, "So I told her I understood and forgave her"' (Schuurman, 2008: 9). He did not tell his father though, because Phillip thought his father would keep asking him to ask questions in his dreams.

Children and Trauma

Trauma occurs when a sudden, unexpected or completely extraordinary event overwhelms the child's ability to cope. Trauma is different from the usual stresses in a child's life because it comes out of the blue and the child has no time to prepare for it. Frequently feelings of helplessness swamp the child and there are no obvious ways that the child can make a difference. Such feelings of powerlessness undermine the child even further. These feelings find their way into the dreams and nightmares of traumatised children.

For children the shock of trauma impacts on them physically and emotionally. It affects their thinking and behaviour. As we saw earlier, trauma produces high levels of stress hormones that are toxic, which is why young children are particularly vulnerable. 'Extreme fear may be somatised, that is experienced in the body, so that frequent illness, failure to thrive and poor cognitive functioning distress the child even further. What is less obvious is the impact such an event has on their sleep. Nightmares and disturbing dreams are characteristic of trauma and can give the child or young person "opportunities to imagine effective ways of responding to the threat"' (Bulkeley et al., 2005: 221), though they may be distressing and disturbing. Grieving is not a linear process (Belicki and Belicki, 2006) and dreams may force us to face emotions repressed or avoided in waking life. They may also serve as a signpost to the need for skilled therapeutic intervention when, for example, post traumatic nightmares impair waking life (Nader et al., 1999).

Vanessa, aged 12, recalled: 'All it is, is people kill me all the time and sometimes, it is that bad, I cry in my sleep. My most frightening dream was when a man stuck a knife in me and killed me. Sometimes I dream that the doctors give me the wrong medicine and I die. I sometimes scream out in my sleep.' When I asked Vanessa about these terrifying dreams that she has almost every night she said, 'I think it is because two of my brothers have died and my mum and dad have split up. I'm not too upset about them splitting up but it's just when I see pictures of my brothers I want to cry but I don't know what my mum would say.'

After trauma children need to gain emotional mastery. In dreams this may involve the child in fully exploring the dream images, correcting mistaken ideas, finding different endings for the dream and drawing, painting or writing about it. The aim is to bring the fears from the dark night of the dream into the light of day where the child can be supported to explore them. As a parent or care-giver, if a child has bad dreams or is fearful about going to sleep because of nightmares, it is helpful to encourage the child to talk about the dreams and to help them dispel them by drawing the dream, for example (Mallon, 2002).

Kristi Mohrbacher was 16 when she was caught up in the massacre at Columbine High School. In 2009, ten years after the attack, she spoke of her recurring nightmare about crawling along the floor of the school auditorium, trying to escape an anonymous sinister presence. She said, 'In the dream I'm trying to hide, trying not to make any noise.' The fear that stalked the students still recurs ten years after the event (Day, 2009).

David's brother was killed in a cycling crash. After this happened he had recurring dreams in which death was the main theme. He told me the most frightening one was one in which all his family were killed in a car crash and he was the only survivor: 'Only I lived and I was paralysed so I couldn't kill myself.' David had faced one of the cruellest blows, the death of his brother in tragic circumstances with no time to prepare. In David's dream he is paralysed which symbolises his utter powerless to prevent his brother's death or to change the circumstances of his life living with his loss.

Emotions such as anger, fear, hatred and despair may be expressed when a child is awake. Where such emotions are not discharged in waking life, when feelings are repressed, they are often expressed in dreams and nightmares.

Deep fear may surface in dreams following traumatic experiences. Though the actual cause of death may not be re-enacted it is often expressed in a symbolic way. Some examples are:

- Being overwhelmed by a flood or tidal wave.
- Being attacked by people or wild animals.
- Being caught in a fire with no obvious escape.
- Being in a plane which is about to crash.
- Being caught in a hurricane.

The underlying sense of the dreams are that events are beyond the control of the dreamers and they are powerless.

Alice, aged seven, was with her five-year-old sister and other members of her family as her mother took them to school. Letting go of her mother's hand, the five year old was hit by a silver car as they were about to cross the road. Alice has had recurring dreams of a silver car since the death of her sister and physically shakes if she sees one on the road. She found it difficult to accept that it was not her fault. She thought she could have done something to save her sister. Alice drew her dreams for me and we looked at where everyone was when the accident happened. By working through the events it became clear to Alice that she was furthest away and she could not have done anything to stop the accident happening. We talked about this over many sessions and gradually the guilt dissipated though her feelings of sadness and wanting to be with her sister continued over a longer period. She also felt bad that after the accident she started to wet the bed again. When she understood that some children go back to earlier behaviour after a traumatic event and that it was not her fault that she wet the bed, she felt more positive and the bedwetting stopped.

What Helps the Child Who has Distressing Dreams and Nightmares?

Parents do not know what they do when they leave tender babes alone to go to sleep in the dark. (Charles Lamb).

The English essayist Charles Lamb (1775–1834) was plagued with nightmares as a child. He said, 'The night-time solitude, and the dark, were my hell.' Many children today will share those feelings. However, nightmares do have a positive role. They are 'wake up' calls to alert us to something we are worried about and which we need to address in our waking lives. A child, who seems fine in the waking hours but wakes from terrifying nightmares, is alerting us to unseen fears. So, what can you do to aid a child who has such sleep experiences?

In working with dreams the essential aspect is to listen to the dream that the dreamer tells you, to explore the connections the dreamer makes to the dream images and waking life, to ask the young person to describe images in greater detail and to collaborate with the dreamer to construct an interpretation. The aim is not to offer your own interpretation but to enable the dreamer to make her own interpretation. The person who holds the key to the meaning of the dream is the dreamer. There are many more techniques you can use in dreamwork but the first step is to be open to dreams, invite your client or patient to tell their dreams and to listen to the dream narrative (Mallon, 2002).

Strategies for working with dreams

- Listen to the story of the dream.

- Don't put your interpretation on the dream. The dreamer is the one who knows what the dream is about.

- Don't dismiss the dream as silly or unimportant. Dreams are not 'right' or 'wrong': they are expressions of the inner world of the child.

- Reassure the child that her disturbing dreams do not mean she is 'mad'. Help her to realise that the dreams are a way of coming to terms with her loss.

- Ask supportive, open questions to explore the dream: Who was in the dream? How did you feel? If the child was frightened, was there anyone who helped? If there was no one, could they think of someone who would have helped?

- Allow the child to go at her own pace. Don't force her to go on talking when she wants to stop.

- Help the child to make links to waking events. If she was frightened by a dog in the dream can she recall being frightened by a dog when she was awake ?

- Some children believe that if they talk about a dream event it will happen in waking life. Help children to understand that dreams communicate feelings and ideas and help you to understand yourself better.

- Respect the child's right to confidentiality. Never talk about a child's dream to another person unless you have their permission.

- If the child wants to, encourage her to draw or paint the dream, then look at the image and talk about it. If there was a frightening monster, could she think of anything or anyone who could help in the dream? If so add them to the image. She might want the offending monster to be cut out or trapped in a strong cage. The aim is to generate positive responses that empower the child.

Dreams and Continuing Bonds

Dreaming is one of the ways in which the bereaved child continues to experience the deceased (Worden, 1996). 'Children who maintained a connection with the parent through dreams and feeling watched knew, for the most part, that these experiences were coming from somewhere inside themselves' (Worden, 1996: 29). The dreams provided a meeting point between the painful reality of their loss and a wished-for state which can never again be realised.

> 'I can remember my Dad by dreaming of him.' Luke, aged nine.

Dreams also show how long the grieving process can last. Mel, was eight when this recurring dream began:

> 'I used to dream of my cousin who was four years old when she died and very close to me. After her death I dreamt that she woke me up and we used to play with her dolls. I was always depressed after that dream. I always wanted to die so I could live with her and play with her. I always played with her in my dreams, for a year after she died. And, now I still occasionally have dreams of walking up steps and meeting her. Sometimes, I still wish I could live with her.'

Adrian, aged 12, described his happiest dream. In it he is in heaven with all his 'dead and live' relations;

> 'We are floating on a bubble of sugar. In the bubble we see a light of blueish colour. I see my face in it and I look happy. Then I wake up.'

These dreams give Adrian a chance to re-experience pleasurable contact with relatives who have died and they are a source of solace.

The Spiritual Dimension of Dreaming

Throughout history dreams have had an impact on spiritual life and such dreams often occur in childhood (Adams et al., 2008; Bulkeley et al., 2005; Mallon, 2006). Spiritual dreams can carry a number of direct and symbolic images, and a variety of themes, many relating to death (Bulkeley and Bulkeley, 2005). Some children dream of heaven, 'the gates of heaven', as in a dream of ten-year-old Claire described by Adams et al. (2008) or 'I dream that I'm going up a ladder to heaven', as one boy recounted to me (Mallon, 1989). These may be influenced by religious education, family faith or the cultural milieu in which the young person lives.

Some dreams are explicitly religious containing imagery of religious figures, spiritual guides and others who are significant to the dreamer. 'Perhaps from a more spiritual perspective, we can see children's dreams as windows looking backward in time, providing evidence of the experience of the soul prior to embodiment. This information may remain fresh and valuable to young children for only a short time, before it is socialized out of their belief system and no longer recognized or acknowledged' (Bulkeley et al., 2005: 220).

In many cultures dreaming is highly valued and talking about dreams with family and friends is the norm (Bulkeley, 2000). For example, in the Gazan and Galilean Arab culture children grow up thinking about and narrating their dreams. Many studies have shown the efficacy of working with dreams (Garfield, 1996; Gogar and Hill, 1992; Keller et al., 1995).

Dreams offer spiritual solace to those have been bereaved. Elisabeth Kubler-Ross called dreams of the dead 'true contacts on a spiritual plane'. Such dreams can bring people closer to the sacred and the transcendent that inspire and guide waking life (Bulkeley, 1995). They can bring some comfort after a seemingly meaningless, random event such as accidental death or murder. Where the dead person is cared for by God or angels or other revered beings in dreams, then the bereaved often feel relieved (Adams et al., 2008; Mallon, 2000b).

Dreams of guidance, of being 'looked after' have ancient roots in beliefs that the ancestors continued to watch over and care for the bereaved from beyond the grave. This is evident throughout the world in ancestor worship, prayers for guidance, shrines erected to the deceased and in spiritualism and mediumship (Picardie, 2001). One female dreamer said that dreams of an afterlife, in which the dead live on often help those 'left behind' to move through their grieving, bonds intact yet free to carry on with their own life.

Reflexive Exercise 1

This exercise is done over a month:

Over the next month record your dreams. Each morning write down the dream(s), give it a title and note any connections you can make to your waking life. In analysing the dream each time ask yourself: Who was in the dream? Where was it set? Was there any other person in the dream? How did you feel? If you were frightened, was there anyone who helped? If there was no one, could you think of someone who could help? Keep notes on your thoughts and feelings.

At the end of the month go through your dream record and see if you can find any patterns and themes:

- What can you learn about yourself from these dreams?
- Did anything about your dreams surprise you?
- What did your dreams tell you about waking concerns?
- Did you have any dreams related to loss?

If you complete this exercise you will be in a much stronger position to work with the dreams of children and young people.

Reflexive Exercise 2

Novelist and travel writer Rosie Thomas was sent to boarding school at the age of ten after the death of her mother. In an article Danny Danziger records her words: 'I was lonely, but I just pretended that everything was all right and sent myself birthday cards every year' and 'You can't forget your unhappiest years: you're not allowed to. I constantly dream about school. I wake up with the smell of it in the back of my throat, a sort of mix of polish and disinfectant, yet with something fetid about it.' ('The Best of Times, Worst of Times', *Sunday Telegraph* April 2001)

- What cumulative losses did Rosie's experience following her mother's death ?
- Why does she have recurring dreams of school?
- How do you feel about Rosie's experience?

10 The Spiritual Dimension of Grief

> It was simple for me, the saints were in heaven and guardian angels had extendable wings like Batman and my dad had died and gone to live in the tree in the backyard. (Pascoe, *My Father Who Art in a Tree,* 2002: 1)

The spiritual aspects of bereavement, mourning and grief are important and relevant to our work with bereaved children and young people (Leighton, 2008). Counsellors and others who support the bereaved may be reluctant to explore spiritual issues yet, as Susan Furr states, 'they are intricately woven into the loss experience' (Burke et al., 2005: 135). The parents and care-giver's values, beliefs and practices are, not surprisingly, the most powerful influences on children's spiritual lives (Coles, 1991). Clearly, your own beliefs will influence your practice, however in ensuring that you maintain beneficence, non-judgemental positive regard and empathy, you can support those whose beliefs are different to your own, though this may be challenging.

Religion and spirituality are sometimes used interchangeably. However, to clarify the use in this chapter we will look at the root of the words. 'Religion derives from the Latin 'religare' or 'religio' which means 'to bind back' or 'to bind together' or 'to be in relation with' (Becker et al., 2007: 214). It refers to being in relation to something or someone behind the visible reality, which in the Christian tradition is known as God. In the present day, religion has become the outward expression of a system of beliefs, values, codes and rituals. Religious groups provide community-based worship and each faith group has its own sacred practices and beliefs to which the communicants adhere (Emblen, 1992). Such communities have special significance to its members and wider society, as sociologist Tony Walter says, 'Religion is in part what glues societies together' (Walter, 2003: 219).

Spirituality is a more elusive and broader term. Spiritual experiences are when we feel most deeply connected to our world, when we feel part of something larger than our own ego. It is related to a person's sense of being connected to self, to others and to the wider universe or cosmos and the meaning and purpose of life (Bosacki, 2001). Haye and Nye describe it as a natural human predisposition (Haye and Nye, 2006; O'Murchu, 2000). Spirituality exists in all people and is not dependent on religious beliefs. It is concerned with feeling meaningfully connected to others and the meaning and purpose of life (Bellous, 2008; Batten and Oltjenbruns, 1999; Leighton, 2008). Murray and Zentner (1989) describe the spiritual aspect of life as that which tries to be in harmony with the universe and seeks answers about the infinite. Spiritual practices may include belonging to a faith group and taking part in services, pilgrimage and retreats, prayer and meditation, carrying out rituals and rites, and reading spiritual works (Culliford and Powell, 2005). Spirituality can be experienced by anyone, including children with intellectual disability, since it is not related to intellectual capacity (Swinton, 2002).

Spiritual beliefs offer comfort for many. Kallenberg found 'a religious attitude to life makes traumatic events easier to bear' (2000: 123). The social network of a faith community and the set of beliefs gives meaning to life and hope. However, traumatic bereavement may bring a crisis of belief as the bereaved try to make sense of what has happened for, as Bellous states, 'Meaning making is a fundamental activity of the human spirit' (2008: 196).

The area of child and adolescent bereavement and the role of spirituality is not widely studied (Batten and Oltjenbruns, 1999). There have been numerous studies into how religious or spiritual beliefs influence adult responses to bereavement but available data does not allow for a definitive answer (Becker et al., 2007). There does seem to be a positive effect in having a religious or spiritual belief following the death of a significant other (Powell et al., 2003). As Walsh and colleagues concluded, 'People who profess stronger spiritual beliefs seem to resolve their grief more rapidly and completely after the death of a close person than do people with no spiritual beliefs' (Walsh et al., 2002: 1554). Spiritual beliefs are associated with resilience (Smith, 2005).

At adolescence, many young people explore the meaning of life and death and some may draw on their spiritual and religious experiences. In a study by Gallup and Lindsay in 1999, they found 76% of adolescents said they believed in God, 29% said they had experienced the presence of God, 42% regularly prayed and 50% had attended religious services in the previous seven days (Hooyman and Kramer, 2006). Where adolescents have such beliefs, evidence indicates they have a greater sense of well-being (Donahue and Benson, 1995). At Winston's Wish, a weekend support group for bereaved children, anonymous questions from the children to the camp doctor often include questions about spiritual issues (Thompson and Payne, 2000).

When working with a child or young person it may be helpful to find out any religious or spiritual practices or traditions that may be important to them (Golsworthy and Coyle, 2001; Hooyman and Kramer, 2006); and, also, to discover any spiritual self-care the young person uses such as prayer, meditation, contemplation and who offers them spiritual care or guidance. Such support may come from an imam, rabbi, priest, chaplain, shaman or pastor. Explore previous losses and how the family or individual managed them and whether their spiritual values helped through that experience. While you are doing this, ascertain how comfortable they feel about talking about it. Clearly, if this is uncomfortable or they are resistant, then move to another area to help them explore their feelings about their loss.

Balk (1999) asserts that all humans are searching for meaning in life and when a bereavement occurs it challenges people's assumptions about existence and the meaning of it. Bereavement can provide an opportunity for spiritual exploration and development as the bereaved reflect on what has happened to transform their life. As people examine and assess their life they may change their values and beliefs. In a study of 42 adolescents following the death of a sibling, Balk (1991) found that prior to the death religion had not played in important part of life for 50% of the participants. When interviewed, nearly 62% said that religion had become important or very important to them. The value of religion as a coping response had increased from 60% around the time of death to 80% after the death (Becker et al., 2007).

In most cultures throughout the world religion plays a major role in dealing with death, mortality, and religious rituals manage transitions a critical points of life. In the religious community children and young people can talk about the meaning of the death: 'Did God want Daddy to be with him?' 'What was plan of the supreme being to take my daddy?' 'Will I be with Daddy when I die?' However, it may be that 'spiritual beliefs may be strengthened because nothing else helps' (Frantz et al., 2001; Hooyman and Kramer, 2006: 74). After death big questions arise for children and young people. They may find comfort in faith or have increased doubts about their faith. They may feel angry with God or whatever name is given to their divine being: 'Why could a just God take my father?' 'How could God let this disaster happen?' David Balk points out the fact that the death of a sibling shatters the idea of the world as a benign, safe place and brings forward intense questioning about religious beliefs and the existence of God or otherwise. Existential questions about the meaning and purpose of life abound, particularly in adolescence (Balk, 1991).

Psychiatrist and author Robert Coles has spent many years interviewing children about their inner lives, including their views on spirituality. He said, 'I worked with children who had their own moral concerns, their philosophical interests, their religious convictions' (1991: 10). Talking with children from America, the Middle East and Latin America, he found great interest in spiritual matters and faith-based views. He wrote of an eight-year-old Jewish girl who had a strong sense of spiritual connectedness and continuity. She told him, she 'could feel Him nearby a lot of times', and that she hoped He'd stay until, 'He's so close I can hear Him', at which point she indicated she'd no longer be here, alive' (Coles, 1991: 36).

Children may have a sense of their own spirit that resides within them. The following example comes from a young girl who was caught in horrendous war conflict:

> 'One dark night me and my family had to sleep in the spooky wood. We tried to escape the war…We were so frightened. There was banging and shooting. My spirit got out of my body because he was scared. We managed to go to England. We were OK but my spirit wasn't. My spirit tried to look for me every day but he did not find me. One sunny morning my spirit came to London and still looked for me. In London there was no shooting or bombs. We were all ok. The next morning my spirit found me and we lived happily ever after.' Ariola. (Smith, 2005: 69)

Ariola explained that her spirit had to flee because he was so frightened and could only return when there was safety and when the sun was out so he could see her. The traumatic experience in the woods was such that Ariola was separated from her parents and 'slept' there for two days surrounded by injured and dead bodies.

Religious and spiritual beliefs influence how children and young people view death and this in turn shapes how they respond to bereavement. Where the young person believes that they will be re-united in the afterlife it may bring comfort but we must remember that this does not lessen the pain of bereavement (Leliaert, 1989). Each person's spiritual and religious preferences need to be respected, and particularly when working with children and young people, the family belief system needs to be recognised (Attig, 1995).

A teenager whose father had died spoke of the importance of faith to him: 'It's important not to give up on your religion. Really, it's the only thing that's been helping me through this. If it wasn't for that, I'm sure I'd just give up on everything' (Worden, 1996: 171).

Palliative Care

> Death often presents nothing short of a spiritual crisis, both for the one
> who is dying and for the companion. (J.S. Holder and J. Aldredge-Clanton,
> 2004: 4)

In palliative care, the spiritual needs of their patients and families play a central role in the care of the holistic patient pathway (Marie Curie Cancer Care, 2003; National Institute for Clinical Excellence, 2004; Wimpenny, 2007; Wright, 2002). A study in 2006 which reviewed the literature of spirituality and palliative care suggests that a more integral approach needs to be developed which included the experiential nature of spirituality in patients and their families (Sinclair and Geraghty, 2002). The hospice movement and palliative care professionals have made a huge contribution to developing childhood bereavement services, particularly in preparing children for an expected death. The video research project carried out by East Berkshire palliative care team under Dr Gillian Chowns, 'No You Don't Know How We Feel', is one example of such excellent work. In it young people express their feelings and thoughts about being bereaved.

Children who are facing severe illness or bereavement may raise questions of a spiritual nature (Hutton, 2006). Children who are living with terminal illness may develop an awareness of a new spiritual dimension in their lives and seek meaning in their life and death. Unmet spiritual needs may cause distress to children so we need to listen to the child's experiences and discover their view of the world and respond to their spiritual needs as they change over time (Culliford, 2002).

> Hope is the thing with feathers
> That perches in the soul
> (Emily Dickinson)

Children and Young People's Views on an Afterlife

Children and young people have thoughts about an afterlife. Lansdown et al., (1997) found 50% of children aged five to eight years of age believed in heaven though they did not always see it as a pleasant place. In *Children and Grief: When a Parent Dies* (1996), William Worden reported that 74% of children in the Child Bereavement Study located the deceased 'in heaven', 'regardless of religious orientation' (Silverman and Worden, 1992: 97). An eleven-year-old girl said, 'At night I think about what heaven would be like. Would it be like fields and flowers, or would it be different for each family so you could see all your other relatives?' (1992: 97–8). 'Whatever their religion, children this age (6–8 year olds) tend to locate the parent who died in a place, usually heaven, and often with a function. Most thought the parent was watching over them' (Christ and Christ, 2006: 205). Many children conceive of heaven as an extension of life on earth, as a continuation of the dead person's existence on a different plane.

Children have a whole range of ideas about heaven and the afterlife. In a survey about children's concepts of the afterlife (Frangoulis et al., 1996), many children had concerns that heaven would be too crowded, or that they might see blood but mainly the children thought of heaven as a pleasant place. One terminally ill girl at St Christopher's hospice asked, 'Are you asleep all the time when you are in heaven or do you wake up?' and 'Can you take your toys to heaven?' When children were asked how the dead person got to heaven, most thought that flying or floating was the usual way, though one five year old said, 'God picks you up, you have to wait twelve days for a flight and the flight takes eight hours' (Black, 1996: 1).

Some young people have a profound faith that sustains them through great physical and emotional pain. Garvan was terminally ill and knew he was dying. He told Sister Dominica:

> 'And when I die, I do believe that Christ will look after my family and whatever they need. He will provide for them. I shall always look down on them if I go before them. I will be there in the midst of my family. They might not see me, but I'll be there, watching them, looking after them, all the time.' Garvan, aged ten. (Driscoll, 2004: 5)

A survey of 500 children and young people in Sweden (Tamm, 1996) found that there were differences in gender responses to what young people thought about what happened after death. Boys were more likely to think that life ends at death, the body decomposes and that is the life finished. However, girls were more likely to believe in an afterlife 'Thoughts about reincarnation and death in the form of "near death experiences" are common among girls aged twelve and older' (Tamm, 1996: 33). One third of the girls in the study saw death as a journey through a dark tunnel towards a golden light whereas such ideas were 'practically non-existent among boys'. When asked about a continued existence after death boys were more interested in hell than heaven. The influence of video designs on covers, CDs and horror films may influence these responses.

The afterlife is often seen as a place where loved ones can be re-united:

> 'When we had the funeral of my Mum, she was buried with my Dad. My uncle released two white doves to show they were flying to heaven to be together because they'll be together there now.' Tom, aged fifteen.

Matthew is 17 now, he was 15 when his grandmother died. Her death changed his views: 'I used to believe in something after death, but now I don't. Her death changed my view. I thought, "If there's a God, why would they let somebody die in such a horrible way?" I believe that the only thing that we have left of her are pictures and your own personal view of what the person was like. I know I've got everything to remember Grandma in here: in my heart and in my mind and in photographs of her when she was well and happy. Providing I don't lose those, I don't lose the feelings, and she's with me' (Jenkins and Merry, 2005: 184).

Talking about death in front of children remains a taboo in many cultures, particularly in Japan where it is one of the greatest societal taboos. However in research carried out by Sagara-Rosemeyer and Davies (2007), they found that Japanese children perceived life as a process that leads to death, and that death is a transitional point to an afterlife. The idea of an afterlife incorporated the tenets of the three main religious traditions in Japan; Shintoism, Buddhism and Confucianism.

Rituals

Glassock (2001) emphasises the importance of rituals in addressing the spiritual aspects of grief. They provide a structure for grief that can be helpful to both children and adults (Stuber and Mesrkhani, 2001). They provide an opportunity for reflection to respect the deep pain of grief. 'Rituals make mountains out of moments' (Grollman, 1997). 'For most of human history… spiritual experiences of individuals were almost completely moulded and intertwined with the symbols, myths, beliefs and rituals of their tribe or nation' (Klass, 1999a: 3). Expressions of the spiritual aspect of life were traditionally prayer, fasting, meditation, pilgrimage, rituals and visions. The process knits the groups together and shows that should anything happen to individuals, they will be helped in the same way (Dyregrov, 1996).

Rituals mark significant transitions in life and they are purposeful activities. 'The function of rituals during death and loss are to regulate behaviour, time and emotions, and, to provide guidance for often fragmented social relationships' (de Vries, 1996: 403). They emphasise the individual's connection to their society and their cultural group. Every documented human society has mourning rituals in which the memories of the dead are visited and re-visited and which often involve public displays that have a societal dimension (Gorer, 1965). Rando (1984) explains how rituals provide the bereaved with a shared, spiritual meaning for death which they can integrate with their belief system.

Rituals allow the community to show their support and care for the bereaved. 'The family's cultural or faith-based strengths can also provide cohesion and encourage internal fortitude' (Ratnarajah and Schofield, 2007: 90). Children are helped by rituals in much the same as adults are. They provide a focus for their grief, while the friends and family and peers show their solidarity with the bereaved, and through rituals they also learn that they are not alone or abandoned. They provide an outlet for grief and a concrete way to say goodbye to the dead person. As Dyregrov says, the ritual of seeing the body can confirm that the person will not come back: 'It wasn't until I saw Daddy lying in the coffin that I really understood what had happened. It was so good to see him lying there so peacefully, seeing that he felt no pain. I touched him. It felt so right and so good to say farewell to him in that way. I became calm, because he was so peaceful' (Dyregrov, 1996: 3).

Children need to be prepared for rituals so that they know what to expect and what will happen. When taking part in viewing the dead, for example, they need information about the room, including decoration and flowers; where the coffin will be placed, whether it will be open or closed; the appearance of the dead person, the colour of the hands and face, and details of the clothes. It is helpful to know that the temperature will be cool and why this is the case. In addition, before the child or young person goes into the room, check whether there is an automatic air freshener. It can be quite daunting if you are having a few moments silence only to be interrupted by a sudden spurt of air that seems to come out of nowhere.

In preparing the child ensure that he or she knows she can react or not react as they wish, that there are no hard and fast rules of what to do (Dyregrov, 1996). Explain that it is an opportunity to say a final 'Goodbye' to the physical body. They may have time alone if they wish to and they can take photographs. Just prior to the viewing, it is helpful if an adult views the body alone to ensure everything is in order as funeral directors have been known to show grieving relatives into a room which did not hold the body of their deceased relative but a stranger bruised and battered from a road traffic collision. After the viewing allow time for the child or young person to talk about their experience, if that is what they want to do. In terms of taking part in rituals Dyrgrov says, 'Children have the right to be included in rituals. If we exclude them, we deny them the opportunity of being part of some of the most important family occasions. Rituals, and having participated in them, will continue to be significant throughout a child's life, and as adults we should regard the involvement of children in them as essential for their future development' (1996: 4).

There are traditional rituals at death such as viewing the body, attending the funeral, and holding a service to remember the dead person; however, people can devise their own rituals (Imber-Black et al., 1988). In recent years bereaved family members have held torch light processions to the place where a death has occurred to lay flowers at the spot where the accidental death took place. Flowers are thrown on the water where a boat sank.

Memorial services and rituals of remembrance are an important means of supporting the bereaved (Rawlings and Glynn, 2002). They may include prayers, recitations, poetry, music and the opportunity for reflection. Children can be part of choosing the music, the flowers, what songs to sing. They may want to give a concrete symbol of their grief, such as a drawing, a poem, a toy or a flower, which they can put in the coffin. If they do not wish to see the body to say goodbye out loud or in their head, they may want to write a card or letter to do so. In some cases the child may want an adult to write the words down for them.

A rite of passage marks a time when a person reaches a new and significant point in his or her life. Rites of passage fall into three main phases: separation, transition and incorporation. Funerals marks the separation the death has brought about, the transition as the bereaved learn new behaviour in the new stage of their life and the last stage is incorporation when the person is admitted into the new role.

Rituals to Remember the Deceased

Rituals allow the bereaved child to stay connected to the person who has died. They maintain continuity for the child by acknowledging and valuing the past and carrying those aspects into their future. 'On anniversaries, rituals are of special importance for the family, as they function as concrete anchor-points for their grief' (Dyregrov, 1996: 4). 'Winston's Wish' holds residential courses for children who have been bereaved. In one ritual they use, each bereaved child lights a candle to remember someone who has died. The candle is blown out at the end of the ceremony and each child keeps it to take home and light again to mark anniversaries, birthdays or special times that are significant. This can be adapted for school ceremonies.

A friend, whose son was eight when her partner tragically died, arranged a picnic a year later for all his father's friends. Each person wrote their name on a postcard, wrote down how they knew his father and one memory they would like to share. Such physical reminders often sustain a child through turbulent times of growth and provide a link for future partners and children as yet unknown.

Rituals help the child or young person make the link between past and present so that funerals and playing a role in them helps them to accept the reality of their loss (Requarth, 2006). As Gamino states following research into the participation in funerals, 'Funeral rites appeared to enhance mourner's comfort at the time of death, both by facilitating social support and by connecting the griever with deeper levels of meaning with which to understand and frame their loss experience' (Gamino et al., 2000: 79).

A personal account

Alana was six. Her father kissed her goodnight but she never saw him alive again. He died suddenly during the night. She didn't go to the funeral because her father's parents couldn't bear the thought of her being there. The family suppressed their grief and clamped down on any overt expression of emotion in the child.

Shortly after the cremation Alana's mother took his ashes home. Later they went to the church where the couple had married so that ashes could be buried. Each year, on the anniversary of his death, they go to the church and each take a rose. One year the mother placed some rosemary with the rose. Alana asked what it was for. 'Rosemary is the herb for remembrance,' she said. Her daughter asked if she could have some and her mother gave her the remainder of the small bunch she had brought. A little while later her mother noticed the eight year old sprinkling rosemary on the graves. In her way she was ensuring that all those who had died would be remembered.

Rites to help a bereaved child

The funeral as rite of passage

The most important public event that follows a death is the funeral. It is a rite of passage that marks a significant life change, both to those directly affected by the loss and their wider community. For children, it can be frightening, comforting, boring or sustaining, so much depends on the reactions of others around them.

Many children's fantasise about funerals and cremations are all too frequently inspired by television and video horrors. This means that some children initially need clear, reassuring explanations about what does and does not happen at this time.

Memorial cards

Funeral directors may have cards which are distributed at the funeral or cremation. These ask for the name of the person attending the event, details of the relationship to the deceased, (relative, friend or colleague) and have a space for a message. Where a child has been bereaved these can be particularly important in enabling him to learn more about the person's life outside his family relationships. Usually the cards are kept by the next of kin and give a physical record that can be kept for the children in the future.

Rites of Grief Around the World

> Death customs are rites of passage and initiate a change in status
> for both the dead and the bereaved. (de Vries, 1996: 405)

In Japanese culture Jizo is the Buddhist deity which guards children and travellers. When a foetus is aborted or miscarried it is called Mizuko. The Misuko Jizo Buddha arose as the diety which protected these in the next world. Japanese Buddhists believe that their offspring live on in the next world and statues of the deity in sacred temples provide a focus for grieving mothers in particular. Mothers have statues made to symbolise their unborn or dead babies and place them next to a statue of the deity in dedicated temples. Sometimes they place shawls around the tiny statue's shoulder to keep them warm or put on bibs to represent feeding. An example is the Misuko Jizo Buddha at Hase Kannon temple, Kamakuru, Japan.

Mother's Day may re-awaken feelings of loss in children whose mother has died. In China, a red rose is given to a living mother on this special day and a white rose is given to children whose mother has died. Mother and children are both honoured in this creative ritual. In Puerto Rico, children whose mother has died wear a pink rose on Mother' Day.

Sense of presence of the deceased

Children and young people may experience the presence of the deceased and are not usually frightened by this because they feel the dead person would not want to hurt them (Cranwell, 2007). Some children interpret sights, sounds and aromas as indications of the presence of the dead person. In many cases, this is a comfort but for some young people, they fear the parent may be watching and disapproving or may suddenly appear and frighten them. Research with adults has found that the sense of the presence of the dead comes unbidden (Bennett and Bennett, 2000; Walter, 2008) and this would seem to be the case with children too. As Worden states, 'Feeling watched by the dead parent was a common experience, particularly in the early months after the death. Those continuing to feel watched one and two years after the death were more likely to have lost mothers' (1996: 28).

Amy Ahmad was five when her grandfather died, though he lived in another city, she had fond memories of their time together. Now aged seven, she recalls: 'I knew he was really close by to us because whenever we were at home – this was after he died – I knew he was really close by. His feelings were landing on me and Emily [her younger sister] in our house. It's like an invisible person by your side. It makes me much happier because I know I've got someone there with me when I feel scared and alone. It's like he's watching over me when I want him to be there and need him' (Jenkins and Merry, 2005: 181–2).

Sister Frances Dominica, founder of the world's first children's hospice, Helen's House in Oxford has spent most of her life working with children with life-threatening illness: 'What the experience of death has taught me is that, regardless of someone's belief or lack of it, you are walking on holy ground' (Driscoll, 2004: 4). 'Five years after her sister died a five year old told God, "You've had my sister long enough now, we need her back please"' (Driscoll, 2004: 5).

Reflexive Exercise 1

'Rippling' is an idea put forward by Irvin Yalom (2008). It refers to the fact that each of us creates concentric circles of influence that may affect others for years if not genera-tions. The influence we have on other people is passed on through them to others, in much the same way as the ripples of a pond go on and on until they are no longer visible. This legacy can be helpful for children and young people struggling with making meaning of their existence and the transience of life. As he says, 'Rippling refers … to leaving behind something of your life experience; some trait; some piece of wisdom, guidance, virtue, comfort that passes on to others, known or unknown' (2008: 9). 'Rippling tempers the pain of transiency by reminding us that something of us persists even though it may be unknown or imperceptible to us' (Yalom, 2008: 10).

- What legacies have you left to family, friends or community that will remain after you die?
- Are there other things you would like to leave that you could be remembered by?
- What legacies or ripples have you received and how do these influence you?

Reflexive Exercise 2

Take some time to reflect on your spiritual and/or religious beliefs.

- Do you have a set of religious or spiritual beliefs that influence your life?
- If so, what are they and how do they influence you?
- Do you go to a place of worship. If so, how does this sustain you?
- How might religious or spiritual beliefs help you when someone close dies?
- What do you think about an afterlife?

Appendix: Resources and Organisations for those Supporting Bereaved Children

ChildLine

Royal Mail Building
Studd Street
London N10 QW
Tel. 0171 239 1000
Free helpline 0800 1111
www.ChildLine.org.uk

ChildLine is a service for children to use if they are worried about any problem whatsoever. It is a confidential telephone helpline, run by trained staff who will do whatever they can to enable the child to resolve his or her difficulties.

The Alder Centre

Royal Liverpool Children's Hospital,
Alder Hey
Liverpool L12 2AP
Tel. 0151 252 5513
Child Death Helpline 0800 282986
www.westlancs.gov.uk

Offers support to anyone who has been affected by the death of a child. Volunteers and trained counsellors provide help for adults and children. There is a telephone helpline available.

The Child Bereavement Trust

Brindley House
4 Burkes Road
Beaconsfield
Bucks. HP9 1PB
Tel. 01494 678088
www.childbereavement.org.uk

Support on all aspects of bereavement which involves children.

Child Death Helpline

York House
37–39 Queen Street
London WC1N 3BH
Tel. 0800 282 986
www.childdeathhelpline.org.uk

Provides help for anyone affected by the death of a child at any age, in whatever circumstances.

The Compassionate Friends

53 North Street
Bristol BS53 1EN
www.tcf.org.uk

This self-help, national organisation offers support to anyone who has lost a child. There are two sub-groups, one for parents of murdered children and one for parents of children who have died by suicide. They also have an extensive library from which you may borrow books and tapes.

CRUSE Bereavement Care

Cruse House
126 Sheen Road
Richmond
Surrey TW9 1UR
Tel. 0870 167 1677
www.crusebereavementcare.org.uk

Bereavement care provided by trained counsellors, plus advice and information on practical problems and befriending. Specialist services for various bereaved groups.

Lesbian and Gay Bereavement Project

Healthy Gay Living Counselling
Unit 4
The Hop Exchange
24 Southwark Street
London SE1 1TY
Tel. 020 7403 5969

Provides advice and support from trained volunteers.

Action for Prisoner's Families (APF)

Tel. 0808 808 2003
Email info@actionpf.org.uk
www.prisonersfamilieshelpline.org.uk

The Prisoners' Families Helpline is a free and confidential service for anyone affected by imprisonment of a close family member or friend. It offers support to adults and children, including when a death has occurred.

National Autistic Society

NAS Autism Helpline 0845 070 4004

The Autism Helpline has a small list of counsellors who have an understanding of autism spectrum disorders and bereavement.

Bereavement Support for People with Learning Disability

www.bereavementanddisability.org.uk

This organisation raises awareness of issues concerning disability. It has a series of excellent guides: a guide for individuals who have experienced bereavement, a guide for carers who are offering support and a guide for professionals offering bereavement support. It also has links to other useful sites such as Mencap.

Brake

PO Box 548
Huddersfield HD1 2XZ
Tel. 01484 559909
www.brake.org.uk

Charity caring for people bereaved or affected by serious injury in a road crash.

Child Bereavement Charity

The Saunderton Estate
Wycombe Road
Saunderton
Bucks. HP14 4BF
Tel. 01494 446648
www.childbereavement.org.uk

Provides specialise support, information and training to those bereaved by the death of a baby or young child. It offers support to children who have been affected by the death.

Child Bereavement Network

8 Wakley street
London EC1V 7QE
Tel. 020 7843 6309
www.childbereavementnetwork.org.uk

National network which offers a directory of local and national support services offering direct support to young people and training for professionals. It also has DVDs, postcards and other resources to provide information and training.

Child Death Helpline

Tel. 020 7813 8550
www.childdeathhelpline.org.uk

Charity which offers support for anyone affected by the death of a child of any age, from pre-birth to adult, under any circumstances. The death does not have to be recent, it can have happened long ago, support will still be offered to bereaved parents.

The Children's Society

Edward Rudolf House
Margery Street
London WC1X 0JL
Tel. 0845 300 1128
www.thechildrenssociety.org.uk

The Children's Society has developed the Disability Toolkit website to help professionals who work with disabled children (symbol resource pack). It includes materials for use with children, case studies, latest research information and policy developments. www.disabilitytoolkit.org.uk

CLINKS

www.clinks.org

Membership charity which supports voluntary and community agencies in prisons and probation services. Provides a directory of services and advice about inter-agency relationships.

Forces Children's Trust

Tel. 01737 361077

Charity devoted to helping dependent children whose parent has died whilst serving with the armed forces.

Gone Forever

www.goneforever.org.uk

The Gone Forever Project was set up in 1990 and began as a collaborative project between Sheffield Hallam University and Sheffield Area Bereavement Forum. They run training courses for teachers to raise awareness of the needs of children and young people who have been bereaved including those with special educational needs.

Healthier Inside

www.ncb.org.uk/healthierinside

Programme based at the National Children's Bureau which is aimed at improving health and well-being outcomes for young people in custody. Downloadable resources to support implementation including magazines, a toolkit and young people's charter.

Mothers Against Violence

Room 113
23 Newmount Street
Manchester M4 4DE
Tel. 0798 5490333

Manchester based support and lobbying group for relatives of young people affected by gangland crime and violence.

Penhaligon's Friends

Cornwall
Tel. 0845 607 1943
www.penhaligonsfriends.org.uk

Telephone support, bereavement days, advice and information leaflets as well as counselling for bereaved children and their families.

RoadPeace

Email info@roadpeace.org.uk
www.roadpeace.org.uk

RoadPeace is a national charity set up in 1992 to support and represent road crash victims. It provides emotional and practical support to those bereaved, injured or otherwise affected by the event.

Winston's Wish

Gloucestershire Royal Hospital
Great Western Road
Gloucester GL1 3NN

Winston's Wish helpline:

> Telephone help for bereaved children
> Monday – Friday 9.00am – 5.00pm
> Tel. 0845 203 0405
> Email info@winstonswish.org.uk
> www.winstonswish.org.uk

This national charity offers a grief support programme for children. It gives children and families the chance to meet others who have experienced bereavement on a 'Camp Winston' residential course. This inspirational organisation also offers ongoing support, training, telephone advice and leaflets.

Rainbows

> Tel. 0114 256 6445

Help for bereaved children or those who are experiencing other forms of loss. Works through schools and family support settings.

Richmond's Hope

> Tel. 0131 661 6818
> www.faithworks.info

Edinburgh bereavement support centre for children aged 4–16 and their families.

Royal Hospitals

Information on children and young people and trauma can be downloaded from www.royalhospitals.org/traumaticgrief. It also includes a guide for relatives and self-care for workers supporting the traumatically bereaved.

St Christopher's Candle Project

> S.E. London
> Tel. 020 8768 4500

Bereavement service which supports children and young people under 18. It offers telephone support, one-to-one and group counselling to children across London.

SOBS (Survivors of Bereavement by Suicide)

Tel. 0844 561 6855

www.uk-sobs.oeg.uk

A national charity which offers support, counselling to those affected by the death of someone who has died by suicide.

Books for Children and Young People

Books, stories, myths and legends offer a diverse source of material on bereavement, separation and loss. These can be used for individual or group reading as well as group activities.

Many children's books and films deal with this theme of loss and restitution: The *Harry Potter* series, *Star Wars, The Wizard of Oz, E.T., Oliver* and *Beauty and the Beast* are just a few. Not all the stories have a happy ending – Darth Vader does not renounce the evil empire until faced with death so hero Luke Skywalker has to live all his life without his natural father. However, in the best of these myths and stories there is some kind of resolution and growth towards maturity and an acceptance that life's lessons are not always easy to learn.

Books for younger readers

Althea (1982) *When Uncle Bob Died*. Dinosaur Publications.
    Aimed at 5–8 year olds, this lovely book talks about fear, anger, sadness and memories.
Briggs, R. *The Snowman*.
    Available as a book and video, *The Snowman* is mainly about how a snowman comes alive and takes a boy on many adventures. At the end he melts and the boy is left with his feelings of loss and wonderful memories of the time they had together.
Brown, L. and Brown, M. (1996) *When Dinosaurs Die*. Little, Brown.
    Well-illustrated book which explores topics and questions about death including saying goodbye, customs and beliefs about death. Religious views are taken into account as are humanistic ones and provides a sound basis for discussion.
Burningham, John *Grandpa*: Puffin Books.
    With gentle, delicate illustrations Burningham tells of the bond between a girl and her Grandfather. At the end there is his empty chair and we know he has died. This book gives an excellent basis for sharing ideas about loss and death in particular. (4+).
Dahl, Roald, (1967) *James and the Giant Peach*. Allen & Unwin.
    James lives with his awful aunts following the death of his parents who were eaten by an escaped rhinoceros. One day a spectacular peach begins to grow in the back garden. The book shows the how the spirit to survive against all the odds, with the help of friends, carries James through his great adventure.
De Paola, Tomie *Nana Upstairs and Nan Downstairs*. Puffin.
    Tommy lives with his family, including his grandmother and great grandmother. The story explains how he copes when both his grandparents die.

Gillespie, Joanne (1989) *Brave Heart: The Diary of a Nine-year-old Girl who Refused to Die*. London: Century.

Joanne's delightful illustrations accompany her text. 'I decided to write this book,' she says, 'because when I was frightened and not sure of myself in hospital there was nothing for me to read. So, I decided to write this book for other children who are like me feeling frightened and ill. And I hope it will help them to feel a bit more sure of themselves.'

Ironside, Virginia *The Huge Bag of Worries*. Hodder Wayland.

Aimed at 5 to 8 year olds, the illustrated book explores anxieties and worries that children may experience.

Kent, Jack *There's No Such Thing as a Dragon*. Happy Cats Books.

Billy's mother just won't accept the existence of a dragon, and as a result the dragon gets bigger and bigger. In much the same way, the topic of difficult feelings may be ignored and as a consequence may increase. This delightful picture book is a useful vehicle for discussing death with children

King-Smith, D. (1998) *The Sheep-Pig*. London: Puffin.

The film *Babe* is based on this story in which a pig talks to the flock of sheep and becomes their leader. The book sensitively handles the death of a sheep mauled by dogs and provides plenty of humour and hope.

Simmonds, Posy *Fred*. Puffin Books.

A wonderfully told story of the death of a cat and his amazing funeral with characteristically quirky illustrations.

Simms, Alicia (1986*) Am I Still A Sister ?* Big A. and Co.

This thoughtful book written by a young person following her baby brother's death, addresses a whole range of emotions and situations following the death of a sibling.

Stickney, Doris (1997) *Water Bugs and Dragonflies*. Mowbray.

A book for younger children which gives a sensitive and straightforward explanation of death. It also deals with the idea of life after death and is a helpful way to introduce the concept of the life cycle.

Varley, Susan (1985) *Badger's Parting Gifts*. London: Picture Lions.

A classic story book for children to help them explore loss and bereavement. It tells how badger's forest friends cope with his death and the memories of the things he taught them. Though aimed at children it is of value to use with any age group and helps explore the idea of continuing bonds and the legacies that are left by those who die.

Vorst, Judith *The Tenth Good Thing About Barney*. Aladdin Publishing Company.

This book looks at how a young boy copes with the death of his cat by remembering the good times they had together.

White, E.B. *Charlotte's Web*. Puffin.

This classic story relates the powerful relationship between Wilber the pig and Charlotte the spider. It beautifully describes the life cycle and the power of love and acceptance in a readily accessible way. (7–12).

Wilhelm, H. (1985) *I'll Always Love You*. Hodder & Stoughton.

A moving story of a boy's love for his dog who he has grown up with. When the dog dies, the boy says though he is very sad, he remembers that he told his dog 'I'll always love you', every night. It gives an opportunity to talk about feelings. (4–8).

Winston's Wish *Muddles, Puddles and Sunshine*.

A workbook for children about their special person.

Books for older readers

Almond, David (1998) *Skellig*. Hodder Children's Books.

> Michael moves house and in the crumbling garage finds a creature. He does not know if it is human or something else. It is a tender story of love and faith. The story is underpinned by the theme of resilience and the need to find resources in the face of uncertainly.

Anderson, R. *Pizza On Saturday*. Hodder.

> Charlotte's world changes suddenly when her father suffers a massive stroke. She learns that nothing stays the same including herself, as she meets new people who have troubles of their own, including a new girl at school whose journey from another part of the world has been anything but easy. Bereavement is central to this short easy-to-read novel aimed at ten year olds and above.

Blume, Judy *Tiger's Eyes* Macmillan Books.

> *Tiger's Eyes* tells the story of a boy who has to cope with intense feelings after the sudden and violent death of his father during a shop raid. (12–18).

Boyce, Frank Cotterell (2004) *Millions*. Macmillan.

> A brilliant story about Damien and his brother who find a sack full of money. Their hilarious adventure leads them to discover what brings happiness and that money can never bring back their mother who has died. It a life-affirming book which was made into a very successful film for children and young people.

Chick, Sandra *I Never Told Her I Loved Her*. Livewire Books for Teenagers.

> When Frankie's mother dies she struggles because all she can remember are the arguments they used to have and the quarrels her parents used to have. Gradually Frankie and her father talk about their loss and plan for the future.

Dowd. S. (2009) *Solace of the Road*. David Frickling Books.

> This road story charts the journey of Holly as she tries to find her mother after a life in care, secure units with key workers and social workers. The bitter sweet story will engage older readers.

Frank, Anne (1954) *The Diary of Anne Frank*. Pan.

> Anne Frank wrote her diary in hiding from Nazi terror in an Amsterdam attic from 1942 to 1944, when she was aged between 13 and 15. As a beacon of hope in the darkest times it portrays adolescent hopes and fears in the face of great loss.

Fuller, Jill *John's Book*. Lutterworth Press.

> When John's father dies suddenly, he and his mother have to find out how they can live without him. The story explores the range of emotions – anger, sadness and bewilderment – that John feels and shows how he begins to plan for the future.

Gaiman, Neil (2008) *The Graveyard Book*. Illustrated by Chris Riddell. Bloomsbury.

> A gripping and chilling story of a boy called Bod who is an ordinary boy; however, he is brought up in a graveyard and nurtured by ghosts after his parents die. Danger lies in the world of the living too and the story shows how Bod's resilience sees him through.

Gibbons, Alan (2004) *The Lost Boys' Appreciation Society*. Dolphin Paperback.

> When Gary and John's mother is killed in a car crash the teenage boys find that their life is wrecked too. Their father struggles to cope and Gary goes off the rails, while John struggles with his GCSEs. This touching, fast-moving and humorous story covers the diverse responses to grief and ends on a positive note.

Gleitzman, Morris *Two Weeks with the Queen.*

An Australian boy, Colin, does not accept that his brother's cancer is incurable. His distraught parents send him to London to stay with relatives and he decides to contact the Queen to ask for help. A friendship with a young man whose companion is dying of AIDS helps Colin accept the inevitability of his brother's death. It's a humorous, sad, touching book which shows how important good communication is in these difficult circumstances.

Holm, Anne (1979) *I Am David.* Methuen.

Prize-winning fiction for older readers, this book is about a boy who escapes from a concentration camp during World War ll and tramps his way across Europe searching for his identity and a family. Full of hope and tenderness.

Lewis, C.S. (1950) *The Lion, the Witch and the Wardrobe.* Geoffrey Bles.

This classic book works well on so many levels that children are enchanted by it. The death of Aslan and the spiritual dimension of the story make it particularly pertinent in exploring loss.

Lowry, Lois *A Summer to Die.* Laurel Leaf Library.

Thirteen-year-old Meg tells the story of the illness and death of her older sister Molly who has leukaemia.

Magorian, M. *Goodnight Mister Tom.*

The book, also available as a film, relates the story of a war-time evacuee, who experiences trauma, physical abuse from his mentally ill mother, loss and separation. He is billeted with the wonderful Mr Tom. The power of love to kindle hope and resilience makes this book very useful in exploring themes related to bereavement.

Mystrom, Carolyn (1990) *Emma Says Goodbye.* Lion Publishing Series.

Aunty Sue is young, strong and lively. Emma finds her way of coming to terms with Sue's illness and death. (12+).

Newman, Marjorie (1995) *Steve: A Story About Death.* Watts.

Steven aged eleven, his nine-year-old sister and their mother face life together after his father is killed at work by a falling wall.

Nicholls, S. (2008) *Ways To Live Forever.* Scholastic.

An excellent book about an eleven-year-old boy Sam, who has leukaemia and charts his illness through lists, drawings and humorous escapades.

Paterson, Katherine (1995) *Bridge To Terabitha.* Puffin.

This is the story of a friendship between two ten year olds. When one dies in an accident, the other has to manage the feelings of grief and loss.

Pullman. P. *His Dark Materials.*

This prize winning trilogy deals with bereavement, relationships, religion and spirituality. Brilliantly written with a fast paced adventure at its heart, the book will appeal to a wide age range.

Rosen, M. *The Sad Book.* Walker Books.

This book, beautifully illustrated by Quentin Blake, shows how people may mask their grief to protect other people. It shows how sad Michael Rosen feels when he thinks about the death of his son Eddie, who featured in many of the books that Rosen wrote for children. This exceptional book can be used with any age group.

Sunderland, M. and Armstrong, N. (2003) *The Day the Sea went Out and Never Came Back.* Speechmark.

A story aimed at helping younger children cope with loss and grief. The main character is a sand dragon called Eric who loves the sea. One day the sea goes out and does not come back. Gradually, he finds the courage to feel and face his grief. Designed to be used in conjunction with *Helping Children with Loss: A Guide Book*.

Wilson, Jaqueline *Vicky Angel*. Delacorte Press.

Jade's best friend Vicky dies in a tragic car accident. Jade is devastated and the story tells how she copes when Vicky appears to her as a ghost. Life starts to unravel and eventually Jade sees a counsellor who helps her find herself and her own life path.

References

Abdelnoor, A. and Hollins, S. (2004a) 'The effect of childhood bereavement on secondary performance', *Educational Psychology in Practice*, 20 (1): 43–54.

Abdelnoor, A. and Hollins, S. (2004b) 'How children cope at school after family bereavement', *Educational and Child Psychology*, 21 (3): 85–94.

Abrams, R. (1999) *When Parents Die*. London: Routledge.

Acheson, D. (1998) *Independent Inquiry into Inequalities in Health*. London: HMSO.

Adams, K., Hyde, B. and Wooley, R. (2008) *The Spiritual Dimension of Childhood*. London: Jessica Kingsley.

Adams, K.S. (1982) 'Loss, suicide and attachment', in C.M. Parkes and J. Stevenson-Hinde (eds), *The Place for Attachment in Human Behaviour*. London: Tavistock, pp. 269–94.

Aitken, A. (2009) 'Online life after death', *Bereavement Care,* 28(1): 34–5.

Alexander, H. (2002) *Bereavement: A Shared Experience*, 3rd edn. Oxford: Lion.

Allison, E. (2009) 'Ben Gunn, the blogging prisoner locked in a struggle', *The Guardian*, Society section, 7 October: 1.

Allison, H.G. (2001) *Support for the Bereaved and Dying in Services for Adults with Autistic Spectrum Disorders*. London: The National Autistic Society.

American Academy of Child and Adolescent Psychiatry (1998) 'Practice parameters for the assessment and treatment of children and adolescents with posttraumatic stress disorder', *Journal of the American Academy of Child and Adolescent Psychiatry,* 37 (10): 4s–26s.

American School Counselor Association (2005) *The ASCA National Model: A Framework for School Counseling Programs*, 2nd edn. Alexandria, VA: ASCA.

Andrikopoulou, A. (2004) 'Studying five-year-olds' understanding of the components of death', *Educational and Child Psychology*, 21 (3): 41–60.

Arnason, A. (2000) 'Biography, bereavement, story', *Mortality*, 5 (2): 189–204.

Attig, T. (1995) 'Respecting the spirituality of the dying and the bereaved', in I.B. Corless, B.B. Germino and M.A. Pittman (eds), *A Challenge for Living: Dying, Death and Bereavement*. Boston: Jones and Bartlett, pp 130–77.

Attig, T. (1996) *How We Grieve: Relearning the World*. New York: Oxford University Press.

Attig, T. (2000) *The Heart of Grief: Death and the Search for Lasting Love*. New York: Oxford University Press.

Axline, V. (1964) *Dibs in Search of Self*. Harmondsworth: Penguin.

Bacon, J.B. (1996) 'Support groups for bereaved children', in C.A. Corr and D.M. Corr (eds), *Handbook of Childhood Death and Bereavement*. New York: Springer, pp. 285–304.

BACP (2010) British Association of Counselling and Psychotherapy Ethical Framework can be downloaded from www.bacp.co.uk

Baker, J.E., Sedney, M.A. and Gross, E. (1992) 'Psychological tasks for bereaved children', *American Journal of Orthopsychiatry*, 62: 105–16.

Baldwin, A.L., Baldwin, C. and Cole, R.E.(1990) 'Stress-resistant families and stress-resistant children', in J. Roll, A.S. Masten, D. Cicchetti, K.H. Nuechterlein and S. Weintraub (eds), *Risk and Protective Factors in the Development of Psychopathology*. Cambridge: Cambridge University Press, pp 257–80.

Balk, D.E. (1991) 'Sibling death, adolescent bereavement, and religion', *Death Studies*, 15 (1): 1–20.

Balk, D.E. (1999) 'Bereavement and spiritual change', *Death Studies*, 23 (6): 485–93.

Balk, D.E. (2008) 'A modest proposal about bereavement and recovery', *Death Studies*, 32 (1): 84–93.

Bannister, A. (2003) *Creative Therapies with Traumatized Children*. London: Jessica Kingsley.

Barber, C. (1999) 'The use of music and colour theory as a behaviour modifier', *British Journal of Nursing*, 8: 443–7.

Barenbaum, J. et al. (2004) 'The psychosocial aspects of children who are exposed to war', *Journal of Psychology and Psychiatry*, 45 (1): 41–62.

Barlow, C. and Coleman, H. (2003) 'The healing alliance: how families use social support after suicide', *Omega*, 47 (3): 187–201.

Barnardo's (1997) *Matters of Life and Death*. Newcastle upon Tyne: LEA.

Barrett, D. (1992) 'Through a glass darkly: images of the dead in dreams', *Omega: Journal of Death and Dying*, 24: 97–108.

Barrett, D. (ed.) (1996) *Trauma and Dreams*. Cambridge, MA: Harvard University Press.

Barrett, D. (ed.) (2001) *Trauma and Dreams*. Cambridge, MA: Harvard University Press.

Batmanghelidjh, C. (2007) *Shattered Lives*. London: Jessica Kingsley.

Batten, M. and Oltjenbruns, K.A. (1999) 'Adolescent sibling bereavement as a catalyst for spiritual development: a model for understanding', *Death Studies*, 23 (6): 529–46.

Baugher, B. and Jordan, J. (2004) *After Suicide Loss: Coping with Your Loss*. Tukwila, WA: The Grief Store.

Beautrais, A.L. (2004) *Suicide Prevention, Support for Families and Significant Others after a Suicide: A Literature Review and Synthesis of Evidence*. Wellington, NZ: Ministry of Youth Affairs.

Becker, G., Xander, C.J., Blum, H.E., Lutterbach, J., Momm, F., Gysels, M. and Higginson, I.J. (2007) 'Do religious or spiritual beliefs influence bereavement? A systematic review', *Palliative Medicine*, 21: 207–17.

Becker, S.H. and Knudson, R.M. (2003) 'Visions of the dead: imagination and mourning', *Death Studies*, 27: 691–716.

Belicki, K. and Belicki, D. (2006) 'Predisposition for nightmares: a study of hypnotic ability, vividness of imagery and absorption', *Journal of Clinical Psychology*, 42(5): 714–18.

Bellous, J.E. (2008) 'Editorial', *International Journal of Children's Spirituality*, 13 (3): 195–201.

Bennett, G. and Bennett, K.M. (2000) 'The presence of the dead: and empirical study', *Mortality*, 5 (2): 139–57.

Berns, C.F. (2003–2004) 'Bibliotherapy: using books to help bereaved children', *Omega: Journal of Death and Dying,* 48 (4): 321–36.

Bertman, S.L. (ed.) (1999) *Grief and the Healing Arts: Creativity as Therapy.* Amityville, NY: Baywood.

Bettelheim, B. (1978) *The Uses of Enchantment: The Meaning and Importance of Fairy Tales.* Harmondsworth: Peregrine Books.

Biddulph, S. (1997) *Raising Boys: Why Boys are Different and How to Help them Become Happy and Well-Balanced Men.* Warriewood, NSW: Finch Publishing.

Bifulco A., Harris, T. and Brown, G.W. (1992) 'Mourning or early inadequate care? Re-examining the relationship of maternal loss in childhood with adult depression and anxiety', *Developmental Psychopathology,* 4: 433–49.

Bird, J. and Gerlach, L. (2005) *Improving the Emotional Health and Well-being of Young People in Secure Care.* London: NCB.

Birenbaum, L.K., Robinson, A.R., Phillips, D.S., Stewart, B.J. and McCown, D.E. (1989) 'The response of children to the death and dying of a sibling', *Omega: Journal of Death and Dying,* 20: 213–28.

Black, D. (1996) 'Childhood bereavement: editorial', *British Medical Journal*; 15 June, 312: 1496.

Black, D. (2002) 'The family and childhood bereavement: an overview', *Bereavement Care*, 21 (2): 24–6.

Black, D. (2007) 'Bereavement in the arts', *Bereavement Care*, 26 (2): 35.

Black, D. and Trickey, D. (2005) 'Children bereaved by murder and manslaughter', 7th International Conference on Grief and Bereavement in Contemporary Society. Kings College, London, 12th July.

Black. D. and Urbanowicz, M. (1987) 'Family intervention with bereaved children', *Journal of Child Psychology and Psychiatry*, 28: 467–76.

Blackman, N. (2003) *Loss and Learning Disability.* London: Worth.

Bolton, G. (ed.) (2007) *Dying, Bereavement and the Healing Arts.* London: Jessica Kingsley.

Bonell-Pascual, E., Huline-Dickens, S., Hollins, S., Esterhuyzen, A. and Sedwick, P. (1999) 'Bereavement and grief in adults with learning disabilities. a follow up study', *British Journal of Psychiatry*, 175: 348–50.

Bonnano, G. (2004) 'Loss, trauma and human resilience: have we underestimated the human capacity to thrive after extremely adverse events?', *American Psychologist*, 59: 20–28.

Bonnano, G. (2009) *The Other Side of Sadness: What the New Science of Bereavement Tells us About Life after Loss.* New York: Basic Books.

Bosacki, S. (2001) '"Theory of mind" or "theory of the soul"? The role of spirituality in children's understanding of minds and emotions', in J. Erricker, C. Ota and C. Erricker (eds.) *Spiritual Education. Cultural, Religious and Social Differences: New Perspectives for the 21st Century.* Brighton: Academic, pp 156–69.

Boswell, G. (1995) *Violent Victims: The Prevalence of Abuse and Loss in the Lives of Section 53 Offenders.* London: Prince's Trust.

Bosworth, K. and Walz, G. (2005) *Promoting Student Resiliency.* Alexandria, VA: American Counselling Association.

Bowlby, J. (1940) 'The influence of early environment in the development of neurosis and neurotic character', *International Journal of Psychoanalysis*, XXI: 1–25.

Bowlby, J. (1951) *Maternal Care and Mental Health.* Geneva: World Health Organization. (WHO Monograph Series, No 2).

Bowlby, J. (1969) *Attachment and Loss: 1. Attachment*. London: Hogarth Press.

Bowlby, J. and Parkes, C.M. (1970) 'Separation and loss within the family' in E.J. Anthony and C.J. Koupernik (eds), *The Child in his Family*. New York/Chichester: Wiley, pp. 197–216.

Bowman, T. (2003) 'Using literary resources in bereavement work: evoking words for grief', *The Forum*, 29 (2): 8–9.

Brake Conference (2009) 'When Someone You Love Dies', 10 June, Manchester.

Braun, M.J. and Berg, D.H. (1994) 'Meaning reconstruction in the experience of parental bereavement', *Death Studies*, 18 (2): 105–29.

Bray, M.A., Lea, A,T., Patwa, S.S., Margiano, S.G., Alric, J.M. and Peck, H.L. (2003) 'Written emotional expression as an intervention for asthma', *Psychology in Schools*, 40: 193–207.

Brent, D.A., Perper, J.A., Goldstein, C.E., Kolko, D.J., Allan, M.J., Allman, C.J. and Zelenak, J.P. (1988) 'Risk factors for adolescent suicide: a comparison of adolescent suicide victims with suicidal inpatients', *Archives of General Psychiatry*, 45: 581–588.

Brewer, J. and Sparkes, A.C. (2008) 'The meaning of sport and physical activity in the lives of bereaved children: insights from an ethnographic study', International Conference on Grief and Bereavement in Contemporary Society. Melbourne, Australia.

Briere, J. (1996) *The Trauma Symptom Checklist for Children*. Odessa, FL: Psychological Assessment Resources.

Broberg, A.O., Dyregrov, A. and Lilled, L. (2005) 'The Goteborg discotheque fire: post-traumatic stress and school adjustment as reported by the primary victims 18 months later', *Journal of Child Psychology and Psychiatry*, 46 (12): 1279–86.

Brooks, R. and Goldstein, S. (2001) *Raising a Resilient Child: Fostering Strength, Hope and Optimism in Our Children*. New York: Contemporary Books.

Brooks, R. and Goldstein, S. (2002) *Nurturing Resilience in our Children: Answers to the Most Important Parenting Questions*. New York: Contemporary Books.

Bryan, E.M. (1995) 'The death of a twin', *Palliative Care*, 9 (3): 187–92.

Budmen, K.O. (1969) 'Grief and the young: a need to know', *Archives of the Foundation of Thanatology*, 1: 11.

Bulkeley, K. (1995) *Spiritual Dreaming: A Cross-cultural and Historical Journey*. New York: Paulist Press.

Bulkeley, K. (2000) *Transforming Dreams: Learning Spiritual Lessons from the Dreams you Never Forget*. New York: Wiley.

Bulkeley, K., Broughton, B., Sanchez, A. and Siller J. (2005) 'Earliest remembered dreams', *Dreaming: Journal of the International Association of Dreams*, 15 (3): 205–22.

Bulkeley, K. and Bulkeley, P. (2005) *Dreaming Beyond Death: A Guide to Pre-death Dreams and Visions*. Boston, MA: Beacon Press.

Bunce, M. and Rickards, A. (2004) *Working with Bereaved Children: A Guide*. London: Children's Legal Centre. Available at http://www.essex.ac.uk/armedcon/unit/projects/wwbc_guide/index.html (last accessed 19 May 2010).

Bunting, M. (2007) 'Immovable force', *The Guardian*, 10 October: 1.

Burke, J. (2008) 'Creative ways of working with non-verbal media', in A. Towers, 'When only an eyelid moves', *CCYP*, June: 29.

Burke, M.T., Chauvin, J.C. and Miranti, J.G. (eds) (2005) *Religious and Spiritual Issues in Counselling: Applications Across Diverse Populations*. New York: Brunner and Routledge.

Cameron, J. (1995) *The Artist's Way: A Course in Discovering and Recovering your Creative Self*. London: Pan Books.

Campbell, F. (1997) 'Changing the legacy of suicide', *Suicide and Life-threatening Behaviour*, 4: 329–38.

Carr, A. (2000) 'Evidence-based practice in family therapy and systemic consultation: 1: child-focused problems', *Journal of Family Therapy*, 22: 29–60.

Carrion, V.G. and Steiner, H. (2000) 'Trauma and dissociation in delinquent adolescents', *Journal of the American Academy of Child and Adolescent Psychiatry,* 39: 353–9.

Carver, C.S. (1998) 'Resilience and thriving: issues, models and linkages', *Journal of Social Issues,* 54: 245–66.

Casdagli, P. (1995) 'Using drama in grief work', in S.C. Smith and M. Pennells (eds), *Interventions with Bereaved Children.* London: Jessica Kingsley, pp. 204–16.

Cattenach, A. (2007) *Narrative Approaches in Play with Children.* London: Jessica Kingsley.

CBN (Child Bereavement Network) (2004) Summary of some of the key issues for bereaved children and young people.

CBN (Child Bereavement Network) (2008) *Bereavement in the Secure Setting: Delivering Every Child Matters for Bereaved Young People in Custody.* London: CBN.

Cerel, J., Fristad, M.A., Weller, E.B. and Weller, R.A. (1999) 'Suicide-bereaved children and adolescents: a controlled longitudinal examination', *Journal of the American Academy of Child and Adolescent Psychiatry,* 38: 672–80.

Cerel, J., Fristad, M.A., Weller, E.B. and Weller, R.A. (2002) 'Suicide of a parent: child and adolescent bereavement', *The Prevention Researcher*, 9 (2): 9–10.

Chaplin, D., Kerslake, D. and Glassock, G. (2008) 'Report: Eighth International Conference on Grief and Bereavement in Contemporary Society', *Bereavement Care*, 27 (5): 55–7.

Charkow, W.B. (1998) 'Inviting children to grieve', *Professional School Counselling*, 2: 117–122.

Christ, G.H. (2000) *Healing Children's Grief: Surviving a Parent's Death from Cancer.* New York: Oxford University Press.

Christ, G.H. and Christ, A.E. (2006) 'Current approaches to helping children cope with a parent's terminal illness', *CA: Cancer Journal for Clinicians*, 36: 197–212.

Christ, G.H., Siegel, K. and Christ, A.E. (2002) 'Adolescent grief: "It never really hit me until it happened"', *Journal of American Medical Association,* 288: 1269–79.

Christ, G.H., Siegel, K., Karus, D. and Christ, A. (2005) 'Evaluation of a bereavement intervention', *Social Work in End-of-Life and Palliative Care,* 1: 57–81.

Chrouso, G., Charmandari, E., Kino, R. and Souvatzoglou, E. (2003) 'Pediatric stress: hormonal regulators and human development' *Hormone Research,* 59 (4): 161–79.

CHUMS, (2005) 'The death of a child', CHUMS Child Bereavement Service for Bedfordshire Conference, October. Hitchen, Herts.

Cicchetti, D., Rogosch, P.A., Lynch, M. and Holt, K.D. (1993) 'Resilience in maltreated children: processes leading to adaptive outcome', *Developmental Psychopathology*, 5: 629–47.

Claire (No Year) 'My sister Joanne', *Treetops: The Child Bereavement Group of the Corrymeela Community*, 10: 1–8.

Clark, J. and Franzmann, M. (2006) 'Authority from grief, presence and place in the making of roadside memorials', *Death Studies*, 30 (6): 579–99.

Cobain, B. and Larch, J. (2006) *Dying to Be Free: A Healing Guide for Families After a Suicide.* Center City, MN: Hazelden Foundation.

Coles, R. (1991) *The Spiritual Life of Children.* Orlando, FL: Houghton Mifflin Harcourt.

Collins, M. (2005) *It's OK to be Sad.* London: Sage.

Cook, K.E., Earles-Vollrath, T. and Ganz, J.B. (2006) 'Bibliotherapy', *Intervention in School and Clinic*, 42: 91–100.

Cooley, J. and McGauran, F. (2000) *Talking About Death: A Bereavement Pack for People with Learning Disabilities, Their Carers and Families.* London: Speechmark Publications.

Cooper, C. (1999) 'Children's dreams during the grief process', *Professional School of Counselling,* 3(2): 137–40.

Cooper, M. (2002) Conference presentation at Childhood Bereavement Network conference, 29 June.

Cooper, M. (2009) 'Counselling in UK secondary schools: a comprehensive review of audit and evaluation data', *Counselling and Psychotherapy Research*, 9 (3): 137–50.

Corr, C.A. (1996) 'What do we know about grieving children and adolescents?', in K.J. Doka (ed.), *Living with Grief: Children, Adolescents and Loss.* Washington DC: Hospice Foundation of America, pp. 21–32.

Corr, C.A. (2000) 'What do we know about grieving children and adolescents?', in K.J. Doka (ed.), *Living with Grief: Children, Adolescents and Loss.* Washington, DC: Hospice Foundation of America, pp. 21–32.

Corr, C.A., Nabe, C.M. and Corr, D.M. (2003) *Death and Dying, Life and Living*, 4th edn. Belmont, CA: Wadsworth.

Cournos, F. (2001) 'Mourning and adaptation following the death of a parent in childhood', *Journal of the American Academy of Psychoanalysis*, 29: 137–45.

Cousins, W., Monteith, M., Larkin, E., and Percy, A. (2003) *The Care Careers of Younger Looked After Children: Findings from the Multiple Placement Project*. Belfast: Queen's University.

Coyne, E. and Ryan, M. (2007) 'Mapping the knowledge bereavement counsellors use in practice', *Grief Matters: The Australian Journal of Grief and Bereavement*, 10 (3): 64–8.

Cozolino, L. (2002) *The Neuroscience of Psychotherapy: Building and Rebuilding the Human Brain*. New York: W.W. Norton.

Cranwell, B. (2007) 'Adult decisions affecting bereaved children; researching the children's perspective', *Bereavement Care,* 26 (2): 30–33.

Crehan, G. (2004) 'The surviving sibling: The effects of sibling death in childhood', *Psychoanalytic Psychotherapy,* 18(2): 202–19.

Crook, T and Eliot, J. (1980) 'Parental death during childhood and adult depression: a critical review of the literature', *Psychological Bulletin*; 87: 252–9.

Culliford, L. (2002) 'Spirituality and clinical care', *British Medical Journal*, 325: 1434–5.

Culliford, L. and Powell, W. (2005) *Spirituality and Mental Health*. Leaflet of the Spirituality and Psychiatry Special Interest Group. London: Royal College of Psychiatrists.

Davidson, J., Lee-Archer, S. and Sanders, G. (2005) 'Dream, imagery and emotion', *Dreaming: Journal of the International Association for the Study of Dreams*, 15 (1): 33–47.

Davies, B. (1999) *Shadows in the Sun: Experiences of Sibling Bereavement in Childhood.* Philadelphia, PA: Brunner/ Mazel.

Davies, B. (2006) 'Sibling grief through childhood', *The Forum*, January/February/March: 4.

Davou, B. and Widdershoven-Zervakis, M. (2004) 'Effects of mourning on cognitive processes', *Educational and Child Psychology*, 21 (3): 61–76.

Day, E. (2009) 'Ten years on and Columbine still feels the pain' *The Observer,* 12 April: 8–10.

Deeken, A. (2004) 'A nation in transition: bereavement in Japan', *Bereavement Care,* 23 (3): 35–7.

Department for Education and Skills (DfES) (2005a) *Common Core of Skills and Knowledge for the Children's Workforce*. London: The Stationery Office.

Department for Education and Skills (DfES) (2005b) *Common Assessment Framework for Children and Young People*. London: The Stationery Office.

Department for Education and Skills (DfES) (2007) *Care Matters: Time for Change*. London: The Stationery Office.

Department of Health (2001) *Valuing People: A New Strategy for Learning Disability for the 21st Century*. London: Department of Health.

DeSpelder, L.A. (2009) 'Cultural Competencies: Teaching Strategies', *The Forum ADEC*, 35 (2): 15.

DeSpelder, L.A. and Strickland, A.L. (2002) *The Last Dance: Encountering Death and Dying*, 6th edn. New York: McGraw-Hill.

De Vries, M.W. (1996) 'Trauma in cultural perspective', in B.A. van der Kolk, A.C. McFarlane and L. Weisaeth (eds), *Traumatic Stress*. London: The Guilford Press, pp. 400.

Di Ciacco, J.A (2008) *The Colors of Grief: Understanding a Child's Journey Through Loss from Birth to Adulthood*. London: Jessica Kingsley.

Dodd, P.C. and Guerin, S. (2009) 'Grief and bereavement in people with intellectual disabilities', *Current Opinion in Psychiatry*, 22 (5): 442–46.

Dogra, N., Parkin, A., Gale, F. and Frake, C. (2002) *A Multidisciplinary Handbook of Child and Adolescent Health for Front-line Professionals*. London: Jessica Kingsley.

Doka, K.J. (ed.) (1989) *Disenfranchised Grief*. Lexington, MA: Lexington Books.

Doka, K.J. (2002) (ed) *Disenfranchised Grief: New Directions, Challenges and Strategies for Practice*. Champaign, IL: Research Press.

Doka, K.J. (2003) *Living With Grief: Coping with Public Tragedy*. Washington, DC: Hospice Foundation of America.

Doka, K.J. and Davidson, J.D. (1998) *Living with Grief*, Washington, DC: Hospice Foundation of America.

Dominica, Sister Frances Children's Hospice (2002) *Whose Side Is God On?* Available at www.guild-of-st-raphael.org.uk/children's_hospice.htm (last accessed 25 March 2008), pp 1–7.

Donahue, M.J. and Benson, P.I. (1995) 'Religion and well-being of adolescents', *Journal of Social Issues*, 51: 145–61.

Donnelly, M. and Rowling, L. (2007) 'The impact of critical incidents on school counsellors: report of a qualitative study', *Bereavement Care*, 26 (1): 11–14.

Dougall, D. (2008) 'Stories of loss and love from families of the army's fallen', *The Observer*, 10 November: 8–9.

Dowdney, L. (2000) 'Childhood bereavement following parental death', *Journal of Child Psychology and Psychiatry*, 41: 819–30.

Dowdney, L., Wilson, R., Maughan, B., Allerton, M., Schofield, P. and Skuse, D. (1999) 'Psychological disturbance and service provision in parentally bereaved children: prospective case-control study', *BMJ*, 319: 354–7.

Dowling, L. (2003) 'Supporting families and children after loss', *Threshold*, 77: 30–32.

Dowling, S.F. (2002) *Bereavement in the Lives of People with Intellectual Disabilities*. Available at http://www.intellectualdisability.info/lifestages/bereavement.htm (last accessed 2 November 2008), pp. 1–7.

Dowling, S., Hubert, J., White, S. and Hollins, S. (2006) 'Bereaved adults with intellectual disabilities: a combined randomised controlled trial and qualitative study of two community-based interventions', *Journal of Intellectual Disability Research*, 50 (4): 277–87.

Downey, J.A. (2002) 'Exploring children's beliefs about educational risk and resilience', *Academic Exchange Quarterly*, Spring: 126–32.

Driscoll, M. (2004) 'Interview: Margarette Driscoll meets Sister Frances Domininica: mum, nun and friend to the dying'. Available at http://www.timesonline.co.uk/tol/news/article1026109.ece (last accessed 19 May 2010).

Dunn, A.A., Oyebode, J.R. and Howard, R.A. (2005) 'Emotional reactions to continu-ing bonds in spousal bereavement'. Presentation at the 7th International Conference on Grief and Bereavement in Contemporary Society, 12–15 July, King's College, London.

Dwivedi, K.N. (ed.) (1993) *Group Work with Children and Adolescents: A Handbook.* London: Jessica Kingsley.

Dyregrov, A. (1996) 'Children's participation in rituals', *Bereavement Care*, 15 (1): 2–5.

Dyregrov, A.(2004) 'Educational consequences of loss and trauma', *Educational and Child Psychology,* 21 (3): 77–84.

Dyregrov, A. (2008) *Grief in Children: A Handbook for Adults.* London: Jessica Kingsley.

Dyregrov, A., Bie Wikander, A.M. and Vigerust, S. (1999) 'Sudden death of a classmate and friend: adolescents' perception of support from their school', *School Psychology International,* 20: 191–208.

Dyregrov, K. and Dyregrov, A. (2008) *Effective Grief and Bereavement Support: The Role of Family, Friends, Colleagues, Schools and Support Professionals.* London: Jessica Kingsley.

Eakon. J.E. (1999) *How our Lives Become Stories: Making Selves.* New York: Cornell University Press.

Eckersley, R. and Dear, D. (2002) 'Cultural correlates of youth suicide', *Social Science and Medicine,* 55: 1819–904.

Edelmen, H. (1994) *Motherless Daughters: The Legacy of Loss.* London: Hodder and Stoughton.

Edwards, D. (2004) *Art Therapy.* London: Sage.

Eke, L. (2009) 'Suicide, survivors and supervision', *Therapy Today*, December: 30–32.

Ekman, P. and Rosenberg, E. (2005) *What the Face Reveals: Basic and Applied Studies of Spontaneous Expression Using the Action Coding System (FACS).* New York: Oxford University Press.

Elizur, E.and Kaffman, N. (1983) 'Factors influencing the severity of childhood bereave-ment reactions', *American Journal of Orthopsychiatry*; 55: 668–76.

Ellenbogen, S. and Gratton, F. (2001) 'Do they suffer more? Reflections on research comparing suicide survivors to other survivors', *Suicide and Life Threatening Behavior,* 31: 83–90.

Emblen, J.D. (1992) 'Religion and spirituality defined according to current use in nursing literature', *Journal of Professional Nursing*, 8: 41–7.

Ens, C. and Bond, J.B. (2005) 'Death anxiety and personal growth in adolescents experi-encing the death of a grandparent', *Death Studies,* 29: 171–8.

Eppler, C. (2008) 'Exploring themes of resiliency in children after the death of a parent', *Professional School Counselling*, 11: 189–96.

Eppler, C. and Carolan, M.T. (2006) 'Biblionarrative: a narrative technique uniting oral and written life-stories*', Journal of Family Psychotherapy*, 16: 31–43.

Eppler, C., Olsen, J.A. and Hidanp. L. (2009) 'Using stories in elementary school coun-selling: brief narrative techniques', *Professional School Counseling.* Available at http://findarticles.com/p/articles/mi_m0KOC/is_5_12/ai_n32149153/ (last accessed 19 May 2010).

Erikson, E.H. (1968) *Identity Youth and Crisis.* New York: Norton.

Eron, J.B. and Lund, T.W. (1996) *Narrative Solutions in Brief Counseling.* New York: Guilford Press.

Evans, C. (1983) *Landscapes of the Night.* London: Gollancz.

Everatt, A. and Gale, I. (2004) 'Children with learning disabilities and bereavement: a review of the literature and its implications', *Education and Child Psychology*, 21 (3): 30–40.

Felner, R., Terre, L. and Rowlison, R.T. (1988) 'A life transition framework for under-standing marital dissolution and family reorganization', in S.A. Wolchik and P. Karoly (eds), *Children of Divorce: Empirical Perspectives on Adjustment*. New York: Garder, pp. 35–65.

Ferrell, B.F. and Coyle, N. (eds) (2001) *Textbook of Palliative Nursing*. New York: Oxford University Press.

Figley, C.R., Bride, B.E. and Mazza, N. (eds.) (1997) *Death and Trauma: The Traumatology of Grieving*. Washington, DC: Taylor and Francis.

Filak, V.F. and Abel, S. (2004) 'Boys don't cry: cartooning, grieving strategies and gender-based stereotypes in the aftermath of September 11', *Grief Matters: The Australian Journal of Grief and Bereavement*, 7 (1): 12–17.

Filipović, Z. (1994) *Zlata's Diary: A Child's Life in Sarajevo*. London: Viking.

Finlay, I. and Jones, N. (2000) 'Unresolved grief in young offenders in prison', *British Journal of General Practice,* 50: 569–70.

Firth, P.H. (2005) 'Groupwork in palliative care', in P.H. Firth, G. Luff and D. Oliviere (eds), *Loss, Change and Bereavement in Palliative Care*. Maidenhead: Open University Press, McGraw Hill Education, pp. 53–65.

Fitzgerald, H. (2000) 'The grieving teen'. Available at http://www.americanhospice. org/index.php?option=com_content&task=view&Itemid=12&id=70&Itemid=12 (last accessed 19 May 2010).

Fitzpatrick, P. (2006) 'How to help children and staff cope with loss', *Youth Justice Board News,* 32: 8.

Fosha, D. (2000) *The Transforming Power of Affect*. New York; Basic Book.

Foulkes, S.H. and Anthony, E.J. (1984) *Group Psychotherapy*. London: Karnac.

Francis, D., Kellaher, L. and Neophytou, G. (2005) *The Secret Cemetery*. Oxford: Berg.

Frangoulis S., Jordan, N., Lansdown, R. (1996) 'Children's concepts of an afterlife', *British Journal of Religious Education,* 18: 114–23.

Frank, A. (1943) 'Never going outside'. Available at http://prev.annefrank.org/content. asp?pid=118&lid=2 (last accessed 19 May 2010).

Frank, A. (1997) *The Wounded Storyteller*. Chicago, IL: University of Chicago Press.

Frantz, T.T., Farrell, M.M. and Trolley, B.C. (2001) 'Positive outcomes of losing a loved one', in R.A. Neimeyer (ed.), *Meaning Reconstruction and the Experience of Loss*. Washington, DC: American Psychological Association, pp. 191–212.

Frayley, R.C. and Shaver, P.R. (1999) 'Loss and bereavement: attachment theory and recent controversies concerning "grief work" and the nature of detachment', in J.Cassidy and P.R. Shaver (eds), *Handbook of Attachment: Theory, Research and Clinical Applications*. New York: Guilford Press, pp 735–59.

Freeman, J., Epston, D. and Lobovits, D. (1997) *Playful Approaches to Serious Problems: Narrative Therapy with Children and Their Families*. New York: W.W. Norton.

Freud, S. (1960) 'Letter to Binswanger (letter 219)', in E.L. Freud (ed.), *Letters of Sigmund Freud*. New York: Basic Books, pp. 386.

Freud, S. (1965 [1900]) *The Interpretation of Dreams* (trans. J. Stracey). New York: Avon Books.

Freud, S. (1971 [1957]) 'Mourning and melancholia', in J. Stracey (ed. and trans.), *The Standard Edition of the Complete Psychological Works of Sigmund Freud,* Vol. 14. London: Hogarth Press, pp 243–58.

Furman, E. (1974) *A Child's Parent Dies*. New Haven and London: Yale University Press.

Furr, S. (2005) 'Spirituality and grief', in M.T. Burke, J.C. Chauvin and J.G. Miranti (eds), *Religious and Spiritual Issues in Counselling: Applications Across Diverse Populations*. New York: Brunner and Routledge, pp. 135–46.

Galassi, J. and Akos, P. (2007) *Strengths-based School Counselling: Promoting Student Development and Achievement*. Mahwah, NJ: Lawrence Erlbaum Associates.

Gallup, G., Jnr., and Lindsay, D.M. (1999) *Surveying the Religious Landscape: Trends in U.S. Beliefs*. Harrisburg, PA: Morehouse.

Gamino, L.A., Easterling L.W., Stirman, L.S. and Sewell, K.W. (2000) 'Grief adjustments as influenced by funeral participation and occurrence of adverse funeral events', *Omega*, 41: 79–92.

Garfield, P. (1996) 'Dreams in bereavement', in D. Barrett (ed.), *Trauma and Dreams*. Cambridge, MA: Harvard University Press, pp. 186–211.

Garfield, P. (1997) *The Dream Messenger: How Dreams of the Departed Bring Healing Gifts*. New York: Simon and Schuster.

Gavron, J. (2009) 'Tell the boys I loved them', *The Guardian, Family,* 4 April: 1–2.

Geldard, K. and Geldard, D. (2000) *Counselling Adolescents*. London: Sage.

Gerhardt, S. (2004) *Why Love Matters: How Affection Shapes a Baby's Brain*. London: Brunner-Routledge.

Gersie, A. (1991) *Storymaking in Bereavement: Dragons Fight in the Meadows*. London: Jessica Kingsley.

Gibbons, M.B. (1992) 'A child dies, a child survives: the impact of sibling loss', *Journal of Paediatric Health Care,* 6: 65–72.

Gil, E. (1991) *The Healing Power of Play*. New York: Guilford Press.

Gilbert, S, (2008) 'Grief's spiral', *Counselling Children and Young People*, BACP, June: 2–8.

Giovanola, J. (2005) 'Sibling involvement at the end of life', *Journal of Pediatric Oncology Nursing,* 22 (4): 222–6.

Gladding, S.T. (1997) 'Stories and the art of counselling', *Journal of Humanistic Education and Development,* 36: 68–73.

Glassock, G.T. (2001) 'The importance of rituals in coping with grief', *Grief Matters: The Australian Journal of Grief and Bereavement*, Summer: 47–50.

Goelitz, N. (2001) 'Nurturing life with dreams: therapeutic dreamwork with cancer patients', *Clinical Social Work Journal*, 29: 375–85.

Goelitz, N. (2007) 'Exploring dream work at the end of life', *Dreaming*, 17 (3):159–71.

Goenjian, A. (1993) 'A mental health relief program in Armenia after the 1988 earthquake: implementation and clinical observations', *British Journal of Psychiatry*, 163: 230–39.

Gogar, A. and Hill, C., (1992) 'Examining the effects of brief individual dream interpretation', *Dreaming,* 2: 239–48.

Gogray, N., Giedd, J.N., Lusk, L., Hayashi, K.M. et al. (2004) 'Dynamic mapping of human cortical development during childhood through early adulthood', *Proceedings of the National Academies of Sciences,* 101 (21): 8174–9.

Goldman, L. (2000) *Life and Loss: A Guide to Helping Grieving Children*. New York: Taylor and Francis.

Goldman, L. (2002a) 'Trauma and children: what can we do?', *Healing Magazine*, Spring/Summer: 1–4.

Goldman, L. (2002b) 'Children living with fear: recognizing and healing trauma', *Healing Magazine*, Fall: 6–7.

Goleman, D. (1996) *Emotional Intelligence*. London: Bloomsbury.

Goleman, D. (2006) *Social Intelligence: The Science of Human Relationships*. New York: Bantam.

Golsworthy, R. and Coyle, A. (2001) 'Practitioners' accounts of religious and spiritual dimensions in bereavement therapy', *Counselling Psychology Quarterly*,14 (3): 183–202.

Goodyer, I.M. (1990) *Life Experiences, Development and Childhood Psychopathology*. Chichester: Wiley.

Gorer, G. (1965) *Death, Grief and Mourning in Contemporary Britain*. London: Cresset Press.

Gopnik, A., Meltzoff, A.N. and Kuhl, P.K. (1999) *The Scientist in the Crib: Minds, Brains and How Children Learn*. New York: William Morrow.

Gough, M.L.K. (2003) 'Photo therapy with the bereaved', *The Forum,* ADEC, April/May/June, 29: 2.

Graham, P. and Orley, J. (1998) 'WHO and the mental health of children', *World Health Forum,* 19: 268–72.

Graves, D. (2008) *Talking With Bereaved People: An Approach for Structured and Sensitive Communication*. London: Jessica Kingsley.

Green, H. et al. (2005) *The Mental Health of Children and Young People in Great Britain 2004*. London: Office of National Statistics.

Greene, G. quoted in A. Storr (1989) *Solitude*. Flamingo Books; London, p. 123.

Grollman, E.A. (1995) *Bereaved Children and Teens*. Boston, MA: Beacon Press.

Grollman, E.A. (1997) *Living When a Loved One Has Died*. Boston, MA: Beacon Press.

Grollman, E.A. (2008) 'Healing with hope' posted on The Grief Blog, 13 March Available at http://thegriefblog.com/grief/healing-the-grieving-heart-radio/healing-with-hope-rabbi-earl-grollman/ (last accessed 19 May 2010).

Groskop, V. (2009) 'Escape from the past', *The Guardian, Family*, 18 April :1–2.

Grubbs, G. (2004) *Bereavement Dreaming and the Individuating Soul*. Berwick, ME: Nicolas-Hays.

Gunnar, M.R. (2006) 'Attachment and stress in early development: does attachment add to the potency of social regulators of infant stress?', in C.S. Carter, L. Ahnert. K.E. Grossman, S.B. Hardy et al. (eds), *Attachment and Bonding: A New Synthesis*. Cambridge, MA: MIT Press, pp. 145–25.

Gupta, L. and Zimmer, C. (2008) 'Psychosocial intervention for war-affected children in Sierra Leone', *The British Journal of Psychiatry*, 192: 212–16.

Gurian, A., Monahan, K., Lurie, A. and Goodman, R.F. (2009) *Helping Children with Developmental Disabilities Cope with Traumatic Events*. NYU Child Study Center. Available at http://www.aboutourkids.org/articles/helping_children_developmental_disabilities_cope_traumatic_events (last accessed 19 May 2010).

Gutierrez, P.M. (1999) 'Suicidality in parentally bereaved adolescents', *Death Studies*, 23: 359–70.

Hall, C. (1984) 'A ubiquitous sex difference in dreams, revisited', *Journal of Personality and Social Psychology,* 46: 1109–17.

Hammer, S. (1991) *By Her Own Hand: Memoirs of a Suicide's Daughter*. New York: Soho Press.

Hand-in-Hand (2007) *Hand-in-Hand: Supporting Children and Young People Who Have a Learning Difficulty Through the Experience of Bereavement*. A Resource Pack for Professionals. Produced by SeeSaw, Grief support for the young in Oxfordshire. Available at http://www.seesaw.org.uk/files/SeeSaw_handinhand.pdf (last accessed 19 May 2010).

Hare, J., Sugawara, A. and Pratt, C. (1986) 'The child in grief: implications for teaching', *Early Child Development and Care,* 25: 43–56.

Harrington, R. and Harrison, L. (1999) 'Unproven assumptions about the impact of bereavement on children', *Journal of the Royal Society of Medicine*, 52, May: 230–33.

Harris, M. (1995) *The Loss That Is Forever*. New York: Dutton.

Harris, T. (2009) 'John Bowlby revisited: a retrospective review', *Bereavement Care*, 28 (1): 27–30.

Harris, T., Brown, G.W. and Bifulco, A. (1986) 'Loss of parent in childhood and adult psychiatric disorder: the role of lack of adequate parental care', *Psychological Medicine*, 16: 641–59.

Harris-Hendriks J., Black. D. and Kaplan, T. (2000) *When Father Kills Mother: Guiding Children Through Trauma and Grief*, 2nd edn. London: Routledge.

Harrison, L. and Harrington, R. (2001) 'Adolescents' bereavement experiences: prevalence, association with depressive symptoms and use of services', *Journal of Adolescence*, 24: 137–42.

Harrison, R. (2002) *Ordinary Days and Shattered Lives: Sudden Death and the Impact on Children and Families*. West Wycombe: Child Bereavement Trust.

Hartmann, E. and Basile, R. (2003) 'Dream imagery becomes more intense after 9/11/01', *Dreaming: the Journal of the Association for the Study of Dreams*, 13 (20): 61–6.

Hawkins, J. (2002) *Voices of the Voiceless: Person-centred Approaches and People with Learning Difficulties*. Ross-on-Wye: PCCS Books.

Hay, D. and Nye, R. (2006) *The Spirit of the Child*, revised edn. London: Jessica Kingsley.

Healy-Romanello. M.A. (1993) 'The invisible griever: support groups for bereaved children', *Special Services in the Schools*, 8: 67–89.

Heath, B. (2009) 'Songs of loss and living', *Bereavement Care,* 28(2): 32–9.

Hedtke, L. (2001) 'Remembering practices in the face of death', *The Forum,* 27 (2): 5–6.

Heegaard, M. (1991) *What to do When Someone Very Special Dies: Children Can Learn to Cope with Grief*. Minneapolis, MN: Woodland Press.

Heikes, K. (1997) 'Parental suicide: a systems perspective', *Bulletin of the Menninger Clinic*, 61 (3): 354–67.

Hemmings, P. (1995) 'Communicating with children through play', in S.C. Smith and M. Pennells (eds), *Interventions with Bereaved Children*. London: Jessica Kingsley, pp 9–23.

Henderson, P. (2009) *Reflections on Supervision*. London: Karnac Books.

Hieb, M. (2005) *Inner Journeying Though Art-Journaling: Learning to See and Record Your Life as a Work of Art*. London, Jessica Kingsley.

Higgins, B. (2001) *The Health Needs of Young People who Offend*. London: Youth Justice Trust.

Higgins, R. (2008) 'The best of times, the worst of time: Sung-joo Kim', *The Sunday Times*, 20 April: 11.

Higson, C. (2008) 'This much I know', *The Observer Magazine,* 31 August: 12.

Hindmarch, C. (2000) *On The Death of a Child*. Oxford: Radcliffe Medical Press Ltd.

Hofer, M.A. (1996) 'On the nature and consequence of early loss', *Psychosomatic Medicine*, 58: 570–81.

Hogan, N.S. (2006) 'Understanding adolescent sibling bereavement', *The Forum*, 32 (1) January/February/ March: 6–7.

Hogan, N.S. and DeSantis, L. (1992) 'Adolescent sibling bereavement: an ongoing attachment', *Qualitative Health Research*, 2: 159–77.

Hogan, N.S. and DeSantis, L. (1994) 'Things that help and hinder the adoescent sibling bereavement', *Western Journal of Nursing Research,* 16, (2): 132–53.

Hogan, N.S. and Schmidt, L.A. (2002) 'Testing grief to personal growth model using structural equation modelling', *Death Studies*, 26: 615–35.

Hogwood, J. (2007) 'Coping with the intensity of child bereavement work: a qualitative study exploring volunteers' support needs', *Bereavement Care,* 26 (3): 54–7.

Holder, J.S. and Aldredge-Clanton, J. (2004) *Parting: A Handbook for Spiritual Care Near the End of Life*. Chapel Hill, CA: The University of Carolina Press.

Holland, J. (2001) *Understanding Children's Experiences of Parental Bereavement*. London: Jessica Kingsley.

Holland, J. (2004) 'Should children attend their parent's funeral?', *Pastoral Care in Education,* 22: 10–11.

Holliday, J. (2002) *A Review of Sibling Bereavement: Impact and Interventions*. Essex: Barnardo's Publications.

Hollins, S., Blackmen, N. and Dowling, S. (2003) *Books Beyond Words: When Somebody Dies.* London: The Royal College of Psychiatrists and St, Georges Hospital Medical School.

Hollins, S. and Esterhuyzen, A. (1997) 'Bereavement and grief in adults with learning disabilities*', British Journal of Psychiatry,* 170: 497–502.

Hollins, S. and Sireling, L. (2004) *Books Beyond Words: When Dad Died*. London: The Royal College of Psychiatrists and St, Georges Hospital Medical School.

Hollins, S., Sireling, L. and Webb, B. (2004) *Books Beyond Words: When Mum Died*. London: The Royal College of Psychiatrists and St, Georges Hospital Medical School.

Homicide Handbook (2002) *Working with Children Traumatised by Homicide*. Available at http://www.avpphila.org/ovcmanual2002/sec11.assess.pdf (last accessed 19 May 2010).

Hooyman, N. and Kramer, B. (2006) *Living Through Loss*. New York:Columbia University Press.

Hospice Foundation of America (2010) 'Interview with Dr. J. William Worden'. Available at http://www.hospicefoundation.org/pages/page.asp?page_id=49427 (last accessed 19 May 2010).

Howard, S., Dryden, J. and Johnson, B. (1999) 'Childhood resilience: review and critique of literature', *Oxford Review of Education*, 25: 307–23.

Howlin, P. (1997) *Autism: Preparing for Adulthood*. London: Routledge.

Huertas, P. (2005) 'Are we hard wired for love and grief?', *Healthcare Counselling and Psychotherapy Journal*, 5 (3): 14–16.

Huline-Dickens, S. (1996) 'Letters: people with learning disabilities also need help in bereavement', *British Medical Journal,* 313: 822.

Hurd, R.C. (2004) 'A teenager revisits her father's death during childhood: a study in resilience and healthy mourning', *Adolescence*, 39(154): 337–54.

Hutton, C.J. and Bradley, B.J. (1994) 'Effects of sudden infant death on bereaved siblings: a comparative study*', Journal of Psychology and Psychiatry*, 35: 723–32.

Hutton, E. (2006) 'Parting gifts: the spiritual needs of children', *Journal of Child Health Care*, 10 (3): 240–50.

Imber-Black, E., Roberts, J. and Whiting, R. (eds) (1988) *Rituals in Families and Family Therapy*. New York: Norton.

Ishii, C. (2008) 'Continuing bonds with the deceased in contemporary Japan', *The Forum,* 34 (1) January.

Jackson, E. and Jackson, N. (1999) *Learning Disability in Focus: The Use of Photography in the Care of People with Learning Disability*. London: Jessica Kingsley.

Janoff-Bulman, R. (1992) *Shattered Assumptions: Towards a New Psychology of Trauma*. New York: The Free Press.

Jenkins,C. and Merry, J. (2005) *Relative Grief*. London: Jessica Kingsley.

Jewett, C.L (1982) *Helping Children Cope with Separation and Loss*. Cambridge, MA: Harvard Common Press.

Jones, E. (2008) 'Bookwork', *Counselling Children and Young People*, June: 20–21.

Jones, E.H. (2001) *Bibliotherapy for Bereaved Children: Healing Reading*. London: Jessica Kingsley.

Jordan, J.R. (2001) 'Is suicide bereavement different? A reassessment of the literature', *Suicide and Life Threatening Behavior,* 31: 91–102.

Jung, C.G. (1965) *Memories, Dreams and Reflections* (trans. R. Winston and C. Winston). New York: Vintage Books.

Juvonen, J., Nishina, A. and Graham, S. (2000) 'Peer harassment, psychological adjustment, and school functioning in early adolescence', *Journal of Educational Psychology*, 92: 349–59.

Kallenberg, K. (2000) 'Spiritual and existential issues in palliative care', *Illness, Crisis and Loss,* 8: 120–30.

Kalter, N., Lohnes, K., Chasin, J., Cain, A., Dunning, S. and Rowan, J. (2002-2003) 'The adjustment of parentally bereaved children: factors associated with short-term adjustment', *Omega*, 46 (1): 15–34.

Kaplan, T., Black, D., Hyman, P. and Knox, J. (2001) 'Outcome of children seen after one parent killed the other', *Clinical Child Psychology and Psychiatry*, 6 (1): 9–22.

Keller, J.W, Brown, G., Maier, K., Steinfirth, K., Hall, S. and Pietrowski, C. (1995) 'Use of dreams in therapy: a survey of clinicians in private practice', *Psychology Reports*, 76: 1288–90.

Kerr, D. (2004) 'Grief and crime', *Community Care*, 13–19 May: 44–5.

Kissane, D.W. (2002) 'Shared grief: a family affair', *Grief Matters: The Australian Journal of Grief and Bereavement*, 5 (1): 7–10.

Kissane, D.W. (2003) 'Bereavement', in D. Doyle, G. Hanks, N.I. Cherny and K. Calman (eds), *Oxford Textbook of Palliative Medicine*. Oxford: Oxford University Press, pp. 1137–50.

Klaassens, M., Groote, P. and Hulgen, P.P.P. (2009) 'Roadside memorials from a geographical perspective', *Mortality,* 14 (2): 187–201.

Klass, D. (1999a) *The Spiritual Lives of Bereaved Parents*. London: Taylor and Francis.

Klass, D. (1999b) 'Developing a cross-cultural model of grief: the state of the field', *Omega*, 39 (3): 153–78.

Klass, D. (2000) 'How self-help and professional help helps', *Grief Matters: The Australian Journal of Grief and Bereavement*, 3 (1): 3–6.

Klass, D., Silverman, P.R. and Nickman, S. (eds.) (1996) *Continuing Bonds: New Understandings of Grief*. Washington DC: Taylor and Francis.

Klicker, R.L. (2000) *A Student Dies, A School Mourns: Dealing with Death and Loss in the School Community*. Philadelphia, PA: Accelerated Learning.

Knudson, R., Adame, A. and Finocan, G. (2006) 'Significant dreams: repositioning the self narrative', *Dreaming,* 15: 215–22.

Kosminsky, P.S. (2008) 'Practice report: promoting resilience in children experiencing traumatic grief', *The Forum,* 34 (3): 9.

Kranzler, E., Shaffer, D., Wasserman, G. and Davies, M. (1990) 'Early childhood bereavement', *Journal American Academy of Child and Adolescent Psychiatry*, 29: 513–20.

Kraus, F. (2010) 'The extended warranty', in B. Monroe and F. Kraus (eds), *Brief Interventions with Bereaved Children*. Oxford: Oxford University Press, pp. 113–124.

Krementz, J. (1988) *How It Feels When A Parent Dies*. New York: Random House.

Kubler-Ross, E. (1969) *On Death and Dying*. New York: MacMillan.

Kubler-Ross, E. (1975) *Death the Final Stage of Growth*. New York: Prentice-Hall.

Kuhn, A. (2002) *Family Secrets: Acts of memory and imagination*. London: Verso.

Kwok, O.M., Haine, R., Sandler, I. et al. (2005) 'Positive parenting as a mediator of the relations between parental psychological distress and mental health problems of parentally bereaved children', *Journal of Clinical Child and Adolescent Psychology*, 34: 260–71.

Lambert, D. (2005) *A Review of the Effectiveness of Operational Procedures for the Identification, Placement and Safeguarding of Vulnerable Young People in Custody*. Norwich: Norfolk Area Child Protection Committee.

Lansdown, R. (1999) 'Fourth International Conference on Children and Death. Editorial', *Bereavement Care,* 18 (3): 43–5.

Lansdown, R. and Benjamin, G. (1985) 'The development of the concept of death in children aged 5–9 years', *Child Care Health Development*, 1: 13–20.

Lansdown, R., Jordan N. and Frangroulis S. (1997) 'Children's concept of an afterlife', *Bereavement Care*, 14 (2): 16–18.

Laor, N., Wolmer, L., Kora, M., Yucel, D., Spirman, S., and Yazgan, Y. (2002) 'Posttraumatic dissociative and grief symptoms in Turkish children exposed to the 1999 earthquakes', *Journal of Nervous and Mental Disease*, 190: 824–32.

Leighton, S. (2008) 'Bereavement therapy with adolescents: facilitating a process of spiritual growth*'*, *Journal of Child and Adolescent Psychiatric Nursing*, 21 (1): 24–34. Available at http://findarticles.com/p/articles/mi_qa3892/is_200802/ai_n24394980/ (last accessed 19 May 2010).

Leliaert, R.M. (1989) 'Spiritual side of good grief: what happened to holy Saturday?', *Death Studies,* 13 (2): 103–17.

Lendrum, S. and Syme, G. (1992) *Gift of Tears*. London: Routledge.

Levy, A.J. and Wall, J.C. (2000) 'Children who have witnessed community homicide: incorporating risk and resilience in clinical work', *Families in Society: The Journal of Contemporary Human Services*, 81 (4): 402–15.

Lewis, C.S. (1961) *A Grief Observed*. London: Faber and Faber.

Lewis, E. and Heer B. (2008) *Delivering Every Child Matters in Secure Settings: A Practical Toolkit for Improving the Health and Well-being of Young People*. London: National Children's Bureau.

Libow, J.A. (1992) 'Traumatized children and the news media: clinical considerations', *American Journal of Orthopsychiatry*, 62 (3): 379–86.

Lin, K.K., Sandler, I., Ayers, T.S., Sharlene, A.W., Wolchik, S.A. and Luecken, L.J. (2004) 'Resilience in parentally bereaved children and adolescents seeking preventive services', *Journal of Clinical Child and Adolescent Psychology*, 33 (4): 673–83.

Linn-Gust, M. (2001) *Do they have Bad Days in Heaven? Surviving the Suicide Loss of a Sibling*. Atlanta, GA: Bolton Press.

Linn-Gust, M. (2006) 'Mode of death and the effects on sibling grief', *The Forum,* 32, (1): 1–2.

Lloyd-Williams, M., Wilkinson, C. and Lloyd-Williams, F. (1998) 'Do bereaved children consult the primary care team more frequently?', *European Journal of Cancer Care*, 7: 120–24.

LoConto, D.G. (1988) 'Death and dreams: a sociological approach to grieving and identity', *Omega: Journal of Death and Dying*, 37: 171–85.

Lohnes, K. (1994) 'Maintaining attachment to a dead parent in childhood: a developmental perspective'. Unpublished doctoral thesis. The University of Michigan.

Love, H. (2006) 'Suicide-bereaved children and young people's experience of a specialist group intervention: an interpretive phenomenological analysis'. Dissertation, University of Exeter.

Lowton, K. (2002) *Supporting Bereaved Students in Primary and Secondary Schools: Practical Advice for School Staff.* London: King's College, London and National Council for Hospice and Specialist Palliative Care Services.

Lowton, K. and Higginson, I.J. (2002) *Early Bereavement: What Factors Influence Children's Responses to Death?* London: King's College, London and National Council for Hospice and Specialist Palliative Care Services.

Luecken, L.J. (1998) 'Childhood attachment and loss experiences affect adult cardiovascular and cortisol function', *Psychosomatic Medicine*, 60: 765–72.

Luecken, L.J. (2000) 'Parental caring and loss during childhood and adult cortisol responses to stress', *Psychology and Health*, 15 (6): 841–51.

Lukas, C. and Seiden, H.M. (2007) *Silent Grief: Living in the Wake of Suicide.* London: Jessica Kingsley.

Luthar, S.S., Cicchetti, D. and Beckerm, B. (2000) 'The construct of resilience: a critical evaluation and guidelines for future work', *Child Development*, 71 (3): 543–62.

Machin, L. (2009) *Working with Loss and Grief.* London: Sage.

Machiodi, C. (1998) *The Art Therapy Source Book.* Los Angeles, CA: Lowell House.

Machiodi, C. (2008) 'When trauma happens, children draw: part 1', *Psychology Today,* 7 May: 1–6.

Mallon, B. (1987) *An Introduction to Counselling Skills for Special Educational Needs: Participant's Manual.* Manchester: Manchester University Press.

Mallon, B. (1989) *Children Dreaming.* Harmondsworth: Penguin.

Mallon, B. (1998) *Helping Children to Manage Loss: Positive Strategies for Renewal and Growth.* London: Jessica Kingsley.

Mallon, B. (2000a) *Managing Loss, Separation and Bereavement: Best Policy and Practice.* Manchester: Education Matters.

Mallon, B. (2000b) *Dreams, Counselling and Healing.* Dublin: Gill and MacMillan.

Mallon, B. (2000c) 'The guiding spirit in dreams', *The Churches Fellowship for Psychical and Spiritual Studies*, Summer (184): 5–7.

Mallon, B. (2002) *Dream Time With Children: Learning to Learn, Dreaming to Learn.* London: Jessica Kingsley.

Mallon, B. (2005/2008) *The Dream Bible.* London: Octopus.

Mallon, B. (2006) 'Dreams and bereavement', *Bereavement Care*, 24: 43–6.

Mallon, B. (2007) *The Mystic Symbols.* London: Octobus Publications.

Mallon, B. (2008) *Dying, Death and Grief: Working with Adult Bereavement.* London: Sage.

Mallon, B., Tufnell, M. and Rubidge,T. (2005) *When I Open My Eyes: A Report on a Three Year Project Exploring Body, Imagination and Health.* Cumbria: Body Stories.

Mandleco, B.L. and Peery, J.C. (2000) 'An organizational framework for conceptualizing resilience in children', *Journal of Child and Adolescent Psychiatric Nursing,* 13 (3): 99–113.

Margolin, G. and Gordis, E. (2000) 'The effects of family and community violence on children', *Annual Review of Psychology*, 51: 445–79.

Marie Curie Cancer Care (2003) *Spiritual and Religious Care Competencies for Specialist Palliative Care.* London: Marie Curie Cancer Care.

Markell, K.A. (2008) 'Symposium: helping bereaved college students, ADEC 30th Annual Conference', *The Forum*, 34 (3).

Markell, K. and Markell, M. (2008) *The Children Who Lived: Using Fictional Characters to Help Grieving Children and Adolescents*. London: Routledge and Kegan Paul.

Marks, N.F., Jun, H. and Song, J. (2007) 'Death of parents and adult psychological and physical well-being', *Journal of Family Issues*, 28 (12): 1611–38.

Marner, T. (2000) *Letters to Children in Family Therapy*. London: Jessica Kingsley.

Martin, T.L. (2000) 'In the aftermath: children and adolescents as survivor-victims of suicide', in K.J. Doka (ed.), *Living with Grief: Children, Adolescents and Loss*. Washington, DC: Hospice Foundation of America, pp. 263–74.

Masten, A.S. (2001) 'Ordinary magic: resilient processes in development', *American Psychologist*, 56 (3): 227–38.

Masten, A.S., Wright, K.M. and Garmezy, N. (1990) 'Resilience and development: contributions from the study of children who overcome adversity', *Development and Psychopathology*, 2: 425–44.

Massimo, L.M. and Zarri, D.A. (2006) 'In tribute to Luigi Castagnetta – drawings. A narrative approach for children with cancer', *Annals of the New York Academy of Science*, Nov.1089: xvi-xxiii.

Maunder, R.G. and Hunter, J.J. (2001) 'Attachment and psychosomatic medicine: developmental contributions to stress and disease', *Psychosomatic Medicine*, 63: 556–67.

McCaffrey, T. (2004) 'Responding to crises in schools: a consultancy model for supporting schools in crisis', *Educational and Child Psychology*, 21 (3): 109–20.

McCarthy, J.R. with Jessop J. (2005) *Young People, Bereavement and Loss: Disruptive Transitions?* National Children's Bureau for the Joseph Rowntree Foundation.

McDougall, T. (2008) 'Safeguarding vulnerable children', *Paediatric Nursing*, 20 (3): 14–17.

McFarland W. and Tollerud, T. (1999) 'Counselling children and adolescents with special needs', in A.Vernon (ed.), *Counselling Children and Adolescents*. Denver, CO: Love Publishing, pp. 215–53.

McGlauflin, H. (1996) 'Training volunteers and professionals to work with grieving children and their families', *American Journal of Hospice and Palliative Care*, 13: 22–6.

McIntyre, B. and Hogwood, I. (2006) 'Play, stop and eject; creating film strip stories with bereaved young people', *Bereavement Care*, 25 (3): 47–9.

McKissock, D. (2004) *Kid's Grief: A Handbook for Group Leaders*. Epping, NSW: National Centre for Childhood Grief.

McLaren, J. (2004) 'The death of a child', in P. Firth, G. Duff and D. Oliviere (eds), *Loss, Change and Bereavement in Palliative Care*. Maidenhead: Open University Press, pp. 80–95.

McLeod, J. (2008) 'Outside the therapy room', *Therapy Today*, 19 (4): 14–16.

McNiff, S. (1992) *Art as Medicine: Creating a Therapy of the Imagination*. Boston, MA: Shambala.

McWhorter, G. (2003) *Healing Activities for Children in Grief: Activities Suitable for Support Groups with Grieving Children, Preteens and Teens*. Texas: Gay McWhorter.

Mearns, S.J. (2000) 'The impact of loss on adolescents: developing appropriate support', *International Journal of Palliative Nursing*, 6 (1): 12–7.

Meltzer, H., Gatward, R., Goodman, R. and Ford, T. (2000) *Mental Health of Children and Adolescents in Great Britain*. London: The Stationery Office.

Meltzer, H., Gatward, R., Corbin, T., Goodman, R. and Ford, T. (2003) *Persistence, Onset, Risk Factors and Outcomes of Childhood Mental Disorders*. London: The Stationery Office.

Meltzer, M. (1999) *The Mental Health of Children*. London: HMSO.

Mitchell, A.M., Sakraida, T.J., Kim, Y., Bullian, L. and Chiapetta, L. (2009) 'Depression, anxiety and quality of life in suicide survivors: a comparison of close and distant relationships', *Archives of Psychiatric Nursing*; 23 (2): 2–10.

Mitchels, B. (2009) 'Safeguarding vulnerable groups', *Therapy Today*, 20 (9): 26–30.

Monroe, R. (2001) 'Children and bereavement', in *K260 Workbook 4. Bereavement: Private Grief and Collective Responsibility*. Milton Keynes: Open University.

Moody, R. (1993) *Reunions: Visionary Experiences with Departed Loved Ones*. New York: Villamy.

Moody, R.A. and Moody, C.P. (1991) 'A family perspective: helping children acknowledge and express grief following the death of a parent', *Death Studies*, 15: 587–602.

Moore, K. (2009) 'One woman and her dog', *Bereavement Care*, 28 (3): 25–8.

Morrison, B. (2001) 'An invisible death', *Independent on Sunday*, 1 July: 19–22.

Mundy, M. (2004) *Sad Isn't Bad: A Good Grief Guidebook for Kids Dealing with Loss*. Newry: Abbey Press.

Murray, R. and Zentner, J. (1989) *Nursing Concepts for Health Promotion*. London: Prentice-Hall.

Murthy, R. and Smith, L. (2009) *Grieving, Sharing and Healing: A Guide to Facilitating Early Adolescent Bereavement Groups*. Champaigne, IL: Research Press.

Nadeau, J.W. (1997) *Families Making Sense of Death*. Thousand Oaks, CA: Sage.

Nadeau, J.W. (2001) 'Meaning making in family bereavement: a family systems approach', in M.S. Stroebe, R.O. Hannson, W. Stroebe and H. Schut (eds), *Handbook of Bereavement Research: Consequences, Coping and Care*. Washington, DC: American Psychological Association, pp. 329–47.

Nader, K., Dubrow, N. and Stamm, B.H. (eds) (1999) *Honoring Differences: Cultural Issues in the Treatment of Trauma and Loss*. London: Taylor and Francis.

NAS (The National Autistic Society) (2003) *Death, Bereavement and Autistic Spectrum Disorders, Information Sheet*. London: NAS.

NASP (National Association of School Psychologists) (2003) *Helping Children Cope with Loss, Death and Grief. Tips for Parents*. Bethesda, MD: NASP.

National Children's Bureau (2008) *Bereavement in the Secure Setting: Delivering Every Child Matters for Bereaved Young People in Custody*. London: NCB.

Neal, L. (2007) *About Our Boys: A Practical Guide to Bringing Out the Best in Boys*. Leighton Buzzard: Neall Scott Partnership.

Neimeyer, R.A. (ed.) (2001) *Meaning Reconstruction and the Experience of Loss*. Washington, DC: American Psychology Association.

Neimeyer, R. (2005) 'Grief, loss and the quest for meaning: narrative contributions to bereavement care', *Bereavement Care*, 24 (2): 27–9.

Neville, R. (1995) 'Making memory stores with children and families affected by HIV', in S.C. Smith and M. Pennells (eds), *Interventions with Bereaved Children*. London: Jessica Kingsley, pp. 267–81.

Newman, T. (2002) *Promoting Resilience: A Review of Effective Strategies for Child Care Services*. Exeter: University of Exeter, Centre for Evidence Based Social Sciences.

Newman, T. (2003) 'Protection racket', *Zero2Nineteen*, January: 6.

NHS Advisory Service (2002) *Together We Stand: The Commissioning, Role and Management of Child and Adolescent Mental Health Services*. London: HMSO.

NICE (National Institute for Clinical Excellence) (2004) *Improving Supportive and Palliative Care for Adults with Cancer*, cited in P. Speck, I. Higginson and J. Addington-Hall, 'Spiritual needs in health care', *British Medical Journal,* 329: 123–4.

Nicholls, S. (2008) *Ways To Live Forever.* London: Marion Lloyd Books, Scholastic.

Nicholson, L. (2006) *Living on the Seabed: A Memoir of Love, Life and Survival.* London: Vermillion.

Noppe, I.C. (2008) 'Dr Gupta's work with the child-survivors of war', *The Forum,* 34 (3): 1–2.

O'Connor, T.G. (2005) 'Attachment and disturbances associated with early severe deprivation' in C.S. Carter, L. Ahnert, K.E. Grossman, S.B. Hardy et al. (eds), *Attachment and Bonding: A New Synthesis.* Cambridge, MA: MIT Press, pp. 257–67.

Oliveri, T. (2003) 'Grief groups on the internet', *Bereavement Care,* 22 (3): 39–40.

Oltjenbruns, K.A. (1996) 'Death of a friend during adolescence: issues and impacts', in C.A. Corr and D.E. Balk (eds), *Handbook of Adolescent Death and Bereavement.* New York: Springer, pp. 196–215.

O'Murchu, D. (2000) *Religion in Exile: A Spiritual Vision for the Homeward Bound.* Dublin: Gateway.

ONS (Office of National Statistics) (2002) *Living in Britain: Results from the 2001 General Household Survey.* London: HMSO.

ONS (Office for National Statistics) (2008) *News Release: Childhood Stress Linked to Emotional Disorders.* Available at http://www.statistics.gov.uk/pdfdir/cpm1008.pdf (last accessed 19 May 2010).

Oppenheim, D., Pittolo, V., Gericot, C., Grill, J., Hatmann, O. and Dauchy, S. (2008) 'A writing workshop for children with cancer', *Archive of Disease in Childhood,* 93: 708–9.

Orton, G.L. (1997) *Strategies for Counselling with Children and their Parents.* Pacific Grove, CA: Brooks/Cole.

Oswin, M. (1981) *Bereavement and Mentally Handicapped People: A Discussion Paper.* London: Kings Fund.

Oswin, M. (1991) *Am I Allowed to Cry? A Study of Bereavement Amongst People Who Have Learning Difficulties.* London: Human Horizons.

Packman, W., Horsley, H., Davies, B. and Kramer, R. (2006), 'Sibling bereavement and continuing bonds', *Death Studies,* 30 (9): 817–41.

Parkes, C.M. (1980) 'Bereavement counselling: does it work?', *British Medical Journal* 281: 36.

Parkes, C.M. (1988) 'Bereavement as a psychosocial transition: processes of adaptation to change', *Journal of Social Issues,* 44 (3): 53–65.

Parkes, C.M. (1996) *Counselling in Terminal Care and Bereavement.* Leicester: BPS Books.

Parkes, C.M. (2009) 'The genocide in Rwanda: meaning making through film', *Bereavement Care,* 28 (1): 18–21.

Pascoe, J. (2002) *My Father who Art in a Tree.* Harmondsworth: Penguin.

Peel, J. (2009) 'What counsellors could do for schools', *Therapy Today,* 20 (7): 49.

Penny, A. (2007) *Grief Matters for Children: Support for Children and Young People in Public Care Experiencing Bereavement and Loss.* London: National Children's Bureau.

Penny, A. (2009a) 'Meeting the Secretary of State', *Childhood Bereavement Network Bulletin,* 13: 2.

Penny, A. (2009b) 'Bereavement in the secure setting', *Childhood Bereavement Network Bulletin,* 13: 3.

Pentland, C. and Druce, C. (2008) *Hand-in-Hand: Supporting Children and Young People Who Have a Learning Difficulty Through the Experience of Bereavement.* Oxford: Seesaw.

Perry, B.D. and Szalavitz, M. (2006) *The Boy Who was Raised as a Dog*. New York: Basic Books.

Perry, B.D., Pollard, R.A., Blakley, T.L., Baker, W.L. and Vigilante, D. (1995) 'Childhood trauma, the neurobiology of adaptation and "use-dependent" development of the brain: how "states" become "traits"', *Infant Mental Health Journal*, 16: 271–91.

Personen, A., Paikkonen, K., Heinonen, K., Kajantie, E., Forsen, T. and Erikson, J.G. (2007) 'Depressive symptoms in adults separated from their parents as children: a natural experiment during World War II', *American Journal of Epidemiology,* 166 (10): 1126–33.

Pert, C. (1997) *Molecules of Emotion*. London: Simon and Schuster.

Pfeffer, C. (2007) 'Bereaved children of 9/11 suffered higher rates of psychiatric illness', *Biological Psychiatry*. Available at www.medicalnewstoday.com/articles/65624.php (last accessed 26 July 2010).

Pfeffer., C.R., Jiang, H., Kakuma, T., Hwang, J. and Metsch, M. (2002) 'Group inter-vention for children bereaved by the suicide of a relative', *Journal of the American Academy of Child and Adolescent Psychiatry,* 41: 505–13.

Pfeffer, C.R., Karus, D., Siegal, K. and Jiang, K. (2000) 'Child survivors of parental death from cancer or suicide: depressive and behavioural outcomes', *Psycho-Oncology*, 9: 1–10.

Phillips, L. (2009) 'My family values, endnotes', *The Guardian,* 14 March: 8.

Picardie, J. (2001) *If The Spirits Move You*. London: Picador.

Pollack, W.S. (2006) 'Creating genuine resilience in boys and young males', in S. Goldstein and R. Brooks (eds)*, Handbook of Resilience in Children*. New York: Springer Science and Business Media, pp. 65–78.

Poussaint, A.F. (1984) 'The grief response following homicide'. Paper presented at the Annual Convention of the American Psychological Association, Toronto, Ontario, August 24–28.

Powell, L.H., Shahabi, L. and Thoresen, C.E. (2003) 'Religion and spirituality: linkages to physical health', *American Psychology*, 58: 36–52.

Price, R. and Iszatt, J. (1996) 'Meeting the needs of refugee children and their families and schools', in A. Sigston, P. Curran, A. Labram and S. Wolfendale (eds), *Psychology in Practice with Young People, Families and Schools*. London: David Fulton, pp. 55–70.

Punamaki, R. (1999) 'The role of culture, violence, and personal factors affecting dream content', *Journal of Cross Cultural Psychology*, 29: 320–42.

Pynoos, R., Goenjian, A., Tashjian, M., Karakashian, M., Manjikian, R. and Manoukian, G. (1993) 'Post-traumatic stress reactions after the 1988 Armenian earthquake', *British Journal of Psychiatry*, 163: 239–47.

Pynoos, R.S. and Nader, K. (1990) 'Children's exposure to violence and traumatic death', *Psychiatyic Annals* 20: 334–344.

Pynoos, R.S., Steinberg, A.M. and Goenjian, A. (1996) 'Traumatic stress in childhood and adolescence: recent developments and current controversies', in B. van der Kolk, A.C. McFarlane and L. Weisaeth (eds), *Traumatic Stress: The Effects of Overwhelming Experience on Mind, Body and Society*. London: Guilford Press, pp. 331–58.

Raji, O., Hollins, S. and Drinnan, A. (2003) 'How far are people with learning disabilities involved in funeral rites?', *British Journal of Learning Disabilities*, 31: 42–5.

Ramachandran, V.S. (2006) 'Mirror neurons and the brain in the vat', *The Edge*, 69.

Rando, T.A. (1984) *Grief, Dying and Death*. Champaign, IL: Research Press Company.

Rando, T.A. (1993) *The Treatment of Complicated Mourning*. Champaign. IL: Research Press Company.

Raphael, B. (1984) *The Anatomy of Bereavement: A Handbook for the Caring Professions*. London: Unwin Hyman.

Raphael, B. (2005) 'After the tsunami–harnessing Australian expertise for recovery'. Presentation at the Shrine Dome, Canberra, 31 March.

Ratnarajah, D. and Schofield, M.J. (2007) 'Parental suicide and its aftermath: a review', *Journal of Family Studies,* 13 (1): 78–93.

Ratnarajah, D. and Schofield, M.J. (2008) 'Survivor's narratives of the impact of parental suicide', *Suicide and Life Threatening Behavior,* 38 (5): 618–30.

Raveis, V.H., Siegel, K., and Karus, D. (1999) 'Children's psychological distress following the death of a parent', *Journal of Youth and Adolescence,* 28: 165–80.

Rawlings, D. and Glynn, T. (2002) 'The development of palliative care-led memorial service in an acute care hospital', *International Journal of Palliative Care Nursing,* 8 (1): 40–47.

Rayner, M. and Montague, M. (2000) *Resilient Children and Young People*. Melbourne, Australia: Deakin University.

Read, S. (1996) 'Helping people with learning difficulties to grieve', *British Journal of Learning Disability Nursing,* 5, (2): 91–5.

Read, S. (1999) 'Creative ways of working when exploring the bereavement counselling process', in N. Blackman (ed.), *Living with Loss: Helping People with Learning Difficulties Cope With Loss and Bereavement*. Brighton: Pavilion Publishers, pp. 9–13.

Read, S. (2003) 'Bereavement and loss', in A. Markwick, and A. Parrish (ed.), *Learning Disabilities: Themes and Perspectives*. Edinburgh: Butterworth and Hineman, pp. 81–109.

Requarth, M. (2006) *After a Parent's Suicide*. Sebastopol, CA: Healing Arts Press.

Revonsuo, A. (2000) 'The reinterpretation of dreams: an evolutionary hypothesis of the function of dreaming', *Behavioural and Brain Sciences,* 23: 877–901, 1063–82.

Ribbens McCarthy, J. (2006) *Young People's Experience of Loss and Bereavement: Towards an Interdisciplinary Approach*. Maidenhead: Open University Press.

Ribbens McCarthy, J., with Jessop, J. (2005a) *The Impact of Bereavement and Loss on Young People*. Available at http://www.jrf.org.uk/publications/impact-bereavement-and-loss-young-people (last accessed 19 May 2010).

Ribbens McCarthy, J, with Jessop, J. (2005b) *Young People, Bereavement and Loss: Disruptive Transitions*. London; National Children's Bureau.

Riches, G. and Dawson, P. (2000) *An Intimate Loneliness: Supporting Bereaved Parents and Siblings*. Buckinghamshire: Open University Press.

Richter, L. (2008) 'Children's perspectives on death and dying in Southern Africa in the context of the HIV/AIDS epidemic', *The Forum,* 34 (1): 7–8.

Robinson, E. (1977) *A Study of the Religious Experience of Childhood*. Oxford: The Religious Experience Research Unit.

Rodgers, B. and Pryor, J. (1998) *Divorce and Separation. The Outcomes for Children*. York: The Joseph Rowntree Foundation.

Rogers, E.J. (ed.) (2007) *The Art of Grief: The Use of Expressive Arts in a Grief Support Group*. New York: Taylor and Francis.

Rosen, E.J. (1996) 'The family as a healing resource', in C.A. Corr and D.M. Corr (eds), *Handbook of Child Death and Bereavement*. New York: Springer, pp. 223–243.

Rosen, M. (2004) *Michael Rosen's Sad Book*. Walker Books: London.

Rosenblatt, P. (1993) 'Cross-cultural variation in the experience, expression and understanding of grief', in D. Irish, K. Lundquist and V. Jenkins-Nelson (eds), *Ethnic Variations in Dying, Death and Grief*. Washington, DC: Taylor and Francis, pp. 13–19.

Rosenblatt, P.C. (2000) 'Parents talking in the present tense about their dead child', *Bereavement Care*, 19 (3): 35–7.

Ross, D. and Hayes, B. (2004) 'Interventions with groups of bereaved pupils', *Education and Child Psychology,* 21 (3): 95–108.

Rothman, J. (1996) *A Birthday Present for Daniel: A Child's Story of Loss*. Amherst, NY: Prometheus Books.

Royal College of Psychiatrists (2004) *Psychotherapy and Learning Disability*. London: Repsych.

Rubey, C.T. (1999) 'Foreword', in M. Stimming and M. Stimming (eds), *Before Their Time, Adult Children's Experiences of Parental Suicide.* Phildelphia, PA: Temple University Press, pp. xiii–xv.

Rutter, J. (2003) *Supporting Refugee Children in the Classroom*. Stoke-on-Trent: Trentham Books.

Sackville, T. (2008) 'An alternative to gang culture, guns and crime', *Healthier Inside*, 3, National Children's Bureau.

Sagara-Rosemeyer, M. and Davies, B. (2007) 'Integration of religious traditions in Japanese children's view of death and afterlife', *Death Studies,* 31 (3): 223–47.

Saldinger, A., Cain, A., Kalter, N. and Lohnes, K. (1999) 'Anticipating parental death in families with young children', *American Journal of Orthopsychiatry*, 69: 39–48.

Saldinger, A., Cain, A. and Porterfield, K. (2003) 'Managing traumatic stress in children anticipating parental death', *Psychiatry*, 66: 168–81.

Salter, A. (2004) 'An internet-based peer support service for young people', *Bereavement Care,* 23 (1): 3–4.

Saltzman, W.R., Pynoos, R.S., Steinberg, A.M., Eisenberg, E. and Layne, C.M. (2001) 'Trauma and grief focused intervention for adolescents exposed to community violence', *Group Dynamics: Theory, Research and Practice*, 5: 291–303.

Sanchez. L., Fristad, M., Weller, R.A. and Moye, J. (1994) 'Anxiety in acutely bereaved prepubertal children', *Annual of Clinical Psychiatry*, 6 (1): 39–43.

Sandler, I.N., Ayers, T. and Romer, A. (2002) 'Fostering resilience in families in which a parent had died', *Journal of Palliative Medicine*, 5 (6): 945–56.

Sandler, I.N., Ayers, T.S., Wolchik, S.A. et al. (2003) 'The family bereavement program: efficacy evaluation of a theory-based prevention program for parentally bereaved children and adolescents', *Journal of Consultant Clinical Psychology*, 71: 587–600.

Sandler, I.N., Wolchik, S.A. and Ayres, T.S. (2008) 'Resilience rather than recovery: a contextual framework for adaptation following bereavement', *Death Studies*, 32: 59–73.

Saner, E. (2009) 'A trouble shared', *The Guardian*, 7 October: 10–11.

Scaer, R. (2005) *The Trauma Spectrum: Hidden Wounds and Human Resiliency*. New York: W.W. Norton.

Schoka Traylor, E., Hayslip, B.J.R., Kaminski, P.L. and York, C. (2003) 'Relationships between grief and family system characteristics: a cross lagged longitudinal analysis', *Death Studies*, 27: 575–601.

Schore, A. (2001) 'The effects of early relational trauma on right brain development, affect and regulation and infant mental health', *Infant Mental Health Journal*, 22: 201–269.

Schredl, M. (2000) 'Book review: "Dreams and Nightmares": the new theory of the origins and meanings of dreams', *Dreaming*, 2 (4): 247–50.

Schut, H.M., Stroebe, M.S., van der Bout, J and Terheggen, M. (2001) 'The efficacy of bereavement interventions: determining who benefits', in M.S. Stroebe, R.O. Hansonn,

W. Stroebe and H. Schut (eds), *Handbook of Bereavement Research*. Washington, DC: American Psychological Association, pp. 705–37.

Schuurman, D.L. (2002) 'The club no one wants to join: a dozen lessons I've learnt from grieving children and adolescents', *Grief Matters: The Australian Journal of Grief and Bereavement*, Winter: 23–5.

Schuurman, D. (2003) *Never the Same: Coming to Terms with a Parent's Death When you Were a Child*. New York: St. Martin's Press.

Schuurman, D. (2008) 'Invited speaker: Valerie Maasdorp on resiliency in palliative care', *The Forum*, 34 (3): 9.

Schwartz, D. and Gorman, A.H. (2003) 'Community violence exposure and children's academic functioning', *Journal Educational Psychology*, 96: 163–73.

Segal, R.M. (1984) 'Helping children express grief through symbolic communication', *Social Casework*, 65: 590–99.

Servaty-Seib, H.L., Peterson, J. and Spang, D. (2003) 'Notifying individual students of a death loss: practical recommendations for schools and school counselors', *Death Studies*, 27: 167–87.

Servaty-Seib, H.L. and Pistole, M.C. (2006–2007) 'Adolescent grief: relationship category and emotional closeness', *Omega*, 54 (2): 147–67.

Sethi, S. and Bhargava, S.C. (2003) 'Child and adolescent survivors of suicide', *Crisis*; 24 (1): 4–6.

Shapland, M. (1976) 'Film review: Lucy, 21 months, in Foster Care for Nineteen Days, a film by James and Joyce Robinson', *Health Education Journal*, 35 (2): 195–6.

Sheldon, F. (1998) 'ABC of palliative care: bereavement (clinical review)', *British Medical Journal*, 316: 456–8.

Shepherd, D. and Barraclough, B.M. (1974) 'The aftermath of suicide', *British Journal of Psychiatry*, 2: 600–603.

Shipman, C., Kraus, F. and Monroe, B. (2001) 'Responding to the needs of schools in supporting bereaved children', *Bereavement Care*, 20 (1): 6–7.

Shohet, R. (ed.) (2008) *Passionate Supervision*. London: Jessica Kingsley.

Siegel, A. and Bulkeley, K. (1988) *Dreamcatching: Every Parent's Guide to Exploring and Understanding Children's Dreams and Nightmares*. New York: Three Rivers Press.

Siegel, D.J. (1996) 'Cognition, memory and dissociation', *Child and Adolescent Psychiatric Clinics of North America*, 5: 509–33.

Siegel, D.J. (1999) *The Developing Mind*. New York: Guilford Press.

Siegel, D.J. (2007) *The Mindful Brain: Reflection and Attunement in the Cultivation of Well-being*. New York: W.W. Norton.

Siegel, K., Karus, D. and Raveis, V.H. (1996) 'Adjustment of children facing the death of a parent due to cancer', *Journal of American Academic Child and Adolescent Psychiatry*, 35: 442–50.

Siegel, K., Mesagno, F.P., Karus, D. et al. (1992) 'Psychosocial adjustment of children with a terminally ill parent', *Journal of the American Academic Child Adolescent Psychiatry*, 31: 327–33.

Silberg, J. (2003) *Guidelines for the Evaluation and Treatment of Dissociative Symptoms in Children and Adolescents*. Northbrook, IL: International Association for the Study of Dissociation.

Silva, E. and Cotgrove, A. (1999) 'Youth suicide and bereavement', *Bereavement Care*, 18 (1): 5–8.

Silverman, P.R. (2000) *Never Too Young to Know: Death in Children's Lives*. Oxford: Oxford University Press.

Silverman, P.R., Nickman, S. and Worden, J. W. (1995) 'Detachment revisited: the child's reconstruction of the dead parent', in L.A. DeSpelder and A.L. Strickland (eds), *The Path Ahead: Reading in Death and Dying*. Mountain View, CA: Mayfield, pp 231–41.

Silverman, P.R., Range, L. and Overholser, J. (1994–1995) 'Bereavement from suicide as compared to other forms of bereavement', *Omega*, 30 (1): 41–51.

Silverman, P.R. and Worden, J.W. (1992) 'Children's reactions in the early months after the death of a parent', *American Journal of Orthopsychiatry*, 62 (1): 93–104.

Simone, C. (2008) 'Parental suicide: The long term impact on children and young people', *Bereavement Care*, 27 (3): 43–46.

Sinclair, R. and Geraghty, T. (2002) *A Review of the Use of Secure Accommodation in Northern Ireland*. London: National Children's Bureau.

Sinclair, S., Pereira, J. and Raffin, S. (2006) 'A thematic review of the spirituality literature within palliative care', *Journal of Palliative Medicine*, 9: 464–79.

Sink, C.A. (eds) (2005) *Contemporary School Counselling: Theory, Research and Practice*. Boston: Houghton Mifflin.

Sjoqvist, S. (2007) *Still Here with Me: Teenagers and Children on Losing a Parent* (trans. M. Myers). London: Jessica Kingsley.

Skylight (2007) 'Stressed out?'. Available at http://www.skylight.org.nz/young-people/stressed-out.aspx (last accessed 19 May 2010).

Smith, G. (2005) 'Children's narratives of traumatic experiences', in A. Vetere and E. Dowling (eds), *Narrative Therapies with Children and their Families: A Practitioner's Guide to Concepts and Approaches*. Hove: Psychology, pp. 61–74.

Smith, S. and Pennells, M. (1995) *Interventions with Bereaved Children*. London: Jessica Kingsley.

Social Services Inspectorate Report (1997) *When Leaving Home is also Leaving Care: An Inspection for Young People Leaving Care*. London: Department of Health.

Sori, C.F. and Hecker, L.L. (2003) *The Therapist's Notebook for Children and Adolescents: Homework, Handouts and Activities for Use in Psychotherapy*. New York: Howarth Press.

Steward, S. (2008) '"So what now?" Adolescents' formation of positive self-concept following parental death', *The Forum*, 34 (3): 13–14.

Stewart, A.E. (1999) 'Complicated bereavement and posttraumatic stress disorder following fatal car crashes: recommendations for death notification', *Death Studies*, 23: 289–321.

Stimming, M. and Stimming, M. (1999) 'Perspectives on a common loss, uncommon grace and endings and beginnings', in M. Stimming and M. Stimming (eds), *Before Their Time: Adult Children's Experiences of Parental Suicide*. Philadelphia, PA: Temple University Press, pp. 111–32.

Stokes, J. (2004) *Then, Now and Always: Supporting Children as They Journey Through Grief*. Cheltenham: Winston's Wish.

Stokes, J. (2009a) 'Resilience and bereaved children: helping a child to develop a resilient mind-set following the death of a parent', *Bereavement Care*, 28 (1): 9–17.

Stokes, J. (2009b) 'As big as it gets, Winston's wish'. Presentation at a conference, 20 January.

Stokes, J.A., Pennington, J., Monroe, B., Papadatou, D. and Relf, M. (1999) 'Developing services for bereaved children: a discussion of the theoretical and practical issues involved', *Mortality*, 4: 3.

Storr, A. (1989) *Solitude*. London: Flamingo Books.

Streeck-Fisher, A. and van der Kolk, B.A. (2000). 'Down will come baby, cradle and all: diagnostic and therapeutic implications of chronic trauma on child development', *Australian and New Zealand Journal of Psychiatry*, 34: 903–18.

Stroebe, M.S. (2009) 'From vulnerability to resilience: where should research priorities lie?', *Bereavement Care,* 28 (2): 18–24.

Stroebe, M.S., Gergen, M.M., Gergen, K.J. and Stroebe, W. (1995) 'Broken hearts or broken bonds: love and death in historical perspective', in L.A. DeSpelder and A.L. Strickland (eds), *The Path Ahead: Reading in Death and Dying.* Mountain View, CA: Mayfield, pp. 231–41.

Stroebe, M.S., Hanssonn, R. and Stroebe, W. et al. (2001) *Handbook of Bereavement Research: Consequences, Coping and Care.* Washington, DC: American Psychological Association.

Stroebe, M.S. and Schut, H. (1999) 'The dual process model of coping with bereavement: rationale and description', *Death Studies*, 23 (3): 197–224.

Stroebe, M.S. and Schut, H. (2008) 'The dual process model of coping with bereavement: overview and update', *Grief Matters: The Australian Journal of Grief and Bereavement*, 11 (1): 4–10.

Stroebe, M., Schut, H. and Stroebe, W. (2007) 'Health outcomes of bereavement', *Lancet*, 370: 1960–73.

Stubbs, D., Ailovic, K., Stokes, J. and Howells, K. (2008) *Family Assessment: Guidelines for Child Bereavement Practitioners.* Cheltenham: Winston's Wish.

Stuber, M.L., and Mesrkhani, H.V. (2001) 'What do we tell the children? Understanding childhood grief', *West Journal Medicine*, 174 (3): 187–91.

Summerhayes, L. (2007) 'We rewrote the book on bereavement', *Edinburgh Evening News,* 17 October. Available at http://edinburghnews.scotsman.com/features/We-rewrote-the-book-on.3471523.jp (last accessed 19 May 2010).

Summers, S.J. and Witts, P. (2003) 'Psychological intervention for people with learning disabilities who have experienced bereavement: a case study illustration', *British Journal of Learning Disabilities*, 31: 37–41.

Sunderland, M. (2000) *Using Story Telling as a Therapeutic Tool with Children.* Bicester, Oxon: Winslow Press.

Swinton, J. (2002) 'Spirituality and the lives of people with learning disabilities', *The Tizard Learning Disability Review,* 7 (4): 29–35.

Talbot, J. (2008) 'Making sense of the situation: young offenders with learning disabilities and difficulties', *Healthier Inside*, Spring/Summer, 2 (13): 13–14.

Tamm, M. (1996) 'The meaning of death for children and adolescents', *Bereavement Care,* 15 (3): 32–33.

Taylor, S.E. (2003) *The Tending Instinct: Women, Men and the Biology of our Relationships.* New York: Henry Bolt.

Taylor, S.E. (2004) 'Between the idea and the reality: a study of the counselling experiences of bereaved people who sense a presence of the deceased', *Counselling and Psychotherapy Research,* 5 (1): 53–61.

Therapy Today (2009) 'Doctors demand action on "pro-ana" sites', *Therapy Today*, 20 (8): 4.

Thompson, B. (2003) 'The expressive arts and experience of loss', *The Forum*, 26 (2): 16.

Thompson, F. and Payne, S. (2000) 'Bereaved children's questions to a doctor', *Mortality* 5 (1): 74–96.

Todd, S. and Read, S. (2009) 'Talking about death and what it means: the perspectives of people with intellectual disabilities'. NNPCPLD (National Network of Palliative

Care of People with Learning Difficulties), Death with a Difference Conference, Keele University.

Tomm. K. (1990) 'Foreword', in M. White and D. Epston (eds), *Narrative Means to Therapeutic Ends*. New York: W.W. Norton, pp. 5–8.

Towers, A. (2008) 'When only an eyelid moves', *Counselling Children and Young People*, June: 25–9.

Traylor, E.S., Hayslip, B., Zaminski, P.I. and York, C. (2003) 'Relationships between grief and family system characteristics: a cross lagged longitudinal analysis', *Death Studies*, 27: 575–601.

Tremblay, G.C. and Israel, A.C. (1998) 'Children's adjustment to parental death', *Clinical Psychology*, 5: 424–38.

Trickey, D. (2005) 'The impact of traumatic bereavement on families'. Presentation at the 12th International Bereavement and Loss Conference, 8 September, Manchester.

Trimble, S. (2000) 'Grace Christ examines how children deal with grief', *Columbia News*, 25 February. Available at http://www.columbia.edu/cu/news/00/02/graceChrist. html (last accessed 19 May 2010).

Trinder, A. (2008) 'The art of the personal in grief therapy', *The Forum*, 2 (3): 1–2.

Tufnell, G. (2005) 'The effects of war on children: working with trauma and bereavement in refugees'. Presentation at 7th International Conference on Grief and Bereavement, Kings College, 12 July, London.

Ulliana, L. (1998) 'Bereavement and children with autistic spectrum disorder', *Keynotes Newsletter,* June. Autistic Association of NSW.

Valentine, C. (2008) *Bereavement Narratives*. London: Routledge.

Valentine, C. (2009) 'Continuing bonds after bereavement: a cross-cultural perspective', *Bereavement Care*, 28 (2): 6–11.

Van der Kolk, B.A., McFarline, A.C. and Weisaeth. L. (2006) *Traumatic Stress: The Effects of Overwhelming Experience in Mind, Body and Society*. New York: Guilford Press.

Van Eerdewegh, M., Clayton, P. and Van Eerdewegh, P. (1985) 'The bereaved child: variables influencing early psychopathology', *British Journal of Psychiatry*, 147: 188–94.

Van Gulden, H. and Bartels-Rabb, L.M. (1999) *Real Parents, Real Children: Parenting the Adopted Child*. New York: Crossroad Publishing.

Vaswani, N. (2008) 'Persistent offender profile: focus on bereavement', *Criminal Justice Social Work Briefing*, 13: 1–7. Available at http://www.cjsw.ac.uk/cjsw/5172.html (last accessed 19 May 2010).

Vernberg, E.M., La Greca, A.M., Silverman, W.K. and Prinstein, M.J. (1996) 'Prediction of posttraumatic stress symptoms in children after hurricane Andrew', *Journal of Abnormal Psychology*, 105: 237–48.

Vickio, C.J. (1998) 'Together in spirit: keeping our relationship alive when loved ones die', *Death Studies,* 21: 134–86.

Volkan (1972) 'The linking objects of pathological mourners', *Archives of General Psychiatry*, 27: 215–22.

Walsh, K., King, M., Jones, L., Tookman, A. and Blizzard, R. (2002) 'Spiritual beliefs may affect outcome of bereavement: prospective study', *British Medical Journal*, 324: 1551–4.

Walter, T. (1996) 'A new model of grief: bereavement and biography', *Mortality,* 1 (1): 7–25.

Walter, T. (1999) *On Bereavement: The Culture of Grief.* Buckingham: Open University Press.

Walter, T. (2003) 'Historical and cultural variants on a good death', *British Journal of Medicine*, 26 July: 218–20.

Walter, T. (2006) 'Telling the dead man's tale: bridging the gap between the living and the dead', *Bereavement Care*, 25 (2): 23–6.

Walter, T. (2008) 'Mourners and mediums', *Bereavement Care*, 27 (3): 47–50.

Ward, H. (2003) 'Solidarity helps a school grieve', *Times Educational Supplement*, 21 November: 3.

Ward-Wimmer, D. and Napoli, C. (2000) 'Counselling approaches with children and adolescents', in K.J. Doka (ed.), *Living with Grief: Children, Adolescents and Loss*. Washington, DC: Hospice Foundation of America, pp. 109–122.

Waskett, D.A. (1995) 'Chairing the child: a seat of bereavement', in S.C. Smith and M. Pennells (eds), *Interventions with Bereaved Children*. London: Jessica Kingsley.

Watts, J. (1988) 'Experts in the end', *The Observer*, 23 October: 36.

Way, P. (2008) 'Michael in the clouds: talking to very young people about death'. *Bereavement Care*, 27 (1): 7–9.

Webb, N.B. (2002) 'Assessment of the bereaved child', in N.B. Webb (ed.), *Helping Bereaved Children: A Handbook for Practitioners*. New York: Guilford Press, pp. 19–42.

Weisler, J. (1993) *Photo Therapy Techniques: Exploring the Secrets of Personal Snapshots and Family Albums*. San Francisco, CA: Josey Bass.

Weller, E.B., Weller, R.A., Fristad, M.A. and Bowes, J.M. (1991) 'Depression in recently bereaved children', *American Journal of Psychiatry*, 148: 1536–40.

Weller, R.A., Weller, E.B., Fristad, M.A., Cain, S.E. and Bowes, J.M. (1988) 'Should children attend their parent's funeral?', *Journal of American Academy Child Adolescent Psychiatry*, 27: 559–62.

Wells, R. (1988) *Helping Children Cope with Grief*. London: Sheldon Press.

Wertheimer, A.A. (2001) *A Special Scar: The Experiences of People Bereaved by Suicide*, 2nd edn. Hove: Brunner-Routledge.

Weymont, D. and Rae, T. (2006) *Supporting Young People Coping with Grief, Loss and Death*. London: Paul Chapman.

White, M. and Epston, D (1990) *Narrative Means to Therapeutic Ends*. New York: W.W. Norton.

Wiener, H. (1989) 'The dynamics of the organism: implications of recent biological thought for psychosomatic theory and research', *Psychosomatic Medicine*, 51: 608–35.

Wilder, T. (1967) *The Bridge of St. Luis Rey*. London: Penguin Books.

Williams, A.L. and Merten, M.J. (2009) 'Adolescents online social networking following the death of a peer', *Journal of Adolescent Research*, 24 (1): 67–90.

Williams, E. (2004) 'Dead serious', *Times Educational Supplement*, 14 May: 6–7.

Williams, R. (2009) 'Hoods down, looking up: with gang tensions simmering inside, how can colleges keep all the students safe?', *The Guardian, Education*, 10 November: 5.

Willis, S. (2004) 'Work with bereaved children', in B. Monroe and F. Kraus (eds), *Brief Interventions with Bereaved Children*. Oxford: Oxford University Press, pp. 1–12.

Wimpenny, P. (2007) 'A literature review on bereavement and bereavement care: developing evident-based practice in Scotland', *Bereavement Care*, 26 (1): 7–10.

Winston's Wish (2002) *Every Thirty Minutes*. Gloucester: Winston's Wish.

Winston's Wish (2008) *Beyond the Rough Rock: Supporting a Child Who Has Been Bereaved by Suicide*. Gloucester: Winston's Wish.

Wolchik, S.A., Tein, J.-Y., Sandler. I.N. and Ayers, T.S. (2006) 'Stressors, quality of the child-caregiver relationship, and children's mental health problems after parental death: the mediating role of self-system beliefs', *Journal of Abnormal Child Psychology*, 34 (2): 212–29.

Wolfe, B. (2008) 'Experimental workshop: multicultural grief counselling', *The Forum*, 34 (3): 11.

Wolfelt, A. (1994) *Healing your Grieving Heart for Teens: 100 Practical Ideas*. Fort Collins, CO: Companion Press.

Wood, K., Chase, E. and Aggleton, P. (2006) '"Telling the truth is the best thing": teenage orphans' experiences of parental AIDS-related illness and bereavement in Zimbabwe', *Social Science and Medicine*, 63: 1923–33.

Wood, M.J.M. (2008) *Mapping the Landscape: A Directory of Arts Therapist and Arts Practitioners Working in Supportive and Palliative Care Settings in the United Kingdom 2007*. London: Creative Response and Help the Hospices Network of Professional Associations.

Woodward, J. (2006) 'Working therapeutically with lone twins', *Therapy Today*, 17 (4): 335–72.

Worden, J.W. (1991) *Grief Counselling and Grief Therapy: A Handbook for the Mental Health Practitioner*, 2nd edn. London: Routledge.

Worden, J.W. (1996) *Children and Grief: When a Parent Dies*. New York: The Guilford Press.

Worden, J.W. (2002) *Grief Counselling and Grief Therapy: A Handbook for the Mental Health Practitioner*. New York: Springer.

Worden, J.W., Davies, B. and McCown, D. (1999) 'Comparing parent loss with sibling loss', *Death Studies*, 23: 1–15.

Worden, J.W. and Silverman, P.R. (1996) 'Parental death and the adjustment of school-age children', *Omega*, 33: 91–102.

Wright, B. and Partridge, I. (1999) 'Speaking ill of the dead: parental suicide as child abuse', *Clinical Child Psychology and Psychiatry*, 4 (2): 225–31.

Wright, M.C. (2002) 'The essence of spiritual care: a phenomenalogical enquiry', *Palliative Medicine*, 16: 125–32.

Yalom. I.D. (2000) 'Religion and psychiatry'. Speech on receiving the 2000 Oscar Pfister prize delivered at the American Psychiatric Association's annual meeting, May, New Orleans. Available at http://www.yalom.com/lec/pfister (last accessed 19 May 2010).

Yalom. I. D. (2008) 'The ripple effect', *Therapy Today*, May: 4–11.

Youth Justice Trust (2001) *A Survey of Some of the General and Specific Health Issues for YOTS*. Manchester: Youth Justice Trust.

Yule, M.W. and Gold, A. (1993) *Wise Before the Event: Coping with Crises in Schools*. London: Calouste Glbenkian Foundation.

Yule, W. (1998) 'Posttraumatic stress disorder in children and its treatment', in T.W. Miller (ed.), *Children of Trauma: Stressful Life Events and Their Effects on Children and Adolescents*. Madison, CT: International Universities Press, pp. 219–53.

Yule, W. (2000) 'From pogroms to "ethnic cleansing": meeting the needs of war-affected children', *Journal of Psychology and Psychiatry*, 41: 695–702.

Zambelli, G.C. and DeRosa, A.P. (1992) 'Bereavement support groups for school-age children: theory, intervention and case example', *American Journal of Orthopsychiatry*, 62: 484–93.

Index